THE
SPIRITUAL
WARFARE
Handbook

THE
SPIRITUAL
WARFARE

Handbook

HOW TO BATTLE, PRAY
AND PREPARE YOUR HOUSE
FOR TRIUMPH

CHUCK D. PIERCE
WITH REBECCA WAGNER SYTSEMA

Chosen

a division of Baker Publishing Group
Minneapolis, Minnesota

Published by Chosen Books
11400 Hampshire Avenue South
Bloomington, Minnesota 55438
www.chosenbooks.com

Chosen Books is a division of
Baker Publishing Group, Grand Rapids, Michigan

Printed in the United States of America

ISBN 978-0-8007-9785-0

Library of Congress Control Number: 2016931545

Names of certain people referred to in illustrations have been changed, but the stories are factual.

Cover design by Rob Williams, InsideOutCreativeArts

16 17 18 19 20 21 22   7 6 5 4 3 2 1

Contents

5

Introduction

The Spiritual Warfare Handbook has been written to help each reader move from any form of desolation into a new level of abundance. From the beginning, when God saw the earth in confusion and chaos, He planned for a people who would move from chaos into multiplication. He spoke! Chaos subsided and abundance began. This is the essence of spiritual life. When Yeshua, Jesus of Nazareth, defined why He came or was sent to earth, He said in John 10:10, "I came that they may have and *enjoy* life, and have it in abundance (to the full, till it overflows)" (AMP). Many Christians, and even those who are seeking to understand their earthly purpose, never realize that the One who was sent to redeem them purposed them to "enjoy life." Prior to this portion of the verse, we find Jesus declaring, "I am the Door; anyone who enters in through Me will be saved (will live). He will come in and he will go out [freely], and will find pasture. The thief comes only in order to steal and kill and destroy" (verses 9–10 AMP). This is meant to help you enter the Door (called Christ) into a new dimension of abundance.

I have come to know the One who paid the price for my freedom. The Father sacrificed the Son to unlock all spiritual blessings in heavenly places. These blessings have amassed through the years of your bloodline dwelling in the earth. Some of your predecessors may have added to these blessings through their obedience. Some may have accessed the blessings that the Father created for them and manifested these blessings on earth. Others may have rejected these blessings and deferred them to your time to be accessed. Whatever the case, He came that you may *enjoy* the *abundance* of His blessings!

This compilation is meant to assist you as you become more and more liberated to experience freedom. When we don't sense the life of Christ flowing through us, we need to ask the Lord, "What has happened to my passion? In the midst of my circumstance, Lord, did I just get tired and quit withstanding?" In truth, we can pray until we are green. We can do all sorts of religious activities. But if we don't resist the enemy in the midst of that trial (the temptation toward passivity and all other temptations), and if we don't let that trial bring the working of the cross into us, then we won't really enter into the passion and fullness of life that the Lord has for each of us. Having God's passion as we walk in wisdom and revelation is the key to protecting ourselves from becoming outwitted by the enemy.

In Matthew 16, when the Father revealed to Peter who Yeshua was, a prophecy came forth. Unlocked revelation releases prophecy. Jesus released a prophecy for ages to come: "Then Jesus answered him, Blessed (happy, fortunate, and to be envied) are you, Simon Bar-Jonah. For flesh and blood [men] have not revealed this to you, but My Father who is in heaven. And I tell you, you are Peter [Greek, *Petros*—a large piece of rock], and on this rock [Greek, *petra*—a huge rock like Gibraltar] I will build My church, and the gates of Hades (the powers of the infernal region) shall not overpower it [or be strong to its detriment or hold out against it]. I will give you the keys of the kingdom of heaven; and whatever you bind (declare to be improper and unlawful) on earth must be what is already bound in heaven; and whatever you loose (declare lawful) on earth must be what is already loosed in heaven" (Matthew 16:17–19 AMP).

Yeshua Himself prophesied that this triumphant people, filled with the Father's revelation, would arise and prevail against hell's gates. These people will do exploits—taking resources and multiplying or changing them into a form to be used today. These people are an apostolic people. They are a modern people who very much look like the people who crossed over the Jordan River after 476 years from the time God spoke them into existence to when He communicated to their father, Abraham. The gates of hell will not be able to withstand this people. They are people who will build a new prototype for today and unlock a Kingdom mentality that hell cannot withstand. They will have centers for gatherings that are filled with the fire of His glory!

I am honored that I am numbered with this people of triumph. I came to know the Father of my spirit when I was a maturing youth. He opened the heavenly vault and gave me a glimpse of His blessings when I was a young man. He showed me the war and the army of darkness that was determined to keep me from accessing these blessings. He taught my hands to war and my heart to worship. His voice has become my life. Daily, He is still teaching me to experience why I am here: *TO ENJOY LIFE!*

I hope this compilation helps you to hear, to understand your dream life, to stay protected from the wiles of the enemy and to outwit him with a wisdom that only you have been given the privilege to gain through the shed blood of the Savior. But most of all, I pray that the words here help you to accomplish your destiny . . . *TO ENJOY LIFE!* with God

Chuck D. Pierce, president, Global Spheres, Inc.; president, Glory of Zion International Ministries, Inc.

11

When God Speaks

How to Interpret Dreams, Visions,
Signs and Wonders

Preface

Hearing the voice of God is not as difficult as some might think. I have found that many of God's people are hearing Him, but they have not perceived that it is His voice. To *perceive* means "to take hold of, feel, comprehend, grasp mentally, recognize, observe or become aware of something by discerning." We must learn to perceive God's voice, which will help us understand His will for our lives. Acting on what we have discerned as His voice, until it becomes a reality, is the key to a successful Christian life.

To commune with a holy God—as you talk to Him and He talks to you—is the highest privilege we have on earth. My own life has become one of hearing the Lord's voice, not just for myself but for others, as well. My greatest desire is for people to hear God's voice, embrace His word and fulfill the destiny God has for them.

I pray that this book will give you the principles of hearing God through prophecy and revelation, show you how to test and evaluate the prophetic word and help you to know what to do with what God has spoken to you. As you read this book, may you recognize the voice that gives you life and life abundantly!

Chuck D. Pierce, Denton, Texas

1

Hear Him!

> Then God said, "Let Us make man in Our image, according to Our likeness; let them have dominion over the fish of the sea, over the birds of the air, and over the cattle, over all the earth and over every creeping thing that creeps on the earth." So God created man in His own image; in the image of God He created him; male and female He created them. Then God blessed them, and God said to them, "Be fruitful and multiply; fill the earth and subdue it; have dominion over the fish of the sea, over the birds of the air, and over every living thing that moves on the earth."
>
> Genesis 1:26–28

From the beginning of creation, humanity was created to commune with God. Because God created us with a body, soul and spirit, we were given a different value from the rest of creation. We were made as spiritual beings. Our human spirit allows us to exercise intelligence, perception and determination, and to make moral choices; and it enables us to exceed above and have dominion over any other creature in the earth realm. This intrinsic worth drives us to know our Creator as well as to know the hope of our calling and why we exist.

Because we are set apart in this way, we also carry an accountability and a responsibility that the rest of creation does not have. We are expected to be faithful stewards of the talents and abilities that God has given us. The only way we can do this is to seek Him, commune with Him and gain the revelation that will enable us to prosper. When we obey this revelation from Him, we please Him.

We Were Created to Commune with Him Daily

The spirit is the highest function of our being. It is through our spirit that we commune with the spiritual world. When we open our human spirit and allow the Holy Spirit to come and reside within us, we come into a holy union with our Creator. It is through our human spirits that the Holy Spirit gives us the revelation necessary to accomplish His will on the earth. Because this is an ongoing process, we should expect God to commune with us daily as we seek Him. He longs for us to draw near to Him so we can know His heart and greatest desire for our lives.

To *seek* means "to diligently look for and search earnestly for until the object of desire is located and found." Psalm 27:4–8 says:

> One thing I have desired of the LORD, that will I seek: that I may dwell in the house of the LORD all the days of my life, to behold the beauty of the LORD, and to inquire in His temple. For in the time of trouble He shall hide me in His pavilion; in the secret place of His tabernacle He shall hide me; He shall set me high upon a rock. And now my head shall be lifted up above my enemies all around me; therefore I will offer sacrifices

of joy in His tabernacle; I will sing, yes, I will sing praises to the LORD. Hear, O LORD, when I cry with my voice! Have mercy also upon me, and answer me. When You said, "Seek My face," my heart said to You, "Your face, LORD, I will seek."

David was known as a man with a heart after God because he was willing to seek God until he received the Lord's mind and strategy for that hour. That is also why Jesus said, "But seek first the kingdom of God and His righteousness, and all these things shall be added to you" (Matthew 6:33).

Moses gives us a beautiful example of and reason why we should be seeking God on a daily basis. In Exodus 29, we find Moses receiving revelation on the daily offerings two times each day. The day is opened and closed with the gift of worship to and communion with God. Verse 42 says, "This shall be a continual burnt offering throughout your generations at the door of the tabernacle of meeting before the LORD, *where I will meet you to speak with you*" (emphasis added). What a wonderful principle for us! If we will come before God on a daily basis, He will meet us, join with us and speak to us. He will set us apart for service. We will begin to sense His presence. We will have assurance that He is with us. He will take a stand against our enemies. "And they shall know that I am the LORD their God, who brought them up out . . . " (v. 46). We will know that He is the God who will keep us safe, deliver us from evil and lead us into all the promises and destiny He has for our lives.

God Speaks

I was eight years old when I first became aware that God had a voice and actually spoke to people. My godly grandmother would take me to a little Baptist church in East Texas, where we lived. A lady named Mrs. Grimes would do a very peculiar thing. Right in the middle of the preacher's message, Mrs. Grimes would stand up and wave her hands. Being a Baptist church, this was very unusual behavior. Yet the preacher would stop his message and ask her what was happening. Mrs. Grimes would say, "The Lord is speaking to me!" Then the pastor would say, "Tell us what He's saying." And Mrs. Grimes would begin to tell us what she was hearing from the Spirit of God and how it affected the church.

It totally fascinated me that God could really speak to people. When the preacher talked about God, it seemed boring and dry. But when Mrs. Grimes would speak up, it was filled with life and vibrancy. I would look up at my grandmother and say, "If God can speak to that woman, I want Him to speak to me." My grandmother would look down at me—a typically wild eight-year-old boy—and say, "You will have to learn to be quiet and sit still for God to ever say anything to you!"

My Day of Salvation

From that point on, there was no question in my mind that God had a voice. I had heard it through Mrs. Grimes and in the Bible stories taught in Sunday school. Still, I never heard Him speak directly to me—until I was eleven years old. One Sunday during a service, the Spirit of the Lord came to me and clearly said, "This is your day." It was as if I followed His Spirit up to the altar and surrendered my life to Him as best as an eleven-year-old child can.

As I studied the Bible later on, it became clear to me that God has a day of salvation for each one of us (see 2 Corinthians 6:2). We all come into our day of salvation by hearing God's voice speak into our spirit, which up to that point is dead in trespasses. As we respond to His voice and allow Him to illuminate truth in our darkened spirit, we come into our day of salvation. In fact, none of us have been saved without the voice of God prompting us. We may not have heard an audible voice, but because only God can illuminate the truth of salvation, all who have had a salvation experience and know Jesus as their Lord and Savior have heard God's voice, whether or not they understood it at the time! It is this same voice that quickens the Word of God to us. Therefore, every time we glean truth from Scripture, we hear God at some level.

"I Will Restore"

Even though I had been saved, I had a difficult and often traumatic and abusive childhood. My family had suffered great loss and anguish. Much of my family fell apart during my teen years as a result of the enemy's inroads into my father's life. He then died under tragic circumstances when I was sixteen. By the time I turned eighteen, my body had begun to suffer from working, going to college and having a fairly ardent nightlife.

Eventually, I wound up in the hospital suffering from exhaustion and double pneumonia. It was while I was in the hospital that the Lord clearly spoke to me in an audible voice and said, "I will restore all that you have lost." With those words He penetrated every part of my being. Though I had suspected it before, I now knew that God had a plan not only to go back and heal the wounds of my past, but also to restore my future.

> *God's voice has great power to bring us out of the ruins of our past and set us on the course He has ordained for our lives.*

I had never before seen the concept of restoration in the Bible, but as I read more deeply, I learned that God's voice had the power to restore (see Joel 2:25). My whole life changed from that moment; and since that time, God has healed, delivered and restored me in miraculous ways.[1] God's voice has great power to bring us out of the ruins of our past and set us on the course He has ordained for our lives, as I learned on that day many years ago.

Your Testimony Is Powerful

As you read, this may be a good place for you to stop and think about how the voice of God has manifested in your life. How were you saved? How has God supernaturally affected your life and your circumstances? You might want to write out your testimony. The reason for writing it out is because there is great power in the word of your testimony; it builds faith as nothing else can.

Our testimony is an important function of the human spirit. Think of the Ark of the Covenant. Several items were in the Ark, one of which was the testament that God gave to Moses. When we commune with God through the Word, we store His precepts and principles down deep in our hearts, where we have established covenant with God. When we obey these precepts and principles and experience God's faithfulness, we develop a testimony that has great power against our enemy. Once we have an established testimony, we can refute the lies of the devil by saying, "God has spoken this to me. Because I have seen His hand move in the past, I know He will do the same now, for nothing is impossible to Him!"

Revelation 12:10 says, "Then I heard a loud voice saying in heaven, 'Now salvation, and strength, and the kingdom of our God, and the power of His Christ have come, for the accuser of our brethren, who accused them before our God day and night, has been cast down. And they overcame him by the blood of the Lamb and by the word of their testimony.'" The enemy cannot withstand the voice of God coupled with the power of our testimony.

God's Voice Is Creative

In the account of creation in Genesis, we see that the creative instrument God used again and again was His voice. God *spoke* into chaos and light came into being. He *spoke* again and light divided from darkness, creating day and night. The power of His voice created the heavens and the earth, and the abundance of creatures filled the earth and seas.

God's voice is so powerful that it can divide substance. From the power of His voice, substance can be made into a different form. God made the ground from His creative voice, and from that ground He formed human beings. Our very being is, therefore, a product of His creative voice.

Jesus Speaks

Jesus was God as man who came to the earth to redeem the human race and to present the full character of God to us. Part of that character was the power of His voice. When Jesus spoke, things happened. His public ministry began in John 2 when He and His mother attended a wedding. When the wedding feast ran short of wine, Jesus' mother told the servants, "Whatever He says to you, do it" (v. 5). It was Jesus' creative voice (the creative voice of God through Jesus as God and man) that changed the water into wine.

Whenever Jesus spoke, He carried great authority. When He raised Lazarus from the dead, Jesus *spoke* to the grave and to the shroud of death surrounding Lazarus and commanded them to loose Lazarus and let him go. Upon Jesus' command, life once again began to flow through Lazarus (see John 11:43). His voice was so powerful that even death and decay were overcome and destroyed.

The Holy Spirit Speaks *To* and *Through* Us

The Holy Spirit was released to operate in greater measure in the transitional chapter of John 20. Jesus had already been crucified, had died and been raised from the dead, but He had not yet ascended to heaven. Jesus knew that He had to equip His disciples with power to accomplish their role on earth, because He was now leaving to be with the Father. In John 20:22, we read, "He breathed on them, and said to them, 'Receive the Holy Spirit.'"

As the Holy Spirit was released to them, He began to speak to them and *through* them on an ongoing basis. The Holy Spirit spoke many times to them, including when He instructed Peter to go to the house of Cornelius (see Acts 10). But prophecy was birthed in a whole new way as the Holy Spirit began to speak *through* them on a consistent basis. In Acts, the account of Stephen records, "And they were not able to resist the wisdom and the Spirit by which he spoke" (Acts 6:10). Here the Holy Spirit spoke *through* Stephen.

The Word Speaks

In addition to each member of the Trinity having a voice, God has also supplied us with His written Word to speak into our lives. God told Joshua:

> Only be strong and very courageous, that you may observe to do according to all the law which Moses My servant commanded you; do not turn from it to the right hand or to the left, that you may prosper wherever you go. This Book of the Law shall not depart from your mouth, but you shall meditate in it day and night, that you may observe to do according to all that is written in it. For then you will make your way prosperous, and then you will have good success.
>
> Joshua 1:7–8

In the New Testament, we find in John 1:14, "And the Word became flesh and dwelt among us, and we beheld His glory, the glory as of the only begotten of the Father, full of grace and truth." This Scripture describes the unique, loving relationship of the Son with the Father and how we understand that relationship through the Word. By meditating on the Word, we reflect, ponder, contemplate and repeat God's will for our lives. We remove all distractions; it's just God and us interacting. His Word becomes a light to our path. As we order our prayers and communion, His Word orders our feet. His truths and principles guide us. By knowing the Word of God, we know Him and can recognize His voice and how He operates in the earth. The Word is the blueprint of heaven and the blueprint of life. "Today, if you will hear His voice, do not harden your hearts as in the rebellion" (Hebrews 3:15).

God's Voice in Our Lives

Every member of the Trinity operates powerfully through speaking. God's voice commands great authority and continues to be creative today, even in the situations that occur in our lives. Whenever our lives are filled with chaos, as the heavens and earth once were, God's voice can come into our situations and bring order, dividing the light from the darkness.

Furthermore, God speaks to us more often than we may be aware. Consider the fact that throughout the Bible, in both the Old and New Testaments, God spoke to His people frequently. He spoke to the kings, the judges, the prophets, the shepherds and the disciples. He spoke to old and young alike. He spoke to those in powerful positions and to those with no social status. He spoke to the righteous and the sinners. From Genesis to Revelation, God spoke to all kinds of people.

There is absolutely no Scripture in the Bible that even suggests that God stopped speaking when the last word of the Bible was written. Throughout the ages, God has continued to speak to His people. If you have accepted Christ as your Savior and Lord, this includes you! He speaks direction, comfort, insight, correction, exhortation, promises and the like to His people today. "Anyone who is willing to hear should listen to the Spirit and understand what the Spirit is saying" (Revelation 2:7 NLT).

Today, because the blood of Jesus has redeemed us, the Holy Spirit is locking us in to the Father's heart. But here again, the Holy Spirit is not only speaking *to* us, He is also speaking *through* us. When God formed us with His creative voice, He made us in His image, according to His likeness, and He gave us dominion over all the earth (see Genesis 1:26). Because we were created in His image and have been redeemed by Christ, we have the ability, through the power of the Holy Spirit, *to be the voice of God on the earth*. The Holy Spirit is speaking *through* us to one another, and to a lost and dying world. That is what it means to be an ambassador for Christ, and that is what prophecy is all about.

Speaking God's Words

Prophecy in Today's World

And it shall come to pass in the last days, says God, that I will pour out of My Spirit on all flesh; your sons and your daughters shall prophesy, your young men shall see visions, your old men shall dream dreams.

Acts 2:17

Is Prophecy for Today?

Most Christians in the United States grew up in churches that did not embrace the idea of God speaking to us today. We were taught cessationism, which means that the power gifts of healing, tongues, interpretation of tongues, miracles and the like all ceased to function in the first century. One of the gifts that supposedly stopped functioning was prophecy. What that basically means is that God said all He had to say by A.D. 95 and has been silent ever since.

Those who hold to this line of thinking believe that prophecy passed away when the Scriptures were completed. They base their belief on 1 Corinthians 13:8–9, which says that prophecy, tongues and knowledge will pass away. However, in the following chapter of 1 Corinthians, Paul encourages us to desire prophecy (see 14:1). He did not say that these gifts would be replaced by any others or that they would pass away before the Second Coming of Christ.

In fact, in Ephesians 4, Paul writes:

> And He Himself gave some to be apostles, some prophets, some evangelists, and some pastors and teachers, for the equipping of the saints for the work of ministry, for the edifying of the body of Christ, *till we all come to the unity of the faith and of the knowledge of the Son of God, to a perfect man, to the measure of the stature of the fullness of Christ.*
>
> vv. 11–13, emphasis added

In this passage, we see that these gifts have been given *until* we come to unity and reach the stature of the fullness of Christ. At no time in the history of the Church have we achieved these things. Therefore, based on Paul's own words, these gifts, including prophecy, are still in operation today.

How Can We Know the Will of God?

The Bible makes it very clear that God has a purpose and a plan for our lives. Any biblical scholar will agree that this did not end in the first century. But if we have a God who doesn't speak to us, it will be hard to discern what that plan is. Many of us have read books or heard messages on knowing the will of God, which are filled with good principles to follow. Yet, the fact remains that the Bible only gives one real principle to follow in trying to determine God's will for our lives. In the Bible, when someone wanted to know the will of God, they asked Him—and He told them!

God *does* speak to His people. But if we are so entrenched in a mindset that says God does *not* speak today, we might as well write it off as our imagination. The truth is that the prophetic is not an optional extra in the Christian life or in the Church. Amos 3:7 goes so far as to say, "Surely the Lord GOD does nothing, unless He reveals His secret to His servants the prophets."

Throughout the Bible, God communicated with His people. In 1 Corinthians 12, Paul reminded the Gentiles that they once worshiped mute idols. What a foolish thing to worship something that cannot communicate! Our God, however, is not like the mute idols. Our God constantly pours out new revelation and is continually speaking to His people. He is a God who loves us enough to want to enter into communication with us.

> *Our God constantly pours out new revelation and is continually speaking to His people. He is a God who loves us enough to want to enter into communication with us.*

What Is Prophecy?

The definition of *prophecy* is simple. Prophecy is speaking the mind and heart of God as revealed by the Holy Spirit. Prophecy is the outflow of the heart and the very nature of God. Revelation 19:10 says that the testimony of Jesus is the spirit of prophecy. Jesus cares about His Church and therefore, has things He wants to communicate to His Church. Those communications come by way of the Holy Spirit. That is prophecy. It is what Jesus is saying to His Church.

The testimony of Jesus, which is prophecy, is not just a corporate promise. Jesus says that His sheep know His voice (see John 10:4). If you are one of His sheep, you have the capability, the capacity and the privilege of hearing the voice of your Shepherd, which comes through the Holy Spirit.

Understanding the Prophets

Several Hebrew and Greek words can be translated as "prophet" throughout the Bible. To understand how prophecy works today, it is helpful to know the different types of prophets and prophecy taught in God's Word. Let's take a look at some of the various names the Bible uses to describe the prophets and their functions:

1. *Nabi.* This is the general Hebrew word for "prophet." It is linked with the word "reveal," and it means one who proclaims, announces, declares or utters communications, or is a spokesman or a herald. This word also implies a supernatural message that bubbles up or springs forth. *Nabi* is the word used in 1 Samuel 3:20: "And all Israel from Dan to Beersheba knew that Samuel had been established as a prophet of the LORD." It can be either masculine or feminine, and can refer to either a prophet of God or a false prophet who brings forth messages contrary to God's character or will.

In John 7:38, Jesus said, "He that believeth on me, as the scripture hath said, out of his belly shall flow rivers of living water" (KJV). Paraphrased, this would mean, "out of your womb, a river of revelation can flow." Proverbs 29:18 says, "Where there is no vision [no redemptive revelation of God], the people perish; but he who keeps the law [of God, which includes that of man]—blessed (happy, fortunate, and enviable) is he" (AMP). Therefore, it is very important that our river remains flowing or that we are in the presence of others who have a flowing river so that revelation does not stop and we lose sight of our direction.

2. *Roeh*. This Hebrew word means "seer." These prophets see the circumstances and gain revelation on how to move past them. An example is found in 1 Samuel 9:9: "Come, let us go to the seer." Perhaps the most misunderstood of the prophetic types, seers are the ones who have visions or visual impressions. These types of prophets can look at something and receive a supernatural message through that image. God asked many of the prophets in Scripture, "What do you see?" The Lord has often used this method of communicating with me.

3. *Chozeh*. This Hebrew word can be translated as a seer who is akin to a watchman. According to the *New Bible Dictionary*, *chozeh* was most often mentioned in association with service to the reigning king.[1]

4. *Shamar*. This is another Hebrew word translated as "watchman." In *Watchman Prayer*, Dutch Sheet writes, "The three primary Hebrew words in the Old Testament for watchmen are *natsar*, *shamar* and *tsaphah*. These words have both a defensive or protective connotation and an offensive or aggressive application, with the defensive aspect being the most prominent in the Scriptures. . . . Combining the definitions of these three words, which are almost used synonymously, their defensive concept essentially means *to guard or protect through watching over or concealing*. While applied to many subjects—crops, people, cities, etc.—the concept is usually *preservation*."[2]

These prophets watched after God's Word and had tremendous wisdom for walking through life. Here are some examples of watchmen: "Also, I set watchmen over you, saying, 'Listen to the sound of the trumpet!'" (Jeremiah 6:17); "Son of man, I have made you a watchman for the house of Israel; therefore hear a word from My mouth, and give them warning from Me"

(Ezekiel 3:17). A watchman sees what is coming and links it to the promise of God, interceding until it is accomplished. In 1 Kings 18, Elijah released the word of the Lord to Ahab, which was that it would not rain for three and a half years. At the end of that time, Elijah went into intercession until he "saw" the cloud that represented God's change of seasons. Elijah was acting as a watchman who prophesied God's will and then interceded to see it accomplished.

5. *Nataph.* This Hebrew word means to preach, to drop as dew from heaven or to speak by (heavenly) inspiration. This type of prophesying is generally done from a pulpit or in a public place, or is a prophetic word given in the form of an exhortation. The word "*nataph*" is used in Ezekiel 21:2, Amos 7:16 and Micah 2:6. This word deals with oozing or gradually dripping like a trickle from a faucet. In Joel 3:18, the prophet predicted there would come a time when "the mountains shall drip with new wine." This is also predicted in Amos 9:13 concerning the restoration of the Tabernacle of David. As we get closer to David's Tabernacle being restored, we will begin to see the heavens open wider and wider and God's people living in revelation.

Eventually, we will not be hearing "cookie cutter" messages from the pulpit, but when we gather together corporately, we will hear a clear revelatory sound from heaven being brought into the earth realm. This will cause us to develop a walk in the Spirit that the Church has not known in the past few generations.

6. *Prophetes.* This Greek word signifies one who speaks for another, especially one who speaks for God. These are prophets who "forthtell," which means that they speak forth a living message from God for the hour. In this context, the prophet is using interpretive gifts to forthtell the will and counsel of God. This word also signifies one who can "foretell" or give insights

into future events. In this context, the prophet is using predictive gifts. This is the kind of prophet mentioned in Matthew 2:5, who had written that the Savior would come out of the city of Bethlehem.

The Key to Prophecy—the Holy Spirit!

The Holy Spirit is our key to hearing God. Throughout the Bible, in both the Old and New Testaments, whenever the Holy Spirit came, prophecy flowed. Here are just a few examples:

> Then the Spirit of the LORD will come upon you, and you will prophesy.
>
> 1 Samuel 10:6

> The Spirit of God came upon the messengers of Saul, and they also prophesied.
>
> 1 Samuel 19:20

> And it happened, when the Spirit rested upon them, that they prophesied.
>
> Numbers 11:25

> And when Paul had laid hands on them, the Holy Spirit came upon them, and they spoke with tongues and prophesied.
>
> Acts 19:6

The Holy Spirit's ministry through prophecy did not end in the first century! In many accounts of revival throughout the Church's history, when the Holy Spirit came in power, prophecy broke loose. In fact, one of the signs of the Spirit's presence is prophecy. Through the Holy Spirit, God acts, reveals His will, empowers individuals and reveals His personal presence. Prophecy is a key element of this process.

Why Is Prophecy Important?

Prophecy is important because God tells us it is. It's that simple. Here are three biblical reasons to help us understand God's heart toward this important gift.

1. We are to seek to prophesy. "Pursue love, and desire spiritual gifts, but especially that you may prophesy" (1 Corinthians 14:1). In the King James Version, verse 39 says that we are to "covet to prophecy." Did you know that prophecy is the only thing in the entire Bible that we are supposed to covet? And what happens when we covet something? We think about it all the time. We desire it. We think about what we could do to get it. That's how we are supposed to seek prophecy.

Revelation 2 and 3 state the words of Jesus to many different churches. Jesus gives different admonishments, different promises and different messages to each of the seven churches listed in those passages. The one thing that does not differ from church to church, however, is Jesus' command: "He who has an ear, let him hear what the Spirit says" (Revelation 2:7). We are to hear what the Spirit is saying. We are to seek prophecy.

2. God warns us not to reject prophecy. "Do not despise prophecies. Test all things; hold fast what is good" (1 Thessalonians 5:20–21). When Paul wrote to the Thessalonians, they were just starting out and still young in the Lord. When something is in the beginning stages, there is often a lack of maturity and a lack of understanding, which can open the door to flakiness. When flakiness springs up, there is a tendency to say that something (in this case prophecy) is more trouble than it's worth. But Paul said not to shut it down. Don't quench the Spirit. Let it happen, test everything and hold on to what is good.

The Bible also tells us not to despise tongues (see 1 Corinthians 14:39). The relationship between prophecy and tongues is often misunderstood. Simply put, when a tongue is interpreted, it becomes prophecy.

3. Prophecy releases the life and power of God. As we saw in chapter 1, the Word of God has creative power. When Ezekiel saw the dry, dead bones, the Lord told him to prophesy to them:

> So I prophesied as I was commanded; and as I prophesied, there was a noise, and suddenly a rattling; and the bones came together, bone to bone. Indeed, as I looked, the sinews and the flesh came upon them, and the skin covered them over; but there was no breath in them. Also He said to me, "Prophesy to the breath, prophesy, son of man, and say to the breath, 'Thus says the Lord GOD: "Come from the four winds, O breath, and breathe on these slain, that they may live."'" So I prophesied as He commanded me, and breath came into them, and they lived, and stood upon their feet, an exceedingly great army.
>
> Ezekiel 37:7–10

When the prophetic Word of God goes forth, it doesn't just enlighten you or give you information—it releases life and power. Prophecy changes situations!

Understanding the Gift of Prophecy

The Holy Spirit equips us to accomplish God's purposes on earth. This is what 1 Corinthians 12–14 is about. All too often these chapters are separated from one another in the teaching we receive. But the fact is that they were written together and they flow together to help give us an understanding of spiritual gifts and how those gifts are to operate in the Body of Christ. Look at this passage as a whole, in light of the gift of prophecy.

The Body of Christ works in just that way—it is a body, each part having a function and purpose that assists the whole in operating correctly (see 1 Corinthians 12:12–26). There are, however, certain gifts to be desired in the Body, one of which is prophecy (see vv. 28–31). From that point, Paul immediately goes into a discourse on the evidences and importance of love. He goes so far as to say, "And though I have the gift of prophecy . . . but have not love, I am nothing" (1 Corinthians 13:2).

Paul moves on to say, "Pursue love, and desire spiritual gifts, but especially that you may prophesy" (1 Corinthians 14:1). Godly prophecy cannot be separated from love. In fact, true prophecy flows from a heart of love, even if the word is one of correction. The basis for understanding the gift of prophecy is, therefore, understanding issues of love.

Five Dynamic Functions of Prophecy

Having laid out a basic understanding of prophecy, let's now take a look at the various functions of prophecy, based on 1 Corinthians 14. Here is a list of five different purposes for prophecy and what they are meant to accomplish.

1. Comfort. To *comfort* means "to soothe, reassure, bring cheer, bring a feeling of relief from pain or anxiety, lessen one's grief or distress and give strength and hope by means of kindness and thoughtful attention."

> [God is] the Father of mercies and God of all comfort, who comforts us in all our tribulation, that we may be able to comfort those who are in any trouble, with the comfort with which we ourselves are comforted by God. For as the sufferings of Christ abound in us, so our consolation also abounds through Christ.
>
> 2 Corinthians 1:3–5

God longs to comfort His hurting children. He longs to speak to them in a way that produces strength and hope. This is one of the very basic functions of prophecy that all believers should both receive and deliver to others. A prophetic word of comfort, spoken at the right moment, can break the back of discouragement, hopelessness and anguish!

2. Edification. To *edify* means "to instruct, benefit, uplift, enlighten or build up." First Corinthians 14 is filled with correlations between prophecy and edification, the building up of Christian character. A prophetic word, therefore, may contain elements of teaching, or it may bring new revelation to our minds and spirits. The word may bring specific instruction or a sense of strengthening a place in our lives that has been in desolation or ruins. All of these types of edification can be received from a prophetic word. First Corinthians 8:1 says, "love edifies." Because love is the basis for prophecy, all true prophecies, therefore, have an element of edification.

3. Exhortation. To *exhort* is "to urge, advise, caution, admonish, recommend or warn." A prophetic word that exhorts can therefore either build up or tear down. Exhortation may be difficult to receive. It may not be the word of comfort we hoped for.

Even so, words of exhortation are vital in that they bring forth the ultimate purpose of God. Even a difficult word of exhortation that is delivered in the right spirit can leave us feeling a sense of relief and freedom. Prophecy should not leave us with a sense of confusion or condemnation, but rather with a sense of direction and a way of escape from bondage.

4. Redemption. One of the most basic and beautiful functions of prophecy is seeing redemption at work in lives. God's heart, revealed throughout the Bible, is to redeem us from the power of sin and death. Since prophecy is speaking forth the mind of God under the inspiration of the Holy Spirit, the logical conclusion is that prophecy should be redemptive.

Several years ago, a young man named Jon received just such a word from my good friend Cindy Jacobs. Jon was a good husband and father, who was responsible and provided well for his family. He attended church every Sunday and tried his best to follow God. Yet Jon was a closet alcoholic. He was a functional alcoholic, which means that even when he was drunk, few around him knew it. Because he could handle liquor well, he was able to keep secret the fact that he could barely make it through a day without drinking. In addition, he was addicted to chewing tobacco. Yet he knew these things were wrong and had sought God for healing.

During this time in his life, he attended a weekend retreat taught by Cindy. One night, Jon sat quietly in the back while Cindy began giving personal words of prophecy. He felt that God would have nothing to say to him. To his amazement, Cindy pointed to him and called him forward. As he walked toward Cindy, Jon felt sure he was in trouble—as though God was going to publicly rebuke him. But as Cindy began to deliver the prophecy, he could barely believe the words! She told of how the Lord had given Jon the heart of a pastor and how He was going to use Jon in days ahead to see mighty things happen for the Kingdom of God!

Jon was stunned. There was no word of rebuke. His secret life was not uncovered. Cindy had prophesied to him about his destiny rather than his addictions. The words were so powerful that Jon was completely delivered that very night from alcoholism and addiction to tobacco. Today, Jon is a governing elder in his church, a cell group leader, a leader of an effective deliverance ministry and an active member in implementing city-taking strategies in the city in which he lives. Jon will tell you that the turning point in his life was the night when God showed him his redemptive purpose rather than condemning him for his shortcomings. That is redemptive prophecy in action!

5. Direction. As we see throughout the Bible, prophets bring direction to God's people. I have known my coauthor, Rebecca Wagner Sytsema, for many years. In the early nineties, we both served on Cindy Jacobs's staff at Generals of Intercession. During that time, Rebecca went through a two-year period of intensive healing in her life over many issues. I knew that the healing process had brought her to a place where she was ready for marriage. In early 1994, we were preparing to go to a conference in California. One day I looked at her and said, "You need to be at that conference. God has your husband waiting there!"

My words confirmed a feeling that she had been having for about a week, but she had not made her hotel reservations. I immediately picked up the phone and called the hotel where the rest of us were staying. I was told there were no rooms left. I simply told the receptionist that, first, Rebecca's father, Peter Wagner, was in charge of the conference, and, second, her husband would be waiting for her there. The woman on the phone checked again and found one room left. It was at that conference that Rebecca met Jack Sytsema, God's perfect match for her. Two years later, I had the privilege of officiating their wedding.

This is a case in which God gave a clear word of direction and then made a way to see His prophesied will come to pass.

The Process of Prophecy

Besides the functions of prophecy, it is important to understand the process of prophecy—that is, how it works in our lives on an ongoing basis. Here are three important elements of the process of prophecy in our lives.

1. Prophecy is progressive. "For we know in part and we prophesy in part" (1 Corinthians 13:9). No personal or corporate word of prophecy is complete in and of itself. In his excellent book *Developing Your Prophetic Gifting,* Graham Cooke says:

> God only reveals what we need to know in order to do his will in that particular time and place. The things that he does not wish us to know, he keeps secret from the one prophesying.

Elisha said, "The LORD has hidden it from me" (2 Kings 4:27). In other words, "I don't know."[3]

God may give us a little bit here and a little bit there. In retrospect, we may wonder why God didn't tell us this or that, or why He did tell us some seemingly unimportant detail. God always knows what He is doing when He reveals His heart to us through prophecy. That is something that we must simply trust. We must bear in mind, however, that we do not know all that we may encounter or how the prophecies may be fulfilled. Prophecy may point out a path, but we must follow the Lord daily and trust in Him as we move forward.

2. Prophecy evolves. As we follow the Lord in obedience, He will give us our next piece. He will not tell us what He wants us to do three steps down the road. He gives it to us step by step. Such was the case with Abraham. God gave him pieces here and there. Each time Abraham obeyed, God would speak to him again until He brought him into the fullness of what He wanted him to do. God confirmed, expanded, gave new insights and moved Abraham on to his next place.

This is the way of prophecy. Each prophetic word is incomplete, yet as we faithfully obey God, we receive new pieces of the puzzle. Prophecies build on earlier prophecies to bring confirmation and fresh understanding.

3. Prophecy is provisional. The key to the process of prophecy is obedience. God will not usurp our wills and force us to follow His will. Mary, for instance, could have said no to the prophetic pronouncement that she would become pregnant. Instead, she responded by saying, "Behold the maidservant of the Lord! Let it be to me according to your word" (Luke 1:38). Had she said no, the Holy Spirit would never have forced her to become pregnant! Although she did not completely understand how this would happen, nor did she probably grasp the magnitude of that for which she had been chosen, she knew, nevertheless, that through the prophetic word, God had revealed His destiny for her life. Through her choice of obedience, the word came to pass and the human race has been blessed ever since.

The Value of Prophecy

Prophecy is a tremendous gift that God has given to His Church. It is full of tremendous benefits both individually and corporately. Here is a list of some of the values of receiving this gift into our lives and churches.

1. Prophecy brings healing. Proverbs 25:11 says, "A word fitly spoken is like apples of gold in settings of silver." Accepting the comfort and edification available through prophecy can heal a broken heart. As Graham Cooke writes:

> Hurts, wounds, rejections and emotional trauma are a part of our lives, both before and after salvation. The Good News is that we serve a God who is committed to our healing at every level (physical, mental, and emotional). The goal of God is wholeness of life and fullness of the Spirit. Prophecy is a wonderful part of that healing and renewing process. Prophecy brings us, by direct verbal communication, into contact with God's real perspective on our lives and current situations.[4]

2. Prophecy deepens our relationship with God. When we ponder how the God of all creation cares enough to send a personal message from His heart, no matter what the function of the prophecy, it causes us to stop and think about what our individual value to Him must be! Receiving His word brings a new appreciation of God's deep love and care for us. It reminds us of our position with Him. As in any relationship, communication is key to reaching deeper levels. When God communicates with us, and we respond to Him, our relationship becomes deeper and more meaningful.

3. Prophecy provides direction and renewed vision. When we receive God's word, we often gain a clearer understanding of where He is leading us. Knowing where we are headed causes us to focus more intently on the plans and goals God has for us. New excitement and vision are often direct results of the prophetic word that brings us direction.

4. Prophecy brings biblical insight. As we will see in the next chapter, prophecy must line up with the written Word of God. This being the case, the revelation that comes through prophecy often opens up new insights and inspires deeper understanding of mysteries in the Bible. Paul says that we can gain "knowledge in the mystery of Christ, which in other ages was not made known to the sons of men, as it has now been revealed by the Spirit to His holy apostles and prophets" (Ephesians 3:4–5). Prophecy often serves as a catalyst for understanding biblical truths that we have not seen or understood before.

5. Prophecy confirms. God uses a number of ways to communicate with us. It may come through reading Scripture or hearing a message or counseling a friend. God delights in confirming His message to us. He often uses prophecy to say something to us that we may have heard in some other form.

6. Prophecy warns. God does not want us ensnared by our own sin or by schemes of the devil. Prophecy, delivered in love, often warns us that our own sin will result in calamity and despair down the road if we do not repent and turn to God. Prophecy also warns us of traps the enemy has set for us. After the birth of Jesus, the wise men were warned not to return to Herod (see Matthew 2:12). Then Mary and Joseph were prophetically warned to flee to Egypt and stay there until the Lord spoke to them, in order to spare Jesus from Herod's plot to kill Him (see v. 13). Paul was warned by Jesus in Acts 22:18: "Make haste and get out of Jerusalem quickly, for they will not receive your testimony concerning Me." Because God sees the destiny He has for us, He often uses the prophetic word to warn us of the snares the enemy has set up to destroy our destined purposes.

7. Prophecy brings salvation. As I mentioned in chapter 1, when I was eleven years old, I clearly heard the voice of the Lord say, "This is your day." That was the day of my salvation. All salvation is a result of hearing the voice of the Lord on some level. Graham Cooke writes, "I have seen many atheists and agnostics persuaded by God through prophecy. It is the work of the Spirit to convict of sin (John 16:8–11). Prophecy can uncover past history which needs to be amended. It can provide an agenda for repentance, restitution, and revival."[5]

8. Prophecy releases new practices into the Church. There is nothing new under the sun, but there are diverse administrations. The administration of the thirteenth century will not work in the twenty-first century. By "new practices," I do not mean a departure from the Apostles' Creed. But there are new methods of operation and administration God is revealing to the Church that will burst us forth into new practices and new strategies that will work for the twenty-first century. Life means movement, so the minute we stop moving forward, we run the risk of facing death. Therefore, one of Satan's greatest strategies is to get us caught up in yesterday's methods. Prophecy breaks us out of the old methods and into new methods that are relevant for today.

9. Prophecy provides insight into counseling. When I am involved in a counseling situation, I rely on the prophetic voice of God to provide me with the understanding I need to give godly wisdom. The Lord often reveals to me what the problem is and what the root is, and then gives me a prophetic word to unlock the strategy that the person needs to move forward in God's plan for his or her life. It has proven to be a very effective method of counseling.

10. **Prophecy shows us how to pray.** At times our prayer lives can be stalled. Yet when we know the will of God in a certain area, we have great fuel for our prayer lives. God's will is made known to us through the prophetic. That knowledge gives us a basis for ongoing prayer to see His will done on earth as it is in heaven.

11. **Prophecy releases strategy for warfare.** Praying through a prophetic word often entails spiritual warfare. First Timothy 1:18 says, "This charge I commit to you, son Timothy, according to the prophecies previously made concerning you, that by them you may wage the good warfare." Joshua also received prophetic instruction on the warfare he was to wage in order to see the walls of Jericho fall (see Joshua 6:1–5). Many times we see the enemy, but we don't wait for God's strategy to find out how to wage war against him. Prophecy provides us with the strategy we need to war against the enemy who strives to keep God's plans from manifesting in our lives. We often gain wisdom for knowing how to wage war.

12. **Prophecy stirs faith.** Prophecy can change things. When our spirits receive a word from the Lord, we know that there is hope and a way to see that prophetic word fulfilled. Remember how Jon was freed from alcoholism when Cindy gave him a redemptive prophecy? Jon's faith for seeing God deliver him and bring him into his destiny skyrocketed that day! That is the power of prophecy. In the next chapter, we will discuss the relationship between prophecy and faith in greater detail.

Ezekiel and the Four Steps to Fulfillment

We must be in a perpetual process of receiving prophetic revelation. Our lives and destinies are on a continuum. As we move through life, we need to constantly seek new direction and revelation from God. We can't just grab ahold of one level of revelation and think that's going to get us through to the end.

In our book *The Best Is Yet Ahead*, Rebecca and I explain the four levels of prophecy that we see working in the life of Ezekiel in his vision of the Valley of Dry Bones (see Ezekiel 37). If Ezekiel had stopped at any point before God's full purpose had been accomplished, he would have failed. Ezekiel went through a four-step process at each new level of prophecy. These four steps are the same ones we need to follow if we are going to stay on track with prophetic fulfillment in our own lives.

Step One: He received prophetic revelation. Ezekiel sought God and was open to receiving prophetic instruction. In fact, he *expected* God to speak to him. How often in our daily lives do we *expect* to hear God? God is speaking to us today! We need to learn how to listen for God's voice and direction in our lives in order to receive the instructions that will move us forward.

Step Two: He obeyed the voice of the Lord. God told Ezekiel what to say and do in order for the next step to be accomplished. This seems so basic, and yet it is a critical step that we must understand. Ezekiel could not have moved to the complete fulfillment of prophecy without first obeying God at the first, second and third levels. If you are having difficulty gaining new revelation and hearing the voice of the Lord, go back and be sure you have done all that the Lord has required of you thus far. For example, if you have fallen out of relationship with someone and the Lord reveals to you that you need to make it right with that person, you should not go back to the Lord looking for new revelation until you have obeyed Him in the last revelation. If you want to continue to move forward toward prophetic fulfillment, you need to obey the current revelation and make it right with that person.

Step Three: He watched God's purpose being accomplished and assessed the situation. At each level of obedience, Ezekiel saw miracles happen as God's will was accomplished. Even so, he knew that all of God's purposes had not been fulfilled. When he prophesied to the dry bones as the Lord commanded him to do, he saw the bones come together. This in itself must have been a great and miraculous sight. But when he looked closer, he saw that even with this great miracle, there was no breath in the bones. When he again obeyed the Lord and prophesied, he saw breath come into the bones. A great army of living, breathing beings replaced a dead pile of dry, useless bones. And yet there was still hopelessness and infirmity. It was not until Ezekiel saw the Lord break infirmity and death off of the great army and bring them into the land He had promised them that the process of prophetic fulfillment was complete. Even though we may see great miracles along the way, we need to be sensitive to the Holy Spirit's leading as to whether or not His will has been fully accomplished.

Step Four: He listened for his next instruction. Miracle after miracle did not stop Ezekiel from seeking God for the next step. He did not bask in the awesome works of God in a way that stopped him from looking forward. Of course, we need to stop and thank God for His great power and allow ourselves to be drawn into worship, but we can't let the glory of something that already has occurred keep us from moving toward a greater level of glory.

Receiving the Word
of the Lord

*Testing and Responding
to a Prophetic Word*

We can receive a prophetic word from the Lord in many different ways: We may have an impression in our spirit; the Lord may illuminate a passage of Scripture that has particular significance in our lives; or we may have a vivid, prophetic dream. Prophecy can also come when someone communicates wisdom and counsel that gives others the direction they are looking for in their lives. Someone may even say, "I believe the Spirit of God is saying this to you." Prophecy can come from God or from angelic beings visiting you and giving you supernatural revelation. These are all sound, biblical methods that God uses at different times to speak to us.

Prophecy Has Boundaries

We must be aware of several things as we begin to move into receiving prophetic words. We must understand that prophecy has boundaries that God has established for our own protection. For instance, in a corporate setting, Paul gives the following guideline: "Let two or three prophets speak, and let the others judge" (1 Corinthians 14:29).

Another boundary is set in 1 Thessalonians 5:19–21, "Do not quench the Spirit. Do not despise prophecies. Test all things; hold fast what is good." The rest of this chapter is devoted to applying tests to prophetic words so that we can hold fast to what is good.

Determining If the Word Is from God

Not every voice we hear is from the Holy Spirit. Satan has the ability to counterfeit gifts in order to bring confusion and get us off-course. His ability to counterfeit includes the gift of prophecy. Jeremiah records the Lord saying, "I have not sent these prophets, yet they ran. I have not spoken to them, yet they prophesied" (Jeremiah 23:21).

This still happens. There are false prophets. This is why we are admonished to test all things and hold on to what is good. Here are some unclean sources of prophetic words that we need to be aware of.

1. The occult. "You are wearied in the multitude of your counsels; let now the astrologers, the stargazers, and the monthly prognosticators stand up and save you from what shall come upon you" (Isaiah 47:13). Occultic sources of prophecy include psychics, tarot cards, Ouija boards, astrology and horoscopes, clairvoyants, mediums, ESP, witchcraft, divination and so forth. These sources of prophetic utterance must be avoided completely!

Saul, for example, gained revelation by visiting a witch. However, because it was an illegitimate source of revelation—not from God—it ultimately resulted in Saul's death.

2. Delusions. "How long will this be in the heart of the prophets who prophesy lies? Indeed they are prophets of the deceit of their own heart" (Jeremiah 23:26). Not everyone that gives you a false prophecy is malicious; they are just confused. Sometimes they are walking in their own delusion, thinking they are hearing God when they are not.

3. Unrestrained desires. Desires are a natural function of the human emotion. Desires are linked with our wishes, aspirations, urges and expectations. Gone unchecked, desires can cause us to rebel against the will of God in our lives. Have you ever heard anyone use the expression "yearning desire"? Many times we can so yearn to have something that we listen for any voice that will align with our desires. False prophecy can, therefore, come through a desire so unrestrained that we can no longer discern the voice of the Lord over the voice of the enemy or our own flesh. Prophecy can come out of the longings of someone's heart, rather than from a pure word from the Lord.

4. Manipulation and control. "Likewise, son of man, set your face against the daughters of your people, who prophesy out of their own heart; prophesy against them" (Ezekiel 13:17). Prophecy has been used to try to manipulate people into taking actions that they might not take otherwise. For instance, someone might want a certain person to marry another person. It seems like a good thing—so good, in fact, that God must want it, too—so they go up to one or the other and say, "The Lord says you are to marry _____." The true origin behind the word was not God, but a manipulative and controlling spirit. We will discuss this further later in the chapter.

5. Immaturity. There are true prophets who have not yet matured in their gifting and may deliver a word from the Lord mixed with their own emotions. Therefore, the word is impure. This is where some sifting needs to take place and where we need to "hold fast what is good."

6. **False dreams.** "Behold, I am against those who prophesy false dreams" (Jeremiah 23:32). The enemy is able to counterfeit prophetic dreams, just as he is able to counterfeit prophetic words. We must realize that when we are asleep, we are not fully active in our spirit. Many times the enemy will use this time to speak false words to us.

7. **Demons.** "And I have seen folly in the prophets of Samaria: they prophesied by Baal and caused My people Israel to err" (Jeremiah 23:13). Just as the Lord can send angels to prophesy, the enemy can send one of his hosts (Baal was sent in the biblical example given) to deliver a demonic prophecy.

Judging Prophecy

There are many origins for what may seem like prophecy from God. How do we know if what is being said is from God? How do we test prophecy? The following list has been compiled partly from Graham Cooke's *Developing Your Prophetic Gifting* and partly from my own experience in judging prophecy:

1. **Does the word you have received edify, exhort and comfort you?** Does it accomplish the basic functions we outlined in the last chapter? First Corinthians 14:3 says that the real purpose of prophecy is to edify, exhort and comfort. If the word leaves you with a sense of uneasiness instead of edification, or if you feel that something is just not right, you should not receive the word without further testing.

2. **What is the spirit behind the prophecy?** Someone might begin to speak a word to you, but the spirit behind the word does not seem right. It may have a spirit of condemnation on it. Even though it could be totally true, if you feel weighted down and

condemned, you may need to judge it further. Remember, the spirit in which all prophecy should be given is love. Therefore, even a word of exhortation or correction should leave you with a freedom to rebuild.

3. Does it conform to Scripture? God is not going to say one thing in the Bible and then tell you the opposite in a prophetic word. The prophetic word of the Lord will *always* line up with the inspired, written Word of God, which has been given to us as a guide and an example. Remember, the Bible has no bounds or time frame; therefore, you will find that the principles and the illumination of the Word of God are just as important for us today as they were when it was written. In other words, your example or scriptural principle may be found in the Old Testament as often as in the New Testament. But if someone gives you a word and you find no scriptural principle, basis or example for it in the Bible, you should not fully embrace the word.

4. Does it display the character of Christ? In *The Voice of God*, Cindy Jacobs says, "Sometimes wolves in sheep's clothing manipulate Scripture for their own purposes. Just because someone is quoting chapter and verse to you doesn't make a prophecy accurate. Even if Scripture is being used, another area to check is to make sure Christ's character shines through the prophetic word."[1] This, again, leads to love. In addition to love, prophetic words should exalt Jesus rather than a person or ministry. They should lead us to His feet rather than to an organization.

5. Is it manipulative or controlling? Even though some words are filled with truth, they can be used by the one giving the word to manipulate or control others. Control and manipulation are used to wield power, abuse, dominate or rule over others. Such a word has no love, much less any of the other fruit of the Spirit, and should be discarded.

6. Does it usurp your will? Does the word say you *must* do this or that? Does it overpower you in such a way that you are not able to exercise your own free will to choose what you will do? If so, that should be a red flag. God gives us all freedom—even the freedom to sin. All prophetic words should leave you the choice to either accept them or reject them.

7. Does it pull rank? In other words, does the word begin to move you out of the authority structure in which God has placed you? Does it breed rebellion against authority or produce suspicion or insubordination? Does it pull you out of the place God has you spiritually? God gave each of His children an authority structure in which to operate. If the word suggests that you supersede biblical authority, reject it!

8. Does it confirm what God is saying to you? God is always willing to confirm His word to you. When God gives a word, He will usually give it over and over again in many forms. Prophetic words often confirm what God has already spoken to you and fit in with what He is doing in your life.

9. Does it allow outside perspective? If someone gives you a word and says that you are not supposed to communicate it with anyone else, be careful. This is a violation of Scripture. First Thessalonians 5:21 tells us that any word of God is to be evaluated. Godly counsel is always in order when you receive a word, particularly when it tells you to do something drastic, like quit your job and move to another city. Proverbs 11:14 tells us there is wisdom in a multitude of counselors, which includes judging the prophetic. In fact, a good test of any prophecy is to take it to a mature spiritual friend or authority figure in your life and ask him or her to help you judge the word.

10. Does it give a dire warning? Warnings are fine, but see what kind of a warning it is. Is the warning so dire that you have no way out, producing hopelessness in you? Or does the warning show you your way of escape? Is there redemption? Cindy Jacobs tells the story of one such warning that I prophesied over Houston, Texas, on September 21, 1994:

> *I would say, the next 24 days are critical.* Though the enemy has stood against you as a city, I have brought you to a crossroads and you are about to make a transition and crossover. My eyes are upon this city and the remnant of this city, and I will overcome the structures that are set against My Spirit in this city. Revelation that has been withheld is going to begin to come down to people like rain. *Look to the river of the east.* As that river rises so will My people.
>
> Watchman, what do you see? He replied, "*I see a fire. It is a literal fire. Fire is on the river.*" Then the Lord said, "My fire will begin to come to this city."
>
> "I would call you to the night watch. Gather together in the night watch. Sing in the night in the hard areas of the city and evil will be uncovered and deliverance will come. If you will enter into the night watch, you will overthrow the impending destruction and doom that is set for the area."
>
> One of the prayer leaders, Deborah DeGar, took the prophetic word from church to church, leading a prayer watch from 3:00 to 6:00 a.m. *At the end of 24 days, it began to rain in Houston.* There had never been a flood exactly like it in the history of the city. Houston was brought before the eyes of the nation. The San Jacinto River (*the river to the east*) began to rise and flood the entire territory. Gas lines erupted underneath the river and the flooded river *literally had a fire that burned in its midst.* In the middle of the chaos, the Church came together in great unity.
>
> In the case of this prophetic warning, the flooding was not averted, but it did not do the damage it could have done.[2]

11. How do you feel about the word in your spirit? God has given each of us discernment in our spirits. If we receive a prophetic word and it just doesn't seem right to us for whatever reason, we have cause to check it out further before we embrace it as a word from the Lord.

12. Is it confirmed by the Church? If a word is given in a corporate setting, there should be instant feedback from the people and the leaders. There should be a corporate "amen" that comes forth. Rebecca Sytsema, my coauthor, was once in a meeting in the Anaheim Vineyard when a man stood up during worship to give a prophetic word. He said that the Lord was longing to fulfill the desire of His children's hearts. He said that God was, in fact, a God who longed to bring even what seemed like fairy tales to pass. He finished his word and sat down. When worship concluded, John Wimber came to the microphone. After a moment of silence, he simply stated, "Our God is *not* a fairy-tale God!" A loud round of applause went up from the crowd, many of whom had discerned that something had not been right with the word. If a word is given in a corporate setting, what is the reaction of the leaders and the congregation?

13. Does it come to pass? "When a prophet speaks in the name of the LORD, if the thing does not happen or come to pass, that is the thing which the LORD has not spoken; the prophet has spoken it presumptuously" (Deuteronomy 18:22). Here is, of course, one of the most basic tests of a prophetic word. Remember, prophecy may be conditional, based upon something we must do. If you read through the list of responses in the next chapter and are satisfied that you have done all that God has required of you concerning the word, but it is still not fulfilled, it may not have been a word from the Lord at all.

14. Does it produce fruit? A true word from the Lord will bear good fruit that you will be able to discern. In his book *Prophecy*, Bruce Yocum writes:

> If we pay attention to the effect that prophetic utterances have, we can judge their worth. A word from the Lord will produce

life, peace, hope, love, and all the other fruit of the Holy Spirit. A word which is not from the Lord will either produce the fruit of evil—strife, anger, jealousy, lust, indifference—or it will have no effect at all.[3]

What kind of fruit has been produced in your life by the prophetic word? This will be a telling factor in whether or not you accept it as a word from the Lord.

Responding to Prophecy

Once we have tested a prophetic word and have come to the conclusion that God has spoken into our lives, we must then understand how to respond to what we have been told. Here is a helpful checklist of proper actions to take.

1. Keep a journal. There is tremendous importance in writing down, tape-recording or keeping some kind of record of prophetic words. We can't rely purely on our memories. Having a record of prophecy helps us remember the whole word, keeps us from adding thoughts to the word and builds our faith when we go back and read the word. We can also see how the word we received fits in with what God has said to us in the past.

There are times, however, when we do not clearly understand all that God is trying to say to us at the time the word is given. Having a record of the word helps us go back and gain fresh understanding at a later time. For example, in June of 1998, I was given a birthday party at the home of C. Peter Wagner. Cindy Jacobs had come to help celebrate. During the party, Cindy began to feel a spirit of prophecy come upon her. Peter, who keeps a full prophetic journal, grabbed a tape recorder. Cindy gave me a beautiful word for the new year I was entering into in my own life. Then she turned to Peter and began to prophesy that God was calling him to raise up a seminary that would gather leaders from around the world. She went on to give several specific details.

At the time, such a thought had never entered Peter's mind. He had no frame of reference for such a concept. Nonetheless, Cindy's word was transcribed and entered on page 67 of the Wagner Prophetic Journal. A few months later, Peter met with several apostles from various streams of Christianity. During that meeting, the Lord spoke to Peter about a whole new concept for training leaders from around the world. It became clear that he was to retire from his position as a professor at Fuller Theological Seminary, where he had taught for thirty years, and begin his own seminary-type school. As he obeyed the Lord, God began pouring new revelation out as to how the school would operate. Later that year, he officially formed Wagner Leadership Institute, and the first student was enrolled that December.

Peter was able to go back to page 67 of his journal and revisit exactly what the Lord had spoken to him. In fact, as he began to seek counsel and set up the leadership for the school, he was able to distribute copies of the word Cindy had given him so that those involved would also know the word God had given over the new venture.

2. Do not interpret the word by the desires of your flesh. Many of God's people have fallen into deception by taking a prophetic word and adding their own interpretation to it, then saying that God promised them this or that. Cindy Jacobs offers the following caution:

> I have had many singles come to me saying God has promised them certain mates because they were told so in prophecies. When I asked them what the prophecies said, they came up with something like, "God said He would give me the desires of my heart and so-and-so is the desire of my heart." [Such an interpretation] may be the desire of their flesh but God may not have anything to do with it at all.[4]

Be very careful not to take a word and run in a direction God has not ordained.

3. Embrace the word. To *embrace* means "to grab hold of something." When we embrace or grab hold of a word, it activates faith to see the word fulfilled. Remember, "faith comes by hearing, and hearing by the word of God" (Romans 10:17). When we embrace a true prophetic word, it brings faith that God has a destiny for us. We must allow ourselves to embrace our prophetic word with the faith that God is well able to do what He said He would do. If God has inspired the word, He will uphold it by the Holy Spirit. Even if we have received a difficult word, if the word is from God, faith will rise within our spirit, because we know that God has a path for us.

When I was eighteen, the Lord spoke to me and said, "I have called you for the healing of the nations." At that time, the only frame of reference I had for a call to the nations was to become a missionary, which was something I did not want to do. Even though I was willing to obey God, I did not embrace His word to me. It was ten years later when God spoke that word to me again. This time I embraced the word fully. He then began to show me that He had not called me to be a missionary, but rather an intercessor, prophet and strategist for the nations He would lay on my heart. He began to open doors for me to travel in and out of nations so that I could bring prophetic words and build up strategic intercession to see His will accomplished. Had I not been willing to embrace this word when He spoke it to me a second time, I would have missed that portion of His destiny for my life.

4. Pray it through. Because prophecy is provisional, once we know what God wants to do in our lives, the best thing to do is to begin to pray along those lines. This will not only help to build our relationship to God and persistence in faith, it will also teach us spiritual warfare. The enemy does not want to see God's will accomplished in our lives; he will do all he can to see that we are not successful in reaching our destinies. That is why we must commit ourselves to praying through the word until we see it come to pass. For instance, I have known many barren couples who have received words about children. Yet they did not conceive immediately. In some cases, it took years. But as they chose to pray through their word with the faith that God is well able to do all that He says, the bondage of barrenness broke off their physical bodies and often their spiritual lives as well.

5. **Obey the word.** As previously mentioned, prophecy is often provisional, which means we must do something to see it come to pass. There are conditions to meet. Here is a good biblical example: "*If* My people who are called by My name will humble themselves, and pray and seek My face, and turn from their wicked ways, *then* I will hear from heaven, and will forgive their sin and heal their land" (2 Chronicles 7:14, emphasis added). Does God want to forgive the sin and heal the land of His people? Of course! But they have to do something in order to see that prophecy occur—namely, humble themselves, pray, seek His face and turn from their wicked ways. Something that has been prophesied to us may never come to pass if we are not faithful to meet the conditions.

In chapter 2, I told the story of how God gave a clear word of direction to Rebecca, instructing her to go to the conference in California in order to meet Jack. Had she not gone to that conference, she could have missed meeting God's chosen mate for her. God surely could have arranged another way for them to meet, but there was a timing issue involved as well. Her obedience to the prophetic word kept her moving forward in God's timing and destiny for her life.

6. **Look for the fulfillment of the word.** Having completed steps one through five, we should look for and expect that the

word will be fulfilled. John 1:14 speaks of the word becoming flesh, which is a good statement for the fulfillment of a prophetic word. God desires that His word be made flesh—that the intangible substance of a prophetic promise becomes a tangible reality in our lives. Many do not see their promise manifested because they do not know how to watch for the fulfillment of their word.

Can We Prophesy?

While it is not within the scope of this book to thoroughly answer this question, the discussion of prophecy would not be complete without a brief look at who can prophesy. While not all of us are called as God's spokespersons on the earth, the fact is that we all prophesy, whether it is through sharing an encouraging word, edifying a friend, giving godly advice or knowingly giving a prophetic word. Romans 12:6 says we prophesy according to our measure of faith. What measure of faith are you operating in? I want to encourage you to ask God right now to increase your faith.

If you are a believer in the Lord Jesus Christ, the Holy Spirit is made resident within you. You can now ask the Spirit of God to begin to speak through you, with the knowledge that He can. You can also give Him liberty to begin to manifest His particular giftings within you, whether they are in prophecy, helping, hospitality, teaching or any of the gifts listed in Romans 12, 1 Corinthians 12 and Ephesians 4. All the gifts are greatly needed in the Body of Christ—including yours!

Warring with a Prophetic Word

This charge I commit to you, son Timothy, according to the prophecies previously made concerning you, that by them you may wage the good warfare.

1 Timothy 1:18

We have talked a great deal about destiny and prophetic fulfillment, but we have not discussed prophecy itself. This chapter is devoted to understanding the role that prophecy plays in our lives, and how to wage warfare with the prophecies we receive.

Understanding Personal Prophecy

The simple definition of *prophecy* is "speaking forth the mind and heart of God under the inspiration of the Holy Spirit." Therefore, to give an accurate word of God we must have both His mind and emotion as we deliver that word. A prophetic declaration communicates God's intent to fulfill His promises to us. Receiving a prophetic word can have a powerful impact on the perception of our prophetic destiny. This word can help shape our vision for the future and bring us into a deeper understanding of God's heart for our lives.

In our book *Receiving the Word of the Lord*, we discuss more fully the value, process and function of prophecy, and offer several ways to test a prophetic word. That book will help anyone needing a basic explanation of personal prophecy. In the context of this book, however, we want to focus on prophecy as it pertains to prophetic fulfillment. To do that, we need to take a closer look at several aspects of how prophecy works in our lives.[1]

Prophecy Is Incomplete

"For we know in part and we prophesy in part" (1 Corinthians 13:9). No personal or corporate word of prophecy is complete in and of itself. In his excellent book *Developing Your Prophetic Gifting*, Graham Cooke says, "God only reveals what we need to know in order to do his will in that particular time and place. The things that he does not wish us to know, he keeps secret from the one prophesying. Elisha said, 'The Lord has hidden it from me!' (2 Kings 4:27). In other words, 'I don't know.'"[2]

Cooke goes on to say, "Oddly enough, a prophecy will give us positive highlights about our future role or tasks, but may say nothing about any pitfalls we may encounter. It may not refer to enemy opposition, people letting us down, or any crushing disappointments that we may experience as we attempt to be faithful to our call."[3]

God may give us a little bit here and a little bit there. In retrospect, we may wonder why God didn't tell us this or that, or why He did tell us some seemingly unimportant detail. God always knows what He is doing when He reveals His heart to us through prophecy. That is something that we must simply trust. We must bear in mind, however, that we do not know all we may encounter, or how the prophecies may be fulfilled. Prophecy may point out a path, but we must follow the Lord daily and trust in Him as we move ahead along that path. Prophetic fulfillment comes in moving down the path that was pointed out through personal prophecy.

Prophecy Evolves

As we follow the Lord in obedience, He will give us our next piece. He will not tell us what He wants us to do three steps down the road. He gives it to us step by step. Such was the case with Abraham. God gave him a piece here and a piece there. Each time Abraham obeyed, God would speak to him again. God would confirm, expand, give new insights and move Abraham on to his next place. One exciting dimension of Abraham's prophetic evolution comes in Genesis 22, when God reveals Himself as Jehovah Jireh to Abraham. This name of God actually means that God will reveal provision that we can't see, so we can advance into our future. Another tremendous concept in this chapter was that God prophesied the next piece of Abraham's destiny into his son Isaac. Therefore, what Abraham could not accomplish or complete was passed on to the next generation.

That is the way of prophecy. Each prophetic word is incomplete, yet as we are faithful to obey God, we receive new pieces of the puzzle. Prophecies will often build on earlier prophecies to bring confirmation and fresh understanding. Cooke writes, "The Lord will never speak the totality of his heart to us in a single prophetic word. Rather he speaks words that will give us a focus for now and the immediate future. As we work within those prophecies and allow our lives to be encouraged and shaped by them, we can see that prophecy builds from one word to another."[4]

Prophecy Is Conditional

The key to the process of prophecy is obedience. God will not usurp our wills and force us to follow His will. Mary, for instance, could have said no to the prophetic pronouncement that she would become pregnant. Instead, she responded by saying, "Behold the maidservant of the Lord! Let it be to me according to your word" (Luke 1:38). Had she said no, the Holy Spirit would never have forced her to become pregnant! Although she did not completely understand how this would happen, nor did she grasp the magnitude of what she had been chosen for, nevertheless, she knew that through the prophetic word, God had revealed His destiny for her life. Through her choice of obedience, the word came to pass and the human race gained access to its full redemptive plan.

The condition of obedience to the Holy Spirit is not a negotiable factor in prophetic fulfillment. In the Old Testament the word "faith" is used only twice. However, we find that the concept of faith is built in to the obedience of God's people based upon the promise that God has spoken to them. As these people obeyed, they became the fathers and mothers of our faith. Therefore, when God's word comes to you, always look for the obedience factor.

Just because we have received a prophetic word does not mean it's a done deal. We are often tempted to believe that the fulfillment of a prophetic word is the next step in our lives, but there may be some things we have to do first in obedience to God. Abraham, for instance, had to be circumcised before he saw prophetic fulfillment. And then there was that big event where he had to put Isaac, his only son, on the altar. "Only son" meant that his entire future was wrapped up in this individual.

However, that was the condition God had placed on him before He could reveal and extend His promise to the next generation.

Let us add one note of clarification: There is some prophecy that is unconditional and that God alone will fulfill. God is sovereign. He can do anything He wishes. But usually in His plan He has made it provisional for us to come into agreement with His sovereign hand. Therefore the words that He chooses to sovereignly accomplish are usually pertaining to the human race as a whole, rather than personal prophecy. This does not remove His sovereign grace to intervene at any time in our life, but it keeps us actively pursuing Him.

Prophecy Has Timing

We must understand the seasons of God and not move out of His timing. Not every prophetic word is given in a *now* time. The prophecy that Daniel uncovered for the children of Israel had to lie dormant for seventy years before its time came!

One of the first prophetic words that ever came over my life was "You will have an anointing to know God's times and seasons. You will move supernaturally in His timing." I had no idea what this word meant. If there has been one anointing God has taught me in my life, it's this one. This anointing has been called by many the Issachar Anointing (see 1 Chronicles 12:32).

Receiving a word about a future ministry might not mean that we run off and start moving in that direction the next day. In misplaced enthusiasm, many people might start doing what they were eventually supposed to do, but because they moved out of God's season, they will never be as effective as if they had waited on the Lord. It is like a baby who is born prematurely. That child may be alive but will have many more weaknesses, complications and developmental obstacles to overcome, and may never reach the potential it would have had if it had been carried to full term. We need to be sensitive to God's development—of training, mentoring and circumstances in our lives that will provide the fertile soil where prophetic fulfillment will blossom to its fullest.

By the same token, we need to know when to move with a prophetic word. When I first met Rebecca Sytsema, she was single. She had promises from the Lord about her husband but had not yet met him. In 1994 several of us were preparing to go to a spiritual warfare conference. Rebecca shared with me she had had a dream that she was going to meet her husband at that conference. I immediately knew that was right. We got on the phone to make her a hotel reservation, but the receptionist told us there was no room available.

Without hesitation I said to the hotel worker, "You must find her a room! Her husband is waiting for her there!" Without any explanation of what I meant by my statement, the people at the hotel were able to find a room. It was at that conference that Rebecca met Jack Sytsema. Two years later I performed their wedding ceremony, and they have since had three children and are on a solid path toward all that God has for them in their lives. But what if she had not gone to the conference? I can't say that she would never have met Jack, but she would have missed a *now* season and would have had to wait longer than God intended to move toward prophetic fulfillment.

This should give great encouragement to those waiting on a similar promise. God has the times and seasons worked out. Do not run ahead of God, but be prepared to move when the time comes!

The Dangers of Presumption

Besides moving out of God's timing, there are other dangers we can encounter with personal prophecy if we move in presumption. In other words, we receive a prophecy and, rather than allowing the Lord to work it out in our lives, we presume we know exactly what the prophecy means and try to make it happen. The word may be accurate, but the interpretation can get us moving in the wrong direction. Jesus overcame the spirit of presumption in the wilderness. Satan would quote Scripture to Him and try and get Him to act on it. But Jesus defied Satan's attempts to get Him moving out of God's timing.

The enemy does not care which end of the continuum he uses to get you into unbelief. He can use doubt and hardness of heart to keep you from moving forward, or he can use presumption to get you to move forward out of season. When we move in presumption, we open up ourselves and our families to needless attacks from the enemy. We need to be careful not to presume when and how God intends to bring prophetic fulfillment. We must remember that we only see a part of the picture. The way to avoid the pitfall of presumption is to obey the Lord in what you know you need to do next. In her book *The Voice of God*, Cindy Jacobs offers the following list of questions to help us stay out of presumption when we are ready to make changes based on a word or prophecy:

- Is this consistent with everything God has been saying about my life?
- How will this affect my current responsibilities? For example, will I be able to take care of my family financially? What kind of stress will this put on my family? Are they willing to sacrifice what will be required if I make these changes in my life?
- Have I reached a maturity level in my life that will enable me to perform with integrity the new tasks and/or changes, or will I flake out because I am not properly prepared?
- Do brothers and sisters in the Lord witness to this word, especially those in authority over me?[5]

Going to War

Having given some basic issues that are important for us to understand when it comes to personal prophecy, let's look at the spiritual warfare often necessary to see prophecy fulfilled. Just as God has a plan for your life, you can be just as sure that Satan also has a plan for your life. Satan considers it his job to thwart every plan and purpose God has for you, for your family and for your territory. That is the very essence of spiritual warfare—whose plan will prevail?

> Timothy, my son, I give you this instruction in keeping with the prophecies once made about you, so that by following them you may fight the good fight, holding on to faith and a good conscience. Some have rejected these and so have shipwrecked their faith.
>
> 1 Timothy 1:18–19 NIV

Do you have a prophetic promise concerning your children, but they are not making wise choices? Do you have prophetic promises concerning ministry, finances, future direction, barrenness breaking off your life or any number of other things? Keeping in mind all we have discussed in this chapter concerning obedience, timing, presumption and prophetic evolution, ask the Lord if the enemy is at work to keep you from prophetic fulfillment. If so, it's time to go to war! As Jim Goll puts it, "Once you have secured an authentic prophetic promise, load it, take aim and shoot! Fight the fight and wage war with the prophetic."[6]

Praying a Prophetic Word

God's word has tremendous power. Remember that it was by His word alone that He created light: "Then God *said*, 'Let there be light'; and there was light" (Genesis 1:3, emphasis added). By His word alone He created day and night, the earth and the heavens, land and sea, vegetation and every living creature. Everything that has been created exists because of the word of God. Furthermore, we see in John 1 that Jesus is the Word of God: "In the beginning was the Word, and the Word was with God, and the Word was God. And the Word became flesh and dwelt among us, and we beheld His glory, the glory as of the only begotten of the Father, full of grace and truth" (John 1:1, 14). God's Word, therefore, not only gives us our being but also provides our redemption and secures our future through Christ.

When God speaks a prophetic promise, there is power within the words. There is power to gain the supply we need. There is power to step into a new level of faith. And there is power to overthrow the enemy. Couple with that the fact that our own words have a certain measure of power in them. Our words have the power to both bless and curse (see James 3:9). Proverbs 18:21 reads that life and death are in the power of the tongue. Our words spoken in prayer can move the very hand of God and can block Satan's destructive maneuvers. Therefore, when we take a prophetic word that God has given us and speak it back to God in prayer, it is a potent combination.

Jim Goll reminds us, "At times we must declare the [prophetic] word to our circumstances and any mountain of opposition standing in the way. We remind ourselves of the promise that lies ahead, and we remind the devil and command any foul spirits—for example, the spirit of discouragement—to back off, declaring what the written and spoken promises of God reveal. Each of us has purposes, promises and a destiny to find, fight for and fulfill. So take your 'Thus saith the Lord' to battle with you and fight."[7]

What Are We Warring Against?

There are five areas we see from the Word of God where we are in conflict:

1. **The devil.** Satan and his demons affect most of us. This includes Christians. He has a hierarchy and a horde underneath him that are confederate to stop the purposes of God.

2. **The flesh.** The flesh tries to hang on for dear life instead of submitting to the power of the cross and being crucified. Galatians 5:24 tells us that we should crucify our flesh each day. The flesh hinders us from obeying God. Without this daily crucifixion, we give the devil the right to tempt and ensnare us.

2. **Enemies.** Many times evil spirits will embed in individuals or groups of individuals collectively. Then they use these individuals to set themselves against God's covenant plan in a person's life.

3. **The world.** The world system is organized and is usually competing contrary to God's will. We are enemies of the world. The god of this world is controlling the world system. Though we are not part of this world's system, we still live in it. The world system has both a religious aspect as well as a governmental aspect that must be understood if we are going to successfully maneuver in the world but never be part of the world.

4. **Death.** Death is our final enemy. Jesus overcame death, and we must war with the strategies of death until we have completed our life cycle on the earth. And through His Spirit we can also overcome.

If we do not war against these things, we will never possess the inheritance God has given us.

A War Strategy

Because of what we are warring against, we must have a war strategy for our life. In addition to the power of praying a prophetic word back to God, the Bible has many other warfare strategies when it comes to prophetic fulfillment. One excellent example of this is in 2 Chronicles 20. In this story a number of Judah's enemies came together to form a confederation against Judah and were planning to invade their God-ordained, God-promised boundaries. In obedience to the Lord, Judah had not previously invaded those who were in the confederation and who were now arising to steal what rightfully belonged to Judah. There was no question that the combined strength of their enemies could easily have overthrown them.

Jehoshaphat, who was a godly king, cried out to the Lord for a strategy for the warfare they faced. As he addressed the people he said, "Believe in the LORD your God, and you shall be established; believe His prophets, and you shall prosper" (2 Chronicles 20:20). He called the nation together and followed these steps:

1. **They fasted** (v. 3). One of the greatest weapons we have in spiritual warfare is fasting. In *Possessing Your Inheritance* we said, "Fasting is a discipline that most religions and cults understand because this sacrifice releases power. For the Christian, fasting is essential. Often you cannot gain the revelation you need for your next step without it. . . . Fasting removes spiritual clutter and positions us to receive from God. By fasting, we make it possible for the Lord to more powerfully reveal Himself to us—not because He speaks more clearly when we fast, but because we can hear Him more clearly."[8]

2. **They inquired of the Lord** (v. 4). This was a strategy David often used when he was about to be overthrown by his

enemies. Each time David inquired of the Lord, he received strategic revelation that led to victory. Like David and like the people of Judah, when we are at war and we inquire of the Lord, we should expect Him to answer in a way that will provide strategy and direction for us.

3. **In faith they declared their God-given boundaries, reminding God of His promises of inheritance to them** (v. 7). As we described above, they prayed the prophecy back to God, and they did so in faith. They let their faith arise. Faith is that pause between knowing what God's plan is and seeing it actually take place.[9] According to Jim Goll, "Take any promises that have been spoken to you by the Holy Spirit and turn them into persistent prayer, reminding God of His word. . . . Use these confirmed, authentic words from heaven to create faith within your heart. Let them pave the way for the entrance of ever-increasing faith in your life."[10]

4. **They acknowledged their own futility and recognized that they needed to keep their eyes on God or be overtaken by the enemy** (v. 12). Even though we may feel powerless and helpless in the face of Satan's onslaughts, we need to remember that our perspective is very different from God's. If we focus purely on our circumstances, Satan can use what we see with our eyes to bring discouragement, bring hopelessness, rob our joy and cause us to be overtaken by fear. But when we keep our eyes on the Lord, we can transcend our circumstances by quieting our hearts and minds and focusing on the Lord and His promises. Psalm 25:15 reads, "My eyes are ever toward the LORD, for He shall pluck my feet out of the net."

5. **They positioned themselves to face the enemy** (v. 17). Positioning is a crucial element of any warfare. If we are not in position when the enemy comes, he can easily overtake us. We must, therefore, be sure that we are in full obedience

to all the Lord has required of us, and that we are walking on the path He has set for us. Then, donning the full armor of God, we will be ready to face the enemy when he attacks. We, therefore, need to ask ourselves, *Are we standing where we need to be? Do we need to change course or direction to get into the right position?*

6. **They sought counsel** (v. 21). It is vitally important for us to be surrounded by those who can give us wise counsel. Satan is such a master of deception that if we are standing alone, we can easily fall into deception. I have often heard Cindy Jacobs say, "If you don't think you can be deceived, then you already are!" If you are not under the spiritual authority of those who are wise in the ways of God and routinely asking for their counsel, ask the Lord to bring you to that place before moving on in warfare.

7. **They worshiped and praised the Lord** (v. 22). There is, perhaps, no stronger weapon of warfare than praise and worship to the Lord. Satan hates our worship to God for many reasons. For one, he is jealous of our worship. He longs to obtain it for himself through whatever means he can. For another, he knows that the weapon of worship is strong and effective. Consider the words of Psalm 149:5–9: "Let the saints be joyful in glory; let them sing aloud on their beds. Let the high praises of God be in their mouth, and a two-edged sword in their hand, to execute vengeance on the nations, and punishments on the peoples; to bind their kings with chains, and their nobles with fetters of iron; to execute on them the written judgment—this honor have all His saints. Praise the LORD!"

Another important reason is explained by Cindy Jacobs, "When we praise God, He inhabits or enters our praises, and His power overwhelms the power of the enemy. He is a mighty

God, and Satan cannot match His strength. Light will dispel the darkness through God's entering into our praise."[11] Through praise, the Lord Himself begins to do warfare on our behalf to silence our enemy, as we shall see.

The Victory

In this story of Jehoshaphat we find the passage, "Stand still and see the salvation of the Lᴏʀᴅ" (2 Chronicles 20:17). As the people of Judah earnestly sought the Lord and followed the strategy that He gave them, the Scripture says that they were to stand still and allow the Lord to battle on their behalf. In the end, it was the Lord who set ambushes against the enemy so that they were utterly destroyed. Verse 24 reads that not one of their enemies escaped!

The Lord will do the same for us. We must seek the Lord, be obedient to His commands and let Him handle the rest for us: "'Not by might nor by power, but by My Spirit,' says the Lᴏʀᴅ of hosts" (Zechariah 4:6). If we are to have prophetic fulfillment in our lives, we have no choice but to believe that God will do what He said he will do!

The Spoils of War

This story does not end with the victory of the people of Judah against their enemies. There is something more that we need to grasp. Their victory was not complete until they gathered the spoils of war. "When Jehoshaphat and his people came to take away their spoil, they found among them an abundance of valuables on the dead bodies, and precious jewelry, which they stripped off for themselves, more than they could carry away; and they were three days gathering the spoil because there was so much" (2 Chronicles 20:25).

Can you imagine so many dead bodies covered in so much wealth that it took the people of Judah a full three days to collect it all—and it was more than they could carry away? God saw to it that not only was their enemy destroyed, but also that the spoils of war were far beyond what they ever expected! God did the same for the children of Israel as they were being set free from their captivity in Egypt. Scripture says the Egyptians loaded them up with articles of gold, silver and clothing after the Lord secured their freedom from slavery. Through the process of obeying God in the warfare, *God gave them much more than was in the original promise.* He not only secured the boundaries He had set for them, but also caused them to gain wealth in the process.

As the Lord brings us into victory, we need to ask Him what spoils of war He has for us to gather. What has the enemy been holding from us that he must now give up as a result of our victory? In some cases it may be literal wealth. In other cases it may be salvation for our loved ones. It could be restoration of destroyed relationships. It could be a physical healing or deliverance from what has been tormenting us. No matter what spoils of war God has for us, we need to understand that the very nature of war is that the one who is defeated must relinquish something to the victor. Be sure that you have gathered all the spoils that the Lord has for you when you come into victory.

In addition to the wealth they gathered, the army of Judah was strengthened for future battles as they were able to gather the swords, shields and other weapons of war from their fallen enemies. This represents a new strength and a new anointing that comes in victory. As we gain each victory in the war over prophetic fulfillment, God releases a new anointing of authority on us that gives us even greater power to overthrow our enemy in the battles that lie ahead.

A Time to War and a Time to Rest

Ecclesiastes 3 reads that to everything there is a season, a time for every purpose under heaven: "a time for war" (v. 8 NIV)! When it is a time for war, we must have a paradigm for war! The Church is being prepared to enter its most dynamic season of warfare, worship and harvest. When it is a time for war— WAR! David's greatest downfall came during his reign, when it was time to go to war and he stayed home. Passivity in a time of war is disastrous.

There are also times of rest. Not every season of our lives is meant to be marked by warfare. There is a time for everything, including rest. In fact, without seasons of rest, we will never be able to quiet our hearts long enough to hear the voice of the Lord, or to gain revelation for how we should move forward. We need to be wise about how the Lord intends to bring prophetic fulfillment into our lives.

Yes, there will be times of war when we need to stand up and fight. However, the enemy will attempt to prolong our seasons of warfare in order to rob us of our strength. God's grace covers our natural lack of strength during seasons of war. But when God is ready to move us on, we are no longer covered by the same measure of grace. We must never get so caught up in our warfare that we take our eyes off of the Lord, and that we do not enter into the rest He has for us so that we can continue moving forward.

Walking in Revelation

> That the God of our Lord Jesus Christ, the Father of glory, may give to you the spirit of wisdom and revelation in the knowledge of Him, the eyes of your understanding being enlightened; that you may know what is the hope of His calling, what are the riches of the glory of His inheritance in the saints.
>
> Ephesians 1:17–18

When God speaks to us, whether by prophecy or any number of other means, His purpose in doing so is to bring a new level of revelation to our lives. Revelation is essential for living a victorious Christian life. We need the Spirit of wisdom and revelation in order to accomplish the hope of God's calling over our lives. We need God not only to reveal what our next step should be, but also the snares the enemy has set for us on the road ahead so that we can walk in wisdom.

Revelation means "to manifest, make clear, show forth, unfold, explain by narration, instruct, admonish, warn or give an answer to a question." When God speaks to us, He brings one or more of these aspects of revelation so that the eyes of our minds may be enlightened to who He is. Throughout the Bible, God actively disclosed Himself to humanity, and He has not wavered in His desire for us to understand Him. He continues to reveal His power, glory, nature, character, will, ways, plans and strategies to His people today.

Revelation from God has three important functions in our lives, as follows:

1. **Revelation causes obscure things to become clear.** Jeremiah 33:3 says, "Call to Me and I will answer you and show you great and mighty things, fenced in and hidden, which you do not know (do not distinguish and recognize, have knowledge of and understand)" (AMP).

2. **Revelation brings hidden things to light.** One important definition of *revelation* is "apocalypse," which means to unveil or reveal something that is hidden so that it may be seen and known for what it is. We need this kind of revelation in our lives to understand how to overcome Satan's attempts to thwart God's plan for our lives.

3. **Revelation shows signs that will point us into our paths of destiny.** We need revelation in order to know God's will for our lives and, as we come into agreement with His will, how to walk it out. Revelation is not a onetime deal. We need fresh revelation on a continual basis in order to keep moving forward in God's plan and timing.

Gaining Revelation

These three functions of revelation help us understand the "why," but an even bigger question is "how." To answer that question, let's look at Ephesians 1:20–23:

Which He worked in Christ when He raised Him from the dead and seated Him at His right hand in the heavenly places, far above all principality and power and might and dominion, and every name that is named, not only in this age but also in that which is to come. And He put all things under His feet, and gave Him to be head over all things to the church, which is His body, the fullness of Him who fills all in all.

This passage tells us that Jesus is able to defeat the enemy's structures in our lives from His position as "head over all things," because all things are under His feet. Because Jesus is Head, we need to think the way He thinks and put on the mind of Christ (see 1 Corinthians 2:16). Our cognitive processes must align with the thoughts of God in order to be successful in the earth realm.

The problem is that our minds are naturally at enmity with God because of our flesh. We must find a way, therefore, to go beyond our brains and move to a place where we have put on the mind of Christ, a place where the Spirit of wisdom and revelation has been activated in our lives. To do this, we need to move into that realm of faith in which God will be able to show us new revelation in a way that we, as individuals, can receive it. The first important step in gaining revelation is to believe that God has revelation for us and that He has a way to communicate it to us. The second step is to be open and aware of what God is saying. The third step is to enter into a new faith realm.

Faith Comes by Hearing, and Hearing by the Word of God!

Faith is the general persuasion of the mind that a certain statement is true. The primary idea behind faith is trust. When we believe that something is true, it is worthy of our trust. Romans

10:16–17 says, "But they have not all obeyed the gospel. For Isaiah says, 'LORD, who has believed our report?' So then faith comes by hearing, and hearing by the word of God."

The Holy Spirit uses the Word of God to awaken a response of faith within us. Our trust in the Word of God is the stable ground on which we stand for salvation. A response of faith produces certain characteristics within us. Here is a list of the characteristics of faith and each one's opposite quality.

Trust versus Mistrust
Belief versus Unbelief
Loyalty versus Betrayal
Fidelity versus Unfaithfulness
Confidence versus Insecurity
Obedience versus Disobedience
Wholeness versus Fragmentation

When I hear a word that I believe is from the Lord or feel that the Spirit of God is quickening His voice within me, I weigh what I hear based on the characteristics of faith. When I hear a voice that represents the opposite of faith to me, I reject that voice. God has given us each a measure of faith. Romans 12:6 says, "Having then gifts differing according to the grace that is given to us, let us use them: if prophecy, *let us prophesy in proportion to our faith*" (emphasis added). Our faith should be ever growing and becoming stronger.

The concept of faith is the keynote, central Christian message. Based upon our faith, we enter into the state of salvation (see Ephesians 2:8–9); our sanctification is linked to faith (see Acts 26:18); our continuing purification is a result of our faith (see Acts 15:9); and we are justified by faith (see Romans 4:5; 5:1). Thank the Lord that we are adopted by Him and through faith gain a supernatural faith structure (see Romans 8:15; Galatians 3:26). Faith is also called a fruit of the spirit. Fruit is something that can be created and seen in a person (see Galatians 5:22–23). Faith is also a supernatural gift that gives us the ability to do great acts for God. Jesus said that through faith we can move mountains (see Matthew 17:20; 1 Corinthians 13:2).

Receiving Revelation

As we mentioned earlier, the primary way God speaks to us on a regular basis is through Scripture. He may use a verse or passage to bring great revelation for a specific situation in our lives. But not everyone who reads the Bible gains revelation. Some read it purely for historical value. Others read it in the same way they would a Chinese proverb—for principles and insight, but nothing more. However, Christians, in whom the Spirit of God is alive and active, can read the same passages and gain incredible, tremendous insight and hear the "now" voice of God for their lives.

Four Greek words describe the functions of the Word of God—how different individuals can read the same passage of Scripture, but each individual receives something different:

1. *Graphe*. This is the written, historical Word of God. Anyone, saved or not, can read and understand the Bible from this perspective. Reading the Bible as *graphe* is like reading a novel. You understand the story and possibly even the historical value, and maybe ponder the characters and settings, but really glean little else.

2. *Logos*. This is seeing the meaning of the principles of the Bible. For instance, it includes understanding the personal value of following the Golden Rule or reaping what has been sown. These are generally good life principles to follow, but can be of value whether saved or unsaved.

3. *Rhema*. This is where the Word of God crosses over into revelation. *Rhema* is when the *graphe* and *logos* are illuminated

to you by the Holy Spirit. *Rhema* brings enlightenment and bears witness in your spirit. No one who is truly saved has been saved without a *rhema* understanding of their need for Christ in their lives.

4. *Zoe.* All Christians have received a *rhema* word from God, or they could not have come into salvation. For some, their revelation from God ends there. However, for those who walk in the Spirit of wisdom and revelation, reading the Word of God becomes a creative, living part of who they are. When the Word of God becomes *zoe*, it dwells within them. The *rhema* becomes sustained, life-giving revelation. God has clear channels to speak revelation to those who read the Bible as *zoe* life.

Having looked at the different functions of the Bible, let's look at one way to move from reading the Bible as *graphe* to gaining *zoe* revelation. Let's take Jeremiah 33:3 as an example:

> Call to Me and I will answer you and show you great and mighty things, fenced in and hidden, which you do not know (do not distinguish and recognize, have knowledge of and understand) (AMP).

Read it out loud. Then write out the Scripture, outlining the main points. For example:

1. Call to Me
2. I will answer you
3. Show you great and mighty things, fenced in and hidden

Then ask God to activate the Spirit of wisdom and revelation in you regarding that passage. Ask Him to show you things that go beyond your brain and things that you do not currently distinguish or recognize. Ask Him to show you things that you have not seen before. Write down any and all impressions you receive as you are meditating on the Scripture. You may want to do this on more than one occasion. As you allow yourself to receive the impressions, trust the impressions enough to write them down, and allow faith, which God is speaking to you, to arise within you. When it becomes alive and you start seeing *rhema* revelation that you have not seen before, ask God how it applies to you and your situation. Ask Him to establish the *rhema* within you, so that it becomes ongoing, sustained *zoe* life.

Of course, we can hear God in many different ways, and God may bring us *zoe* revelation without going through this process. But for those who are not used to receiving revelation from God, this simple formula is one place to start.

Some Ways God Speaks

Hearing the voice of God and receiving revelation is not as difficult as some might think. Many of God's people hear Him, but have not learned how to perceive His voice. As we have said before, to *perceive* means "to take hold of, feel, comprehend, grasp mentally, recognize, observe or discern." Learning to perceive God's voice and act upon it is a key to living a successful Christian life. How does God speak to us? There are several ways. While this list is not exhaustive, it shows some of the ways God speaks to His people today.

We should never underestimate the power of Scripture as an instrument of God to speak to us in a personal way.

1. The Bible. We have said this before, but it bears repeating: The first and foremost way we hear God speak to us is through the Bible—Holy Scripture, which is His written revelation to humanity. When reading the Bible, has a verse ever just seemed to jump off the page? When that happens, it is often God communicating a particular truth to us for our particular situation.

82

We should never underestimate the power of Scripture as an instrument of God to speak to us in a personal way. In fact, the Bible is our litmus test for any other kind of revelation we feel we are receiving. If we think we have heard God, but what we hear contradicts the Bible in any way, we can be sure it's not God's voice we are hearing!

2. God's still, small voice. When God speaks to us in this way, we know something is right. We have a strong feeling to move ahead in one direction, or we find an issue in our heart has been settled and the answer is clear to us. Some may call this intuition or even a sixth sense, but it is often an inaudible voice of God speaking directly into our spirits.

3. Other people. God can and often does speak a very direct prophetic word to us through other people. Some biblical examples include:

- King David expressing, "The Spirit of the LORD spoke through me; his word was on my tongue" (2 Samuel 23:2 NIV).
- Peter saying, "But men spoke from God as they were carried along by the Holy Spirit" (2 Peter 1:21 NIV).

This can happen in the preaching and teaching we receive, in conversations we have with others, in the prophetic word or a word of knowledge or wisdom we receive or through tongues and interpretation. No matter the method, when the Lord uses someone to speak His words to us, they hit us in a deep and profound way—like someone turning on the lights in the midst of darkness.

4. God's creation. "For since the creation of the world God's invisible qualities—his eternal power and divine nature—have been clearly seen, being understood from what has been made, so that people are without excuse" (Romans 1:20 NIV). Have you ever felt the presence of God in a sunset, a flower or even a raging thunderstorm? At times, great beauty in nature or even in a moral truth can be a vehicle for a direct word from God. In the Bible, God used a rainbow as a sign of His covenant with Noah (see Genesis 9:9–17). He used dew on a fleece to help guide Gideon (see Judges 6:36–40). He caused a fig tree that did not bear fruit to wither and die (see Matthew 21:19–21). The righteousness He makes available to you is likened throughout Scripture to white snow (see Isaiah 1:18). If you take the time to stop and look around you, you may be surprised to find that God speaks through His creation.

5. Dreams and visions. "'We both had dreams,' they answered, 'but there is no one to interpret them.' Then Joseph said to them, 'Do not interpretations belong to God? Tell me your dreams'" (Genesis 40:8 NIV). We see many biblical examples of God speaking to His people in dreams and visions. He spoke to Joseph, Solomon, Pharaoh, many prophets and kings and Joseph (Jesus' earthly father) by this means. Joel 2:28 says, "And afterward, I will pour out my Spirit on all people. . . . Your old men will dream dreams, your young men will see visions" (NIV). God still speaks through dreams today. If we awake from a dream that seems unusually vivid and very real, we may want to ask the Lord if He is trying to speak something to us through that dream. We will take a much closer look at this in the next two chapters.

6. Experiences or circumstances. There may be times when God speaks to us through very specific incidents. Sometimes this happens in prayer at home. Sometimes this happens when we respond to an altar call. Often this will occur when people first become saved. It may be a moment when tremendous clarity comes as a result of some incident. When God speaks to us through a specific experience, we will be able to point back to that moment in time as a benchmark for a shifting in our lives. Many times perplexing circumstances arise in our lives.

However, we need to look deep into these circumstances so we can hear clearly God's voice.

7. Angels. Throughout the Bible, God sent angels as His messengers to speak something to His people. This method of communication is still one He chooses to use from time to time, and it's one that you cannot discount. One day God may surprise you!

8. Audible voice. Sometimes God chooses to speak in an audible voice. He did so to young Samuel as well as to many others in the Bible. Genesis tells us that it was by His audible voice that God created all of heaven, earth and every creature that has breath. Can God not use that same voice to speak to His creation?

Barriers to Revelation

Looking at some of the ways God speaks to us poses the question, Why don't we hear Him more often? Of course, God can choose when, where, how and to whom He will speak. But assuming that He attempts to communicate with us, what are some of the issues in our lives that can prevent us from gaining revelation? Here is a list of some barriers many of us have dealt with or are dealing with today.

1. Distractions. Have you ever found it difficult to pray? Or once you set your mind to it, you became bored and distracted? We often miss what God may be trying to say to us simply because we are unable to focus on Him. If we are having a phone conversation with someone while trying to do three other things, chances are we don't absorb all of the conversation. This is one of the reasons why we are exhorted by Scripture to meditate on God and His Word. If we can find a strategy to minimize our distractions, we may be amazed to hear God speaking to us.[1]

2. Disinformation. Often, as Christians, we look to our churches and our colleagues to build our theology rather than base our doctrinal stand on what God's Word says. This is why many have come to believe that God does not speak to His children today—not because of anything the Bible has said, but because of disinformation they have received somewhere along the line. God has given us His Word and His promises, and He expects us to check our decisions and our beliefs with Scripture so that we will not get tripped up with disinformation. We are always correct to ask God to renew our minds so that we conform to Him rather than to the beliefs of the world (see Romans 12:2).[2]

3. Disbelief. Many cannot and will not hear the voice of God in their lives because they simply do not believe. They may have come to salvation and even pray from time to time, but they really expect little or nothing to come of it. If we truly believed that every time we pray, God—who has control of everything in and around us—not only listens to us, but also desires to converse with us, we would pray every chance we got. However, because we often don't see immediate (or what we consider to be adequate) answers to our prayers, we fall into unbelief. We must remember that we serve an all-powerful, all-knowing God whom we can trust to give us the very best in spite of what we ask for or in spite of how we interpret His answer. If we have fallen into unbelief, our first prayer back toward God should be, "I do believe; help me overcome my unbelief!" (Mark 9:24 NIV).[3]

In our book *Possessing Your Inheritance*, Rebecca and I point out the following progression that can lead to missing God's revelation. When God does speak, we must realize that we have an enemy who immediately tries to steal from us what is rightfully ours. Satan will always attempt to thwart God's plans. Such was the case for the Israelites. When they were coming out of their captivity in Babylon, they received a revelation from the Lord (see Jeremiah 29:10). The Israelites knew God's will for them was to return and rebuild the destroyed Temple of the Lord. They had heard clearly from God. But as they began working toward the restoration God had for them, the enemy resisted their efforts. Instead of fighting for what they knew they were to do, the children of Israel gave in. As the people allowed the enemy to take a foothold, three things happened.

1. **They fell into *discouragement*.** They began to ask why God was calling them to rebuild the Temple in the first place.
2. **They fell into *disillusionment*.** Things weren't going well, so they began to wonder if God had really told them to build at all.
3. **They fell into *disinterest*.** As the situation progressed, they decided they would build their own houses and leave His in disrepair. They stopped caring.

This progression of events is often a pattern for what can happen in our own lives if we do not guard what the Lord has told us and seriously pursue His will. It takes an act of our own will to choose God's plan for possessing our inheritance.[4]

Processing Revelation

God had a purpose in having the Israelites rebuild His Temple. It was not because God was being selfish. Rebuilding had a direct effect on restoring to the Israelites what had been lost through their captivity in Babylon. It was important for their future. When God brings revelation into our lives, it is not an end in itself. Instead, it is part of a process intended to move us toward our potential and our destiny. In this book, we have looked at the value of prophecy in our lives. Prophecy, as well as the majority of revelation we receive, moves us through the following process:

1. **God tells us about Himself.** Often, God will use the Bible as His means of communicating with us about who He is. Even when He uses other methods, they will always align with what the Bible says. Therefore, it is imperative that we become as familiar as we can with the Word of God.
2. **God tells us what He has planned.**
3. **God tells us that we are a part of the plan.**

Not everyone is open to receiving what God has to say. This is because whenever revelation comes from God, it directly confronts us. When we are confronted with truth from God, we must deal with it on some level. Revelation from God requires a response. While God is sovereign, we must respond to His sovereignty in order for His will to be done.

God's revelation comes to us not as information for our brains to process, but as a mandate for our faith to arise and as a guide to conduct our lives. Without faith it is impossible to please God. Equally true, however, is that faith without actions is dead. Revelation challenges us on both levels. Once we gain revelation, we are obligated to that revelation. We become accountable for what God has revealed to us. In order to reach our destiny, we must receive revelation from God and then act accordingly. Of course, sometimes the most appropriate reaction is to wait on God with expectancy, but the principle remains the same. It is when we do not act upon the revelation we receive that windows of opportunity can close—sometimes forever. Walking in revelation and reaching our destiny in God can be summed up very simply: In every circumstance in which we find ourselves, we must find God's sovereign plan within that circumstance and be faithful to walk in His will.

Hearing God
through Dreams
and Visions

Then He said, If there is a prophet among you, I, the
LORD, make Myself known to him in a vision; I speak
to him in a dream.

Numbers 12:6

We concluded the last chapter by saying that in every circumstance in which we find ourselves, we must find God's sovereign
plan within that circumstance and be faithful to walk in His
will. One of the primary ways God communicates with His
people is through dreams and visions, yet those dreams and
visions are often misunderstood, dismissed or ignored. Dreams
particularly can seem foolish or strange. But as Ira Milligan
points out:

89

Paul said that God chose the foolish things of the world to confound the wise (see 1 Cor. 1:27). Although many dreams are foolish or senseless to the world, they are precious to those who understand "the hidden wisdom" from above (1 Cor. 2:7).[1]

Fiona Starr and Jonny Zucker point out:

The Old Testament is laden with dream scenes and interpretations. One of the best known is the story of Jacob's son, Joseph. Joseph was said to hold the power of forecasting through his dreams. Joseph's dream analyses were often the cause of much sibling rivalry, not only because of the unique power that Joseph possessed, but also because of the content of the dreams. In many of his dreams Joseph dreamt of himself as the superior brother. The others grew angry with Joseph's seeming arrogance and tried to exile him while convincing Jacob that his favorite son was dead. Joseph's power, however, helped him find his way out of a dangerous situation when he was able to help Pharaoh of Egypt interpret his own dreams.

Jacob's ladder is another well-known biblical dream story. Some say that the dream of the ladder resting on earth but leading up to the heavens is a symbol for higher communication between God and humans on earth.[2]

The Lord uses dreams and visions to guide, warn, direct, help and communicate His heart. God has not stopped communicating to humanity by these means.

In the Bible, there are over fifty references for God sending messages through dreams and visions to both the righteous and the unrighteous. The Lord used dreams and visions to guide, warn, direct, help and communicate His heart. God has not stopped communicating to humanity by these means. In fact, God often uses dreams and visions to reach unsaved individuals with the Gospel, particularly in closed parts of the world. In Global Harvest Ministries, where I serve as vice president, we recently reported one such story:

An Iranian living near Kassel told a Christian worker of a dream he recently had: "I was standing on the roof of my house when a bright light like a spotlight shone on me. This light then moved down to illuminate a stream, which seemed to be made of light. I don't know what it means. I have consulted books and visited dream interpreters, but I can find no answer." "Only God can interpret dreams," the Christian visitor told him, telling him that Jesus is the light of the world. "The light shining on you means that Jesus is calling you, and the stream may be an indication that you should be baptized." The Iranian was convinced and agreed to follow Jesus and be baptized.[3]

We have scores of similar testimonies of dreams and visions being used by God to draw individuals, families and entire communities to Himself. Similarly, the Lord uses this method of revelation in the lives of most, if not all, believers.

What Is a Dream?

A dream is a release of revelation (whether natural or spiritual) that comes at a time when your body is at peace and you are settled. Sometimes this is the only way God can communicate with you, because your soul is quiet enough for the Lord to speak deeply into your spirit. A dream is like a snapshot of something you can relate to in picture form. Ecclesiastes 5:3 speaks of a dream coming when there are many cares. It may be a subconscious response to the circumstances of your life or the Holy Spirit communicating to you. As Jane Hamon states in her book *Dreams and Visions*:

Dreams are formed in the subconscious mind of a man or woman based on images and symbols which are unique to the individual, depending on his or her background, experience and current life circumstances. Dreams can communicate to us truth about ourselves—or others—which our conscious mind may have failed to acknowledge.

Dreams can originate strictly within the natural mind or can be given as messages from God's Spirit and received within the mind of man. . . . If we compare the communication of the Spirit of the Lord through dreams to other methods of divine communication mentioned in Scripture—prophecy, a word of knowledge, etc.—the primary difference is that dreams are given first to our subconscious minds before being perceived by our conscious minds.[4]

In the ancient eastern world, dreams were treated as reality. Dreams were considered to be the world of the divine or the demonic, and they often revealed the future. Dreams could be filled with revelation that would cause the dreamer to make the right decision for his or her future.

Israel was forbidden to use many of the same type of divining practices as Egypt and other neighboring countries and peoples. However, God would visit them in the night to communicate His will and way to them. This continued throughout the Bible. In the first two chapters of the New Testament alone, God gave direction through prophetic dreams five times.

We as Christians can receive revelation from dreams that are inspired by the Holy Spirit as well. For instance, I once had a dream when I was in prayer for a trip to Israel. My good friend and colleague Bobbye Byerly and I were going to be leading prayer for a meeting facilitated by Peter Wagner that would reconcile Arab Christian leaders and Messianic leaders. Quite a bit of warfare surrounded this meeting. I became very troubled while praying and called Bobbye to tell her that we should pray and fast for three days before going. Bobbye was having the same burden and agreed immediately.

On the second day of the fast, I fell asleep and dreamed that Barbara Wentroble, a well-known prophet, asked me, "So, you are going to Israel. There are two ways. Which way are you taking?" I told her the way we were going. In the dream it was as if I showed her a map and we wandered through the Arab desert to get to Israel. She then said, "You may go that way, but if you do, you will experience much warfare. There is a better way for you to take." I said, "Oh, what is that way?" She replied, "Go straight to Israel and meet with the leadership you know. Then, have your meeting with everyone else." I woke up and knew that God had revealed to me the direction Peter Wagner should take as he proceeded in pulling together this meeting. I encouraged him to first have a meeting with the leaders of Israel whom we knew. Then we could have the overall meeting and reconciliation time. This proved to be a direct revelation from God and had a significant impact on the overall outcome of our mission.

What Is a Vision?

The easiest way to describe a vision is to imagine you are having a dream, but you are awake. To those experiencing a vision, it often seems as if they have entered into a different reality, since they are seeing images of items and events with their spiritual eyes that are not physically there. Others in the room may not see what is going on because the person having the vision perceives a spiritual event.

Sometimes differentiating between vision and dream is difficult to determine, if not impossible. For instance, the circumstances in which the revelatory visions came to the seers of the Bible vary. They came in waking hours (see Daniel 10:7; Acts 9:7), by day (see Acts 10:3) and by night (see Genesis 46:2). But the visions had close connections with the dream state (see Numbers 12:6; Job 4:13).

In the Old Testament, the recipients of revelatory visions were the prophets, "writing" (see Isaiah 1; Obadiah 1; Nahum

1) and "non-writing" (see 2 Samuel 7:17; 1 Kings 22:17–19; 2 Chronicles 9:29), the outstanding examples being Ezekiel and Daniel. Some would write their visions. Other prophets would have other individuals record their visions. Habakkuk 2:1–4 (KJV) says, "I will stand upon my watch, and set me upon the tower, and will watch to see what He will say unto me, and what I shall answer when I am reproved. And the LORD answered me, and said, Write the vision, and make it plain upon tables, that he may run that readeth it. For the vision is yet for an appointed time, but at the end it shall speak, and not lie: though it tarry, wait for it; because it will surely come, it will not tarry. . . . The just shall live by his faith." Many times, prophets need to write their visions so that anyone going by can understand what God is saying and the direction He is giving. In the New Testament, Luke manifests the greatest interest in visions, reporting the visions of Zechariah (see Luke 1:22), Ananias (see Acts 9:10), Cornelius (see 10:3), Peter (see 10:10) and Paul (see 18:9). We find Paul treating visions with much reserve (see 2 Corinthians 12:1). The book of Revelation is the ultimate vision.

In *The Future War of the Church*, Rebecca and I share an in-depth vision that the Lord gave me on December 31, 1985. Even though I dream often, I have only had five visions that were significant enough for me to record. This detailed vision gave direction for the changes in the Church of the future. It also warned of militant Islam and lawless acts coming against the Church. You can read the details of this in chapter 1 of *The Future War of the Church*.[5]

My pastor is Robert Heidler. His wife, Linda, is a wonderful prophetic prayer leader and minister. She had the following vision:

In March of 1997, we were in a Sunday morning church service. I began to have a vision. In this vision, I knew that the Lord was coming to visit my house. I had cleaned everything cleaner than ever before. My carpets were cleaned, my curtains were washed and ironed, and everything was dusted and polished. I had fresh flowers on the table. I could not think of anything else to do to make my house ready for the Lord to come. It was the best it could possibly be.

All at once, the Lord was standing in my house. He had not come to the door; He just appeared. I did not know what to say or to do. He looked around and then pointed to one wall of my living room and said, "That whole wall has to go." I was in shock. That wall was the one between my living room and garage. My washer and dryer were on the other side of that wall. I wanted to protest, but as the Lord spoke the words, the wall shattered. Sheetrock, two-by-fours and wires protruded from the wall, and the room was covered in plaster dust.

Before I could recover from that, the Lord pointed to a room off the back of my house. In reality, I did not have a room like this, only in the vision. This room had all kinds of awards, pictures, trophies, medals and so on. It also had family heirlooms. The Lord pointed to that room and said, "That whole room has to go." Immediately, I thought of getting all my treasures out, but the Lord said, "And don't try to get anything out either." As I looked, a huge crane appeared in my backyard and a wrecking ball swung across and demolished the room.

My house was a wreck, I was in shock and I didn't know what to do. This was not what I had anticipated, but it was very clear what the Lord knew needed to happen in my house.

I love this vision. It speaks for itself. The Lord is saying, "Even though you've got everything in order, get ready for the changes I am bringing!"

What Is a Night Vision?

The Scriptures refer to night visions several times. A night vision occurs when we are not sure if we are asleep or awake, and it tends to be right to the point.

In Acts 16:9–10 we read:

And a vision appeared to Paul in the night. A man of Macedonia stood and pleaded with him, saying, "Come over to Macedonia and help us." Now after he had seen the vision, immediately we sought to go to Macedonia, concluding that the Lord had called us to preach the gospel to them.

Ira Milligan offers this insight:

There is a difference between a dream and a night vision. A night vision requires little or no interpretation. In addition to the actual vision seen, a night vision usually has a voice speaking that gives the primary meaning of the vision. In contrast, a dream seldom lends itself to self-interpretation.[6]

Discernment Is Key!

Whether we are talking about dreams, visions or night visions, we need to recognize that not all revelation communicated through these means is necessarily inspired by God. There are three different categories of dreams and visions, each of which can be traced to different sources:

1. Spiritual dreams and visions, which are inspired by God's Spirit
2. Natural, or soulful dreams and visions, which are produced by the natural processes of a person's mind, will and emotions
3. False or occultic dreams and visions[7]

It is important for us to exercise discernment in determining the source of dreams and visions. If not, we may base our life decisions on soulful desires, or the enemy may gain a ready inroad to thwart us in our destiny. Adapted from Jane Hamon's book *Dreams and Visions*, the following is a list of questions to ask ourselves as we determine what is behind a dream or vision:

1. **Is the message of the dream or vision consistent with the teachings, character and nature of Jesus?** All revelation from spiritual dreams and visions will lead us into a closer, more committed relationship with God.

2. **Does the message of the dream or vision lead to righteousness?** If the message of the dream is more self-serving or speaks to soulful desires, it may not be a spiritual dream.

3. **Is the message of the dream or vision consistent with doctrine, teaching and principles from the Word of God?** All spiritual dreams or visions will support and emphasize biblical truths.

4. **Do you feel a stirring of your spirit or emotions upon awakening?** In the book of Daniel, we see that the king had a greatly disturbing dream. When you feel impacted by a dream, it could be an indication that God is speaking to you.

5. **Does the dream or vision cause you to search your soul? Have pressing questions been answered within the context of the dream?**

6. **Is the dream recurring or similar to others you've had?** While this alone is not an indicator of a spiritual dream, in the context of the other questions posed here, it could offer a clue that the Lord is trying to get your attention repeatedly.[8]

Always Talk to God about Your Dreams

If, after reading these questions and applying your God-given discernment, you determine that your dream is more of a natural or soulful origin, or more demonic in nature, do not be discouraged.

No matter what the origin of the dream, you can and should always talk to the Lord about what you have dreamed. You should not ignore what a dream may reveal about your emotions, and you can always ask God to clarify puzzling or disturbing dreams so He can bring His comfort and healing to your mind, will and emotions. If you discern that a dream is demonic in nature, it might be an indication of how the enemy is working to thwart your destiny, or it could be a call to a new level of spiritual warfare. All dreams have some level of significance in your life, and it is important to invite the Lord into the process of determining what each dream's level of significance may be.

Lean Not on Your Own Understanding

Many of us have been in very difficult places. There was a particular time in my wife, Pam's, and my own life where we had almost insurmountable issues surrounding us. One night, Pam had a dream. In the dream, she was on a path that led through a wooded area, yet she could still see the sun. As long as she kept her eyes on the sun, she continued moving forward. Even though the light got brighter and brighter, when she got close to the end of the path, a huge boulder extended itself out from the forest, completely blocking the path. During the dream, she began to think, *How can I get past this? I must get out to the other side.* She then heard a voice say, "Don't try and go around this blockade. Don't try and go over it. Don't try and go through it. Speak to it and tell it to move." When she got up that morning, she said, "We are going to speak to the issues that are coming against us." We began to speak to each one, making prophetic declaration to it, and we watched changes begin to take place.

Proverbs 3:5–6 says, "Trust in the LORD with all your heart, and lean not on your own understanding; in all your ways acknowledge Him, and He shall direct your paths." Seek God.

Listen carefully. Let Him speak to you. Lean not on your own understanding, but let Him give you the way through your circumstance.

Now let's take an in-depth look at interpreting dreams and visions.

Interpreting Dreams and Visions

> For God may speak in one way, or in another, yet man does not perceive it. In a dream, in a vision of the night, when deep sleep falls upon men, while slumbering on their beds, then He opens the ears of men, and seals their instruction.
>
> Job 33:14–16

Whether or not we are aware of it, God often reveals instructions to us through dreams. We may not even remember the dream, but often we will awaken with a new sense of clarity because God has spoken to us in the night. Because God often seals our instructions through dreams, we need to know how to properly interpret them.

In the Bible, prophecy and dreams were to be tested in the same way. And according to Numbers 12:6, we find that prophecy and dreams were treated equally. Saul complained that God would not speak to him or answer him "by dreams or by Urim or by the prophets" (1 Samuel 28:6). By this we can infer that these were normal ways that people heard from God. We find three types of dreams in the Bible:

1. **A simple message dream.** In Matthew 1–2, Joseph understood the dreams concerning Mary and Herod. There was no real need for interpretation. These dreams were direct, to the point and self-interpreted.

2. **The simple symbolic dream.** Dreams can be filled with symbols. Oftentimes the symbolism is clear enough that the dreamer and others can understand it without any complicated interpretation. For instance, when Joseph had his dream in Genesis 37, he fully understood it, as did his brothers, to the point that they wanted to kill him, even though it had symbols of the sun, moon and stars.

   It is our job as ambassadors for Christ to be carriers and interpreters of God's revelation in this age.

3. **The complex symbolic dream.** This type of dream needs interpretative skill from someone who has unusual ability in the gift of interpretation or from someone who knows how to seek God to find revelation. We find this type of dream in the life of Joseph, when he interprets Pharaoh's dream. In Daniel 2 and 4, we find good examples of this type of dream. In Daniel 8, we find a dream for which Daniel actually sought divine interpretation.

Understanding symbols is important not only to interpret our own dreams, but also to give some direction to those who come to us. As we mentioned in the last chapter, God speaks to unbelievers through dreams. I would prophetically say that this is only going to increase in the days ahead, and God will need believers who know how to discern and interpret in order to lead many to Christ. It is our job as ambassadors for Christ to be carriers and interpreters of God's revelation in this age.

Daniel's Model of Interpretation

As we think about the process of dream and vision interpretation, the book of Daniel provides us with a good pattern to follow. The following is the story of King Nebuchadnezzar's dreams and the process through which Daniel interpreted them:

1. **Daniel determined the source of the dreams and knew they were a message from God.** This is the first step, which we discussed in chapter 5.

2. **Daniel asked for time to interpret the dream (see 2:16).** First Corinthians 2:6 says, "We do, however, speak a message of wisdom among the mature, but not the wisdom of this age or of the rulers of this age, who are coming to nothing" (NIV). In other words, we have wisdom that no one else has access to—wisdom that comes from the Lord. We often need time to seek the Lord for His interpretation, as well as wisdom from those whom God has placed in our lives.

3. **Daniel gathered intercession by urging his friends to seek the Lord (see 2:18).** At times, we need to soak the dream or vision in prayer and ask those around us to intercede on our behalf until clear interpretation of the vision comes from God.

4. **Daniel gained revelation from the Lord (see 2:19).** As we pursue an interpretation, we can ask certain questions that will help us gain revelation over the dream or vision. These include:

- To whom does the dream refer?
- What is it really about?
- What is the setting(s)?
- What is the symbolism in the dream? (There will be more about this later in the chapter.)

- What are the current circumstances and history of the one who received the dream or vision?
- What is God's timing in fulfilling the dream or vision? (Ask this question once there is a handle on the interpretation.)
- Based on this dream, what responsibility does the one who received the dream or vision have?

5. Daniel worshiped God (see 2:20–23). It is so important to give God glory and to worship Him for both the dream or vision and the interpretation. When we miss this, we miss the next step of revelation in our lives.

6. Daniel explained the dream (see 2:36–45). When we interpret a dream for someone else, we need to be sensitive as to how the Lord would have us explain the interpretation.

Modern-Day Dreams and Interpretations

When I was coming into the things of the Lord and the Spirit, the Lord placed a wonderful mentor in my life. Lacelia Henderson was a teacher in the public school system and a wonderful Bible teacher as well. Most importantly, she understood the spiritual realm in which I was just learning to maneuver. I want to encourage each of you reading this book to find someone who can help you as you move into receiving supernatural revelation. Lacelia had a dream that really has stuck with me through the years.

> In the dream, I had gone with friends (Charles and Charlene) to a cabin they had in the woods. We were dressed for bed when someone knocked at the door. Charlene started to answer the door, and I waited in the bedroom. I said I would hide back there while she answered the door. If it was a friend, I would come out, and if not, I would jump out the window and run for help. When she opened the door, these men came in who were dressed in army fatigues. They came in like the Gestapo

and took the place by storm (captured it). In the meantime, I had jumped out of the window in my nightgown. When they saw the open window, they knew that I had escaped. Some of them ran outside and got in a vehicle (like a Jeep) to look for me. It was very, very dark; I was alone and vulnerable (in my nightgown). Their eyes pierced the night as they scanned to and fro trying to spot me. When they were not looking my way, I ran from tree to tree. It was all very intense, and I had very little time to get behind the next tree before they looked back my way. Finally, I came to a clearing and saw some houses. I knew I had to choose the house to run to very carefully. It had to be someone who knew me and trusted me. I knew that once I stepped out into the clearing I would be spotted. I also knew that when I ran to a house to use the telephone to call for help I would not have time to explain the situation to get permission to use the telephone. If I took time to explain I would be caught and stopped by the enemy. Once I got to the house, I had to be able to run straight to the phone to make the call for help.

When I asked Lacelia to write this dream down, she commented to me, "After all these years (it's been fifteen years so far), I can still remember every detail of this dream vividly." This dream was a warning! Not only did it warn of the need to know our relationships in the future, it explained that Christians would go into a new dimension of persecution. This was a dream that activated discernment and wisdom. A Scripture reference very appropriate for this dream is found in 1 Samuel 18:14–15: "And David behaved wisely in all his ways, and the LORD was with him. Therefore, when Saul saw he behaved very wisely, he was afraid of him." First Samuel 20:3 says, "But truly, as the LORD lives and as your soul lives, there is but a step between me and death." This dream revealed a changing government status, and from a spiritual standpoint showed that the "Saul government" of the Church would persecute those who were moving into a new wineskin.

In *The Future War of the Church*, Rebecca and I shared this when we listed the guidelines that will assist us in maintaining our spiritual focus and knowing the times we live in:

> We must know how to get in touch with each other immediately. Maintaining our connections and relationships with each other is another key to securing our future. God sovereignly connects and aligns us with one another, so we can function effectively. Know with whom God has connected you and how to let them know what God is saying to you. This will keep God's warning system in proper order. One way that we remain connected is through frequent gatherings. In Genesis 49, we read that Jacob called his sons together and revealed their futures to them. The Lord is using prophetic gatherings today in much the same way. As we come together corporately, God will speak to us and reveal things we may not see on an individual basis. Another method God is raising up to maintain connections is through organizations like the World Prayer Center in Colorado Springs. The World Prayer Center uses state-of-the-art communications technology to both gather and disseminate information to praying people throughout the world on urgent matters that require immediate, fervent prayer. This is one way God is connecting the Body of Christ in order to secure the future harvest.[1]

Kristine Herman, who works for Wagner Leadership Institute, had the following dream:

> In my dream, I was seated in a large room with tables, and people were eating and fellowshipping. I was seated and a man in a short-sleeved white sweater came up to me and told me that he thought the Lord wanted him to give me some money, so he gave me some cash. He ended up coming back several times and giving me more money. I didn't look to see how much he had given me. I got up from my chair and was walking away, looking in my wallet to see how much money he had given me. I

found two 100 dollar bills along with some smaller bills totaling $250 to $300. I also found a blank check that he had signed. His name (Larry) and his wife's name were at the upper left corner of the check. I also had a credit card form with his credit card information on it and Larry, too, signed this.

Kristine interpreted this dream immediately:

My understanding while I was looking at the check and the credit card form was that I could purchase whatever I desired and there was no limit to the amount I could spend. I could pay off my mortgage with his personal check and that would be just fine.

I think God would give a dream like this to someone who is in a difficult place financially, or perhaps they are moving forward into an expanded vision and need to know that God is going to provide for them.

Interpreting Symbolism

In most dreams recorded in the Bible, God used a tremendous amount of symbolism to convey His message. Jesus often used parables when making His points. This has not changed through the years. The vast majority of dreams and visions are laden with symbolic imagery. It is often helpful, therefore, to have a basic understanding of symbolism and to have reference books on hand with helpful, biblically based lists of symbols and types.[2] (See the appendix for a list of basic symbols.)

Snails and Turtles

I once had a dream about a friend in McAllen, Texas. In the dream, my friend was walking along a path filled with snails. If he did not stomp on the snails, they would turn into snakes that hissed and bit. There were also many turtles, and if my friend kept in line with the turtles, they would lead him safely to his destination.

As God showed me the interpretation, I realized the snails represented my friend's business associates who were linked with legal entities that had the ability to turn and bite. Through the turtles, God was saying that my friend needed to slow things down in order to prosper. As I shared this with my friend, he was amazed. At that time, he was involved in three separate lawsuits, and there were many "snails" in his life. The dream gave him wisdom as to how to proceed with these associates. Also, because he heeded the warning of the turtles and slowed things down, he did prosper and was ultimately successful in all his lawsuits and business ventures.

Symbols Are Flexible

Ira Milligan adds the following thoughts on interpreting symbols:

Almost all symbols can have both positive (good) and negative (bad) meanings. . . . The most important thing to remember about interpreting symbols is, *never be narrow-minded*. Symbols, like words, are very flexible. When one knows the context of a dream and the circumstances of the dreamer's life, one can properly assign the right meanings. Without this knowledge one can only guess.

For instance, it is possible for an ant in a dream to mean several different things . . . [these include] industrious; wise; diligent; prepared for the future; nuisance; stinging or angry words. When one dreams of ants at a picnic, the context would obviously lean toward "nuisance" as the meaning of the symbol, even though it is their industrious nature that makes them such a nuisance! To dream of ants gathering food would relate directly to the key word definition of industrious, diligent preparation for the future. Likewise, dreaming of being bit or stung by ants would fit the "stinging or angry words" definition.

Sometimes a symbol has a meaning to one person that would not fit another. . . . When trying to decipher a symbol, the first question we should ask is, "What does this symbol mean to [*the dreamer*]?"[3]

A Complex Dream

In the spring of 1996, Linda Heidler had this dream while I was in Israel:

In the dream, I was with a large group of people out in a desert place. There was a lot of sand blowing, which would get into your eyes. I remember that my hair kept blowing into my face. We were all watching a woman who was seated at a large machine. She was sitting on a high stool behind the machine. The machine had lots of levers, pulleys, gears, buttons, pedals and so on. One by one the people from the crowd would stand in front of the machine and the woman would begin to talk to them. As she talked to them, she would start working the pedals and pulling the levers. She was moving constantly as she spoke to them. She would tell them things they needed to let go of and things they needed to increase in. As she spoke and worked the machine, the people all turned into triangles. When she was finished, she would put the people into clear plastic containers like Tupperware and seal them. When she had finished with two people, she would put them together and they would form a Star of David, then they would go off together as happy as could be.

As we watched, we would look at the person she was working on and say, "There is no way she can make them into a triangle." But one after another they would all form into triangles. Then when we saw who she was going to pair up to form the Star of David we would say, "There is no way those two will ever match up." But when she finished, they were perfectly matched and very happy.

When it was my turn to stand in front of the machine and she began to talk to me and operate the machine, it was just wonderful! Everything she said made so much sense. It was so wise and freeing and practical. I loved it! When she finished, I was a triangle. She then put me in the Tupperware and sealed me. I could not feel anything different, but I noticed that the sand was not blowing in my eyes anymore and my hair was not blowing in my face. I do not remember who I was matched up with to form the Star of David, but I felt complete.

This is a great example of a complex symbolic dream. First, it had relevance in Linda's life. Second, it applied to my trip in Israel. (See chapter 5 for my explanation of this dream of Israel that Barbara Wentroble was in.) And third, it had a great relevance concerning covenant alignment. To fully interpret the dream, I used Scripture as well as an understanding of symbols. I used several Scriptures to help in the interpretation of this dream along with the word of wisdom:

1. **Workmanship.** "For we are His workmanship, created in Christ Jesus for good works, which God prepared beforehand that we should walk in them" (Ephesians 2:10).

2. **Sealed.** "Who also has sealed us and given us the Spirit in our hearts as a guarantee" (2 Corinthians 1:22). "And do not grieve the Holy Spirit of God, by whom you were sealed for the day of redemption" (Ephesians 4:30).

3. **Joined.** "Now I plead with you, brethren, by the name of our Lord Jesus Christ, that you all speak the same thing, and that there be no divisions among you, but that you be perfectly joined together in the same mind and in the same judgment" (1 Corinthians 1:10). "But he who is joined to the Lord is one spirit with Him" (1 Corinthians 6:17).

"From whom the whole body, joined and knit together by what every joint supplies, according to the effective working by which every part does its share, causes growth of the body for the edifying of itself in love" (Ephesians 4:16).

4. **Transformed.** "I beseech you therefore, brethren, by the mercies of God, that you present your bodies a living sacrifice, holy, acceptable to God, which is your reasonable service. And do not be conformed to this world, but be transformed by the renewing of your mind, that you may prove what is that good and acceptable and perfect will of God" (Romans 12:1–2).

It would take quite a bit of space to write the full interpretation of this dream. But I think when you read the dream along with these Scriptures, you will find application to your life as well.

Symbolic Language

When we sleep, we are set aside from the contact of the culture and world around us. Therefore, if we dream, we sometimes can seem less civilized than our surroundings, but we also can seem wiser in our dreams than when we are awake. A world of pictures, images and silence exists that we really do not perceive in fullness many times when we are awake.

In his book *Dreams*, Rabbi Shmuel Boteach states:

Symbolic language is a language in which inner experiences, feelings, and thoughts are expressed as if they were sensory experiences or events in the real world. It is a language which has a different logic from the one we use while awake. By this logic, it is not time and space which are the ruling categories, as they are in the real world. Rather, symbolic language is governed by categories of intensity and association. It is a language with its own grammar and syntax, as it were, and a language one must understand if one is to comprehend the meaning of Midrashim, myths, and dreams. Symbolic language is the one universal language the human race has constantly developed. Yet it has been forgotten by modern man. Although he may still write his dreams with it, he is at a loss to decipher it when he awakens.[4]

Replacing Symbols with Key Words

Once we have an idea of what the symbols represent, we can follow Daniel's example of interpreting the king's dream. He simply replaced the symbols with the key words or patterns that they represented in order to decipher the message in the dream. Referring again to the dream I had of my friend in McAllen, Texas, the simple interpretation would be that he was moving along in business (represented by the path) and that certain business associates surrounding him (represented by the snails) would turn and bite him (represented by the snakes) if he did not deal with them appropriately (represented by the stomping). Then the dream shifted to reveal that he would have to get in step with God's timing, which was slower than he was going (represented by following in line with the turtles) in order to prosper (represented by the safe destination).

When interpreting symbols for others, it is important to remember that we should not impose our interpretation of symbols if it does not bear witness with the dreamer.

Your Sons and Your Daughters Shall Prophesy . . .

My children have many dreams. Most of them have a real prophetic bent to them. They have been taught to listen carefully for the voice of God in their dreams. Pam and I try to let them share their dreams, good or bad, and then discuss various spiritual insights with them. Daniel, one of our older sons, had a dream a few years ago of watching the Chinese army muster to invade our nation. We had many discussions about this. Our daughter, Rebekah, had the following dream when she was sixteen:

My friend Randi and I were driving in the Expedition (our family vehicle). Randi was actually driving, and I was in the front passenger seat. I looked out the window and saw debris all around us. We were in a suburban area that had been blown up. I was probably in my early 20s (three or four years older than when I had the dream). I saw children playing in the debris. I also saw a family with a father and three boys. The boys were likely 17, 13 and 10 years old. They all looked alike. The four of them were holding hands as they walked through the debris. As they walked up to the car, Randi introduced me. The father recognized me and said, "It's nice to meet you. My wife used to be a big fan of yours." I was perplexed at why he used the past tense in referring to his wife. I next shook hands with the oldest son and felt like I knew him. Then we said we'd see them at the Love Feast at the church and drove off.

When we arrived at the church, the church itself was completely intact, but everything around it was blown up. I saw my friend Micah in the welcome center. As I walked over to see him, I passed the area where brochures were displayed. Underneath the announcement center at the church was a family photograph. It had matting and three photos of the same family that I had just seen on the drive to church. In the first picture, they were happy and content. There was a woman in the picture who was smiling. The second picture was just of the father and boys. They looked very different. The third picture was just of the oldest son. In the photo, it appeared as if he had his hands pushing away the camera. I did not understand why this picture was included. As I visited with another friend at church, I kept thinking that I needed to help my friend Heather, but I didn't know where she was. I seemed to get distracted in conversation, but my overriding thought was that I needed to help Heather.

At this point, the whole dream repeated itself a second time. The dream then repeated itself a third time; however, this time, the atmosphere had changed for the worse. At the church, I went into the nursery to help Heather, but the nursery was completely destroyed. In this portion of the dream, I was 10 years older, and I was a doctor. I turned to a lady and told her that her child would be fine. Heather was at the opposite door in the nursery. She had a baby who I knew would be fine. Upon leaving the nursery, I was much younger again. Things had not been destroyed and looked as they presently are today. I met someone in the hall who shared they were happy for me. I noticed Mom was in the church entrance. I overheard her say there was a new family coming to the church whose mother was really sick. At this point, that family entered the building and I realized it was the family at the beginning of my dream. The mother had cancer and was dying. When I saw and shook the oldest boy's hand, I asked him if we met before. He said, "No." Then the dream ended.

This is a very interesting dream with great spiritual significance. The dream is a three-tiered dream, which reveals three stages of Rebekah's life and three stages of the family's life. The dream also reveals three stages of destruction resulting in future restoration, and three stages of the Church in days ahead. Notice that the dream repeated itself three times. Generally, if a dream is repeated, it becomes a very sure and necessary revelation for the future. I could take this dream and prophesy tremendously to us, saying, "Fear not the devastation ahead, for God has a restorative plan. He will be bringing in many who are sick and afflicted. He will be restoring families. If we will follow Him and feast with Him, we will always be successful in the destiny of our lives."

How Do We Prepare to Receive Dreams from God?

Chances are that whether or not you are aware of it, you have received messages from God in your dreams. Now that you have a bit more understanding, the following is a list of practical things you can do to prepare yourself for future occurrences:

1. **Keep an open mind.** Don't be frightened about receiving God-inspired dreams.

2. **Make sure your bedroom is in peace and conducive to hearing the Spirit of God.** If you have ungodly objects, such as gargoyle statues or Ouija boards in your bedroom (or anywhere in your home for that matter), the Spirit of God will not be able to flow as freely because you have an open door to demonic activity. Do all you can to invite the Holy Spirit into your bedroom.[5]

3. **Ask what your sleep habits are like.** Do you have sleep deprivation? Is your sleep frequently interrupted? Often the enemy will attempt to keep you from being refreshed so that it will be difficult to perceive what God is saying. Try to get your sleep patterns in good order so your sleep is refreshing and rejuvenating.

4. **Pray before you go to sleep and ask the Lord to speak to you, and expect to receive spiritual dreams.**

5. **Have a pen and notebook near your bed to write down impressions.** If it is easier, keep a tape recorder nearby. Record every detail you can remember. If you can remember it, there may be a good reason why. Record the setting, progression, symbols, colors, people—everything you can remember. Also, if your dream changes scenes, continue to record it as one dream because, even though it may have different scenes, it is probably all one message. It is also a good idea to keep a dream diary so you have a record to refer to in days ahead. Often the Lord will use a series of dreams to convey a message. It is possible to miss the full impact of what God is saying without this kind of record.

6. Ask the Lord to help you remember your dreams. Dreams are fleeting. Job 20:8 says, "He will fly away like a dream, and not be found; yes, he will be chased away like a vision of the night." There is often a short span of time in which you can clearly recall your dreams. Also, we have not trained ourselves to remember dreams because few of us understand their true significance. Of course, there will be times when we still cannot remember our dreams, but the Lord can help us with our recall.

7. Give yourself time when you awaken to record your dreams and meditate before the Lord. Because you generally have a short window of time upon awakening to record dreams when they are more vivid, I recommend giving yourself about a half hour between the time you awaken and the time you get out of bed in which to meditate on what the Lord may have been speaking to you in the night. This is a good time to ask God to begin giving you an interpretation of your dream.

8. Be sure you respond to the revelation God gives you through your dreams in the same way you would to a prophetic word or to other Holy Spirit–inspired revelation in your life. As we have stated throughout this book, all revelation from God requires a response from you.

God Is Ready
to Perform His Word!

You will be a joy to all generations, for I will make you so. . . . You will know at last that I, the LORD, am your Savior and Redeemer, the Mighty One of Israel. . . . Salvation will surround you like city walls, and praise will be on the lips of all who enter there. . . . All your people will be righteous. . . . The tiniest group will become a mighty nation. I, the LORD, will bring it all to pass at the right time.

Isaiah 60:15–22 NLT

When we hear God's voice, we should allow our expectations in Him to arise! In our book *The Best Is Yet Ahead*, Rebecca and I explain that "future" and "expectation" are synonymous. Our future is linked with an expectation of God moving. This is a time for the Church to have its expectation level renewed and raised to another level. Isaiah 59 and 60 are wonderful prayer guides to see this happen in our lives. Hope must transcend and move into faith. Faith then produces overcoming, and overcoming leads to a demonstration of God's power and a manifestation of His promises:

> Therefore prophesy and say to them, "Thus says the Lord GOD: 'Behold, O My people, I will open your graves and cause you to come up from your graves, and bring you into the land of Israel. Then you shall know that I am the LORD, when I have opened your graves, O My people, and brought you up from your graves. I will put My Spirit in you, and you shall live, and I will place you in your own land. Then you shall know that I, the LORD, have spoken it and performed it,' says the LORD."
>
> Ezekiel 37:12–14

Notice that the phrase "I will place you in your own land" was the prophetic fulfillment released in Ezekiel 36, where the Lord said, "But you, O mountains of Israel, you shall shoot forth your branches and yield your fruit to My people Israel, for they are about to come" (Ezekiel 36:8). The word of the Lord had come full circle! As we explained in chapter 2, four levels of agreement and prophesying were necessary for Ezekiel to see the fulfillment of God's word. What if Ezekiel had stopped pressing forward after the bones came together, but there was no breath in them? That's what we tend to do in the Body of Christ. We think we've heard God prophesy, but when things don't turn out as we thought, we too often give up and end up falling short of reaching our prophetic destiny. We do not see the word that God has spoken to us coming to fulfillment. As Ezekiel prophesied through to the end, resurrection power was released so that the graves opened and the people were set in their own land.

I love this phrase, "'Then you shall know that I, the LORD, have spoken it and performed it,' says the LORD" (Ezekiel 37:14).

It's one thing for there to be a promise in our lives that we know is from God, but it's another thing for that promise to be performed in our lives. We cannot be a people who faint easily. Discouragement has no place in us as God's people. If we choose not to back up or stop, but to keep moving forward through the levels of prophecy, God will perform His will in us and bring about prophetic fulfillment!

In Jeremiah 1, we see God calling and commissioning Jeremiah to go forth to bring restoration through change and warning. Verses 11 and 12 summarize what I feel the Lord is saying as we enter the next season ahead:

> Moreover, the word of the LORD came to me, saying, "Jeremiah, what do you see?" And I said, "I see a branch of an almond tree." Then the LORD said to me, "You have seen well, for I am ready to perform My word."

Perhaps these verses will enable us to pray and trust the Lord to enter into the fullness of His plans concerning our lives.

He Causes Eyes to Open!

The phrase "What do you see?" appears throughout the Bible in places where the Lord asks this question of His people. In Luke chapter 2, when Jesus Christ was born of Mary and the glory of the Lord manifested in the earth, the shepherds out in the fields, keeping watch over their flocks by night, were startled and even fearful of this manifestation. The angel of the Lord came to them and said not to be afraid, for great joy had entered the earth realm. He actually said, "Rejoice, for the unlocking redemptive force for your life has now come to the earth" (paraphrased).

Suddenly, all the heavenly hosts began to praise God. Once this host departed, the shepherds talked among themselves and said, "Let us now go to Bethlehem and see this thing that has come to pass, which the Lord has made known to us." And when they had seen Him, they told everyone what the angels had said to them (see Luke 2:8–17).

In days ahead, there will be times of manifestation of the Lord's glory. Do not fear this manifestation. Be willing to open your eyes to what the angelic hosts are doing around you. See your provision manifest! See your joy restored! See change come into your sphere of authority! Once you see, be willing to declare what the Lord is doing!

He Is the Branch

"I see a branch of an almond tree," Jeremiah replied to the Lord. The branch was a symbol of kingship and prosperity (see Daniel 11:7; Job 8:16). The Lord is described as *the* Branch, both righteous and beautiful (see Isaiah 4:2; Jeremiah 23:5; Zechariah 3:8; 6:12). *The* Branch produces branches, and we are branches of the true Vine (see John 15:5–6).

Branches of trees (palm, myrtle, willow and others) were used ceremonially at the Feast of the Tabernacles for making booths (see Nehemiah 8:15). This symbolically shows us that eventually we, as His branches, will overlay each other to form a covering of safety as we participate in His glory in the earth. Those who understand the Branch will rule.

As the Lord speaks to you, you need to wake up and watch for things to intensify in your life. Watch for a new blossoming!

Back to Jeremiah's response to the Lord—he specifically saw an almond tree. The almond was significant in that it was the first tree to bloom. It also was used as a breeding device to increase Jacob's herds (see Genesis 30:38). It was one of the best fruits of the land that was given as a gift (see Genesis 43:11). Aaron's rod produced ripe almonds, signifying the priesthood to come (see Numbers 17:8). The early appearing white bloom of the almond was linked to the graying head that signifies wisdom. Jeremiah was called to watch, and when he saw the almond, it meant that spring was coming. The almond symbolized "wakeful hastening." As the Lord speaks to you, you need to wake up and watch for things to intensify in your life. Watch for a new blossoming! Do not fear pruning, for the Branch has come for you to "branch out" and be fruitful. Declare this over your life.

He Comes to Affirm His Glory

The promises of God are "yea and amen." Once we see what God would have us see, He begins to put a "yes" down deep within us. The affirmation of God also is linked with favor. The favor of God upon us causes us to experience pleasure, desire and delight. He delights in us when we see His path for us and move accordingly.

Favor also is linked with a manifestation of God's glory. God's glory (Hebrew, *chabod*) means His weightiness. We experience God's glory when we see His honor, splendor, power, wealth, authority, magnificence, dignity, richness, fame and excellence. Knowing His will and experiencing His glory breaks us out of naïveté, instability, vanity and the thought processes that assume everything is temporary. Once we experience this affirmation of God's will and glory, we will hear God saying to us, "For with God, nothing will be impossible." The affirmation of God causes His glory to be seen.

He Was and Is Our "I AM"

"I AM" was God's response to Moses' request in Exodus 3:13–14. This means, "I AM who I AM"; "I will be who I will be";

or even "I cause to be that which is." God's response is not a name that limits God in any way. Rather, it is an affirmation that God is always free to be and act as He wills.

Jesus' I AM responses in several New Testament passages suggest more than the simple, identifying "I am He." The I AM of Mark 6:50 means, "I AM Jesus and not a ghost." It suggests the divine I AM who alone "treads on the waves of the sea" (Job 9:8; see Mark 6:48–49) and makes the waves hush (see Psalm 107:28–29; compare Mark 4:39). John 8:24 helps us see that Jesus as the I AM is a matter of eternal life and death for us: "For if you do not believe that I am He, you will die in your sins."

Many of us never recognize what His true identity of I AM means to us:

- I AM is **Jehovah** (*Jeh hoh' vuh*). Declare Him as "LORD."
- I AM is **Jehovah-Jireh** (*Jeh hoh' vuh-ji rehh*). Declare, "Yahweh will provide" (see Genesis 22:14). It is the name Abraham gave to the place where the Lord provided a sacrifice in place of Isaac. He made Abraham "see" His provision.
- I AM is **Jehovah-Rapha** (*Jeh hoh' vuh-ray' fuh*). Declare, "He has healed." In Exodus 15, He is the One who healed the children of Israel so they could move forward toward the promise. He really was saying, "You need a healer. I AM He who heals."
- I AM is **Jehovah-Nissi** (*Jeh hoh' vuh-nihs' si*). Declare, "Yahweh is my banner." Moses declared Jehovah as banner and built an altar to Him after defeating the Amalekites (see Exodus 17:15). This name is linked with deliverance and miracles.
- I AM is **Jehovah-Shalom** (*Jeh hoh' vuh-shah luhm*). Declare, "Yahweh is peace." Gideon built an altar to the

God of peace (see Judges 6:24). I AM is the One who can make you whole. Once Gideon understood this part of His character, he was released to go to war against his enemies. I AM is the strategy to defeat your enemies.

- I AM is **Jehovah-Shamma** (*Jeh hoh' vuh-shuhm' maw*). Declare Him as "The Lord is there." The Jerusalem of Ezekiel's vision was known by this name. Compare Isaiah 60:19–20 and Revelation 21:3. May you sense, feel and know His presence.

- I AM is **Jehovah-Tsidkenu** (*Jeh hoh' vuh-tsihd kee' new*). Declare Him as "The LORD [is] our righteousness" (Jeremiah 23:6; 33:16). The name is applied to a future Davidic king who would lead his people to do what is right, thus bringing peace (23:6) and restoring the city of Jerusalem (33:16). You are the righteousness of God in Christ Jesus!

Know I AM as the Prince of Peace

Peace is a state of rest, quietness and calmness. Peace is an absence of strife leading to tranquility. Peace denotes wholeness—body, soul and spirit—and perfect well-being. Peace includes harmonious relationships between God and humans, between one another and between nations and families. Jesus, the Prince of Peace, gives peace to those who call upon Him for personal salvation.

Luke 1:79–80 says He came "'to give light to those who sit in darkness and the shadow of death, to guide our feet into the way of peace.' So the child grew and became strong in spirit." I believe this is the will of the Prince of Peace in our lives. Matthew 10:34 says, "Do not think that I came to bring peace on earth. I did not come to bring peace but a sword." These two statements seem contrary. However, what the Lord is saying is, "Let Me cut away every earthly tie that distracts you from *My* best will in heaven for your life. I long to see you whole and filled with peace. So let Me cut away that which will keep you from being whole and experiencing My covenant blessings."

God Is Ready to Perform His Word!

When God is ready to move, it means He is watching, waking, hastening and anticipating the perfect time to align with His saints in the earth and release His will to be manifested in our midst. To be ready means that He is sleepless, alert, vigilant and on the lookout to cause the supernatural door in heaven to open and pour out His will in the earth. To be ready means He is watchfully looking for the opportunity to care for us in a new way. To be ready means He is watching to begin to build and plant in the earth that which He has blueprinted in heaven.

When God was ready to move to give His Son to you as a gift, He began to order and orchestrate events for that release. He does the same thing in your life. Watch for the ordered events. Be assured that He is watching over you. Watch with Him so that when He opens doors for you, you enter into a new dimension of freedom, victory and glory.

Once you abide in Him, He can accomplish, confirm and continue His will in your life in order to bring you into His full plan. He can cause you to endure your circumstances and enemies so that they do not stop you from advancing into the ultimate victory He has for your life.

To *perform* means "to stir up, strengthen, succeed, accomplish, advance and appoint." To perform means He will release industrious ability within us, so that as we journey on the path He has given us and sacrifice before Him, we will feel His presence and power. To *perform* also means "to assemble, fight, muster together and wait upon the war ahead." In waiting, He comes to our aid to demonstrate His love and ability in our lives. When He performs, He fulfills, finishes, gathers, governs and grants to us that which we need to complete our assignments victoriously.

> Blessed is she [or we] that believed: for there shall be a performance of those things which were told her [or us] from the Lord.
>
> Luke 1:45 KJV

> He was sent "to perform the mercy promised to our fathers and to remember His holy covenant."
>
> Luke 1:72

> And being fully convinced that what He had promised He was also able to perform.
>
> Romans 4:21

> Being confident of this very thing, that he which hath begun a good work in you will perform it until the day of Jesus Christ.
>
> Philippians 1:6 KJV

There will be a performance! Let Him be the performance of your life. Lay down your own performance and enter into His!

In Closing

We hope this book has helped you recognize when God is speaking and also to embrace the voice of God in your life. May the Lord richly bless you as you seek to hear His voice and obey His will for your life! We are praying for you to hear the voice of God in a new way.

Appendix

Dream Symbol Interpretation

As you will notice, many of the following symbols have conflicting interpretations assigned to them, some positive and some negative. This list is only meant to be a general guide. The symbol always needs to be interpreted in light of the context of the dream or vision, in light of what the symbol means to the dreamer and by the guidance of the Holy Spirit.[1]

Numbers

One. Unity, God, beginning, first, rank, order, new

Two. Division, judge, separate, discern, agreement, witness; union (two becoming one)

Three. The Trinity, deity, conform, obey, copy, imitate, likeness, tradition, completeness, perfect, testimony; connected with the bodily resurrection of Christ and His people

Four. The earth (four winds, four corners), reign, rule, kingdom, creation; unsaved or fleshly man; boundaries

Five. Grace, redemption, atonement, life, the Cross, government (fivefold gifts), works, service, bondage (including debt, sickness, phobias and so on), taxes, prison, sin, motion

Six. Humanity, the beast, Satan, flesh, carnal, idol; manifestation of sin

Seven. Complete, all, finished, rest, perfection

Eight. Put off (as in putting off the old self), sanctification, manifest, reveal, new beginnings, resurrection, die, death; new order of things

Nine. Manifestation of the Holy Spirit, harvest, fruitfulness, fruition, fruit of the womb, finality, fullness; perfection or divine completeness

Ten. Judgment, try or trial, test, temptation, law, order, government, restoration, responsibility, tithe; Antichrist kingdom; testimony

Eleven. Mercy, end, finish, last stop, incompleteness, disorganization, disintegration, lawlessness, disorder, the Antichrist; judgment

Twelve. Joined, united, govern, government, oversight, apostolic fullness, the holy city of God; governmental perfection

Thirteen. Rebellion, backsliding, apostasy, revolution, rejection, double blessing, double cursing; depravity

Fourteen. Passover, double, re-create, reproduce, disciple, servant, bond slave, employee; deliverance or salvation

Fifteen. Free, grace, liberty, sin covered, honor; rest

Sixteen. Free-spirited, without boundaries, without law, without sin, salvation; love

Seventeen. Spiritual order, incomplete, immature, undeveloped, childish; victory

Eighteen. Put on (as in the Spirit of Christ), judgment, destruction, captivity, overcome; bondage

Nineteen. Barren, ashamed, repentant, selflessness, without self-righteousness; faith

Twenty. Holy, tried and approved, tried and found wanting; redemption

Twenty-one. Exceeding sinfulness, of sin

Twenty-two. Light

Twenty-three. Death

Twenty-four. Priestly courses, governmental perfection

Twenty-five. The forgiveness of sins

Twenty-six. The Gospel of Christ

Twenty-seven. Preaching of the Gospel

Twenty-eight. Eternal life

Twenty-nine. Departure

Thirty. Consecration, maturity for ministry

Thirty-two. Covenant

Thirty-three. Promise

Thirty-four. Naming of a son

Thirty-five. Hope

Thirty-six. Enemy

Thirty-seven. The Word of God

Thirty-eight. Slavery

Thirty-nine. Disease

Forty. Probation, testing, ending in victory or defeat; trials

Forty-two. Israel's oppression, the Lord's advent to the earth

Forty-five. Preservation

Fifty. Pentecost, liberty, freedom, jubilee; Holy Spirit

Sixty. Pride

Sixty-six. Idol worship

Seventy. Prior to increase, multitude; universality, Israel and her restoration

Seventy-five. Separation, cleansing, purification

One hundred. Fullness, full measure, full recompense, full reward; God's election of grace, children of promise

One hundred nineteen. The resurrection day; Lord's Day

One hundred twenty. End of all flesh, beginning of life in the Spirit; divine period of probation

One hundred forty-four. God's ultimate creation and redemption; the Spirit-guided life

One hundred fifty-three. God's elect, revival, ingathering, harvest; fruit bearing

Two hundred. Insufficiency

Six hundred. Warfare

Six-Six-Six. Antichrist, Satan, mark of the damned, mark of the man who is a beast; the number of the beast

Eight-Eight-Eight. The first resurrection saints

One thousand. Maturity, full stature, mature service, mature judgment; divine completeness and the glory of God

Colors

Amber. The glory of God

Black. Lack, sin, ignorance, grief, mourning, gloomy, evil, ominous, famine, burned, death

Blue. Spiritual, divine revelation, visitation, authority, Holy Spirit, depressed (as in feeling blue), male infant, hope; medium or dark blue can be God's Spirit or Word, blessing, healing, goodwill; very light blue can be spirit of man, evil spirit, corrupt

Brown. Dead (as in plant life), repentant, born again, without spirit

Crimson. Blood atonement, sacrifice, death

Gray. Unclear, vague, not specific, hazy, deception, hidden, crafty, false doctrine; gray hair can be wisdom, age or weakness

Green. Life, mortal, flesh, carnal, envy, inexperienced, immature renewal; evergreen can be eternal life or immortal

Orange. Danger, great jeopardy, harm; a common color combination is orange and black, which usually signifies great evil or danger; bright or fire orange can be power, force, energy

Pink. Flesh, sensual, immoral, moral (as in a heart of flesh); chaste, a female infant

Purple. Royal, kingship, rule (good or evil), majestic, noble

Red. Passion, emotion, anger, hatred, lust, sin, enthusiasm, zeal, war, bloodshed, death

White. Pure, without mixture, light, righteousness, holiness of God, Christ, the angels or saints, blameless, innocence

Yellow. Gift, marriage, family, honor, deceitful gift, timidity, fear, cowardliness

Creatures

Alligator. Ancient, evil out of the past (through inherited or personal sin), danger, destruction, evil spirit

Ant. Industrious, wise, diligent, prepared for the future, nuisance, stinging, angry words

Ass (donkey). Lowliness, patience, strength, endurance, service

Ass (wild mule). Untamed human nature, stubborn, self-willed, unsubdued, depraved, obnoxious, unbelief

Bat. Witchcraft, unstable, flighty, fear

Bear. Destroyer, evil curse (through inheritance or personal sin, including financial loss or hardship), economic loss, danger, opposition, evil, cunning, cruel, strong, ferocious

Beaver. Industrious, busy, diligent, clever, ingenious

Bees. Produce sweetness, power to sting, host of people, affliction, busybody, gossip

Bird. Spirit, Holy Spirit, demon, man, gossip, message (see crow, dove, eagle, owl, vulture)

Bull. Persecution, spiritual warfare, opposition, accusation, slander, threat, economic increase

Butterfly. Freedom, flighty, fragile, temporary glory

Calf. Increase, prosperity, idolatry, false worship, stubbornness, prayers, praise, thanksgiving, enlargement (e.g., when a calf breaks out of a stall)

Camel. Burden-bearer, servant, endurance, long journey, ungraceful

Cat. Self-willed, untrainable, predator, unclean spirit, bewitching charm, stealthy, sneaky, crafty, deception, self-pity, something precious in the context of a personal pet

Chicken. Fear, cowardliness; hen can be protection, gossip, motherhood; rooster can be boasting, bragging, proud; chick can be defenseless, innocent

Crow (raven). Confusion, outspoken, operating in envy or strife, hateful, direct path, unclean, God's minister of justice or provision

Deer. Graceful, swift, sure-footed, agile, timid

Dog. Strife, contention, offense, unclean spirit, unbelievers; pet dog can be something precious, friend, loyal; dog wagging tail can be friend, acceptance; dog biting can be rewarding evil for good, betrayal, unthankful; barking dog can be warning, incessant nuisance, annoyance; dog trailing game can be persistent, obsession; rabid dog can be single-minded pursuit of evil, contagious evil, persecution, great danger; bulldog can be unyielding, stubborn; watchdog can be watchman, elder, minister (good or bad), alert, beware

Dove. Holy Spirit, gentleness, sacrifice

Dragon. Satan, evil spirits, Antichrist forces

Eagle. Leader, prophet (true or false), minister, fierce predator, sorcerer, strength, swift

Elephant. Invincible or thick-skinned, not easily offended, powerful, large

128

Fish. Souls of humanity (both clean and unclean), character, motive

Fox. Subtlety, deception, cunning, false prophet, wicked leader, hidden sin, sly and evil people

Frog. Demon, witchcraft, curse, evil words, puffed up, unclean

Goat. Sinner, unbelief, stubborn, argumentative, negative person, accuser, Satan

Hawk. Predator, sorcerer, evil spirit, warrior, unclean

Horse. Strength, swiftness, power, spiritual support, power of the flesh, spiritual warfare, age

Lion. Dominion, Christ, king, regal, bold, power, Satan, religious tradition, courage, royalty

Mice. Devourer, curse, plague, timid

Monkey. Foolishness, clinging, mischief, dishonesty, addiction

Moth. Deterioration, destructive, deceitful, undetected trouble, corruption

Owl. Circumspect, wisdom, demon, curse, night bird

Pig. Ignorance, hypocrisy, religious unbelievers, unclean people, selfish, gluttonous, vicious, vengeful

Rabbit. Increase, fast growth, multiplication; hare can be Satan and his evil spirits

Raccoon. Mischief, night raider, rascal, thief, bandit, deceitful

Rat. Unclean, wicked person, jerk, devourer, plague, betrayer

Roach. Infestation, unclean spirits, hidden sin

Scorpion. Sin nature, lust of the flesh, temptation, deception, accusation, destruction, danger, a whip

Serpent (snake). Curse, demon, deception, threat, danger, hatred, slander, witchcraft, wisdom

Sheep. Chant, the people of God, innocent

Spider. Evil, sin, deception, false doctrine, temptation; spiderweb can be snares, lies

Tiger. Danger, powerful minister (both good and evil)

Vulture. Scavenger, unclean, impure, evil person or spirit, all-seeing, waiting for evil opportunity

Wolf. Predator, devourer, false prophet, personal gain, wicked and false teachers, destroyer of God's flock

Other

Acid. Bitter, offense, carrying a grudge, hatred, sarcasm

Apples. Fruit, words, sin, temptation, appreciation, fruit of the Spirit

Arm. Strength or weakness, savior, deliverer, helper, aid, reaching out, striker

Ashes. Memories, repentance, ruin, destruction

Automobile. Life, person, ministry

Autumn. End, completion, change, repentance

Baby. New beginning, new idea, dependent, helpless, innocent, sin

Bed. Rest, salvation, meditation, intimacy, peace, covenant (marriage, natural or evil), self-made

Bicycle. Works, works of the flesh, legalism, self-righteousness, working out life's difficulties, messenger

Blood. Life of the flesh, covenant, murder, defiled, unclean, pollution, purging, testimony, witness, guilt

Boat. Support, life, person, recreation, spare time, personal ministry

Brass. Word of God or man, judgment, hypocrisy, self-justification, fake, human tradition

Brother-in-law. Partiality or adversary, fellow minister, problem relationship, partner, oneself, natural brother-in-law

Clouds. Change or covering, trouble, distress, threatening, troubling thoughts, confusion, hidden

Dancing. Worship, idolatry, prophesying, joy, romance, seduction, lewdness

Diamond. Hard, hardheaded, hardhearted, unchangeable, eternal, gift of the Spirit, something valuable or precious

Door. Entrance, Christ, opportunity, way, avenue, mouth

Dreaming. A message within a message, aspiration, vision

Drowning. Overcome, self-pity, depression, grief, sorrow, temptation, excessive debt

Drugs. Influence, spell, sorcery, witchcraft, control, legalism, medicine, healing

Earthquake. Upheaval, change by crisis, repentance, trial; God's judgment, disaster, trauma, shock

Eating. Partake, participate, experience, outworking, covenant, agreement, friendship, fellowship, devour, consume

Elevator. Changing position, going into the spirit realm, elevated, demoted

Eyes. Desire, covetousness, passion, lust, revelation, understanding

Falling. Unsupported, loss of support (financial, moral, public), trial, succumb, backsliding

Father. Authority, God, author, originator, source, inheritance, tradition, custom, Satan, natural father

Father-in-law. Law, authoritative relationship based on law, legalism, problem authoritative relationship, natural father-in-law

Feet. Heart, walk, way, thoughts (meditation), offense, stubborn (unmovable), rebellion (kicking), sin

Finger. Feeling, sensitivity, discernment, conviction, works, accusation (as in pointing a finger), instruction

Flowers. Glory, temporary, gifts, romance

Foreigner. Alien, not of God, of the flesh, demonic

Forest. Foreboding, fearful place, often associated with confusion or without direction

Friend. Self; the character or circumstance of one's friend reveals something about oneself; sometimes one friend represents another (look for the same name, initials, hair color); sometimes represents actual friend

Gold. Glory or wisdom, truth, something precious,

righteousness, glory of God, self-glorification

Grandchild. Heir, oneself, inherited blessing or iniquity, one's spiritual legacy, actual grandchild

Grandparent. Past, spiritual inheritance (good or evil), actual grandparent

Grapes. Fruit, spirit of promise, fruit of the Spirit, promise of wrath

Hair. Covering, covenant, humanity, doctrine, tradition, old sinful nature

Hands. Works, deeds (good or evil), labor, service, idolatry, spiritual warfare

Iron. Strength, powerful, invincible, stronghold, stubborn

Kiss. Agreement, covenant, enticement, betrayal, covenant breaker, deception, seduction, friend

Knees. Submission, obey, worship, service, stubborn, unyielding

Lead. Weight, wickedness, sin, burden, judgment, fool, foolishness

Mechanic. Minister, Christ, prophet, pastor, counselor

Mirror. God's Word or one's heart, looking at oneself, looking back, memory, past, vanity

Miscarriage. Abort, failure, loss, repentance, unjust judgment

Money. Power, provision, wealth, natural talents and skills, spiritual riches, power, authority, trust in human strength, covetousness

Mother. Source, Church, love, kindness, spiritual or natural mother

Mother-in-law. Legalism, meddler, trouble, natural mother-in-law

Nudity. Uncovered or flesh, self-justification, self-righteousness, impure, ashamed, stubborn, temptation, lust, sexual control, exhibitionism, truth, honest, nature

Oil. Anointing; clear oil can be the Holy Spirit anointing, healing; dirty oil can be unclean spirits, hate, lust, seduction, deception, slick, danger of slipping

Pen/pencil. Tongue, indelible words, covenant, agreement, contract, vow, publish, record, permanent, unforgettable, gossip

Pregnancy. In process, sin or righteousness in process, desire, anticipation, expectancy

Pumpkin. Witchcraft, deception, snare, witch, trick

Rain. Life, revival, Holy Spirit, Word of God, depression, trial, disappointment

Silver. Knowledge of God (redemption), knowledge of the world (idolatry)

Sister. Spiritual sister, Church, self, natural sister

Spring. New beginning, revival, fresh start, renewal, regeneration, salvation, refreshing

Stone. Witness, word, testimony, person, precept, accusations, persecution

Storm. Disturbance, change, spiritual warfare, judgment, sudden calamity or destruction, trial, persecution, opposition, witchcraft

Summer. Harvest, opportunity, trial, heat of affliction

Table. Communion, agreement, covenant, conference, provision;

under the table, can be deceitful dealings, hidden motives, evil intent

Tin. Dross, waste, worthless, cheap, purification

Train. Continuous, unceasing work, connected, fast, Church

Tree. Person or covering, leader, shelter, false worship, evil influence; oak can be strong shelter; willow can be sorrow; evergreen can be eternal life

Tunnel. Passage, transition, way of escape, troubling experience, trial, hope

Van. Family (natural or Church), family ministry, fellowship

Water. Spirit, Word of God, the spirit of man or the spirit of the enemy, unstable

Wind. Spirit or doctrine, Holy Spirit, demonic or strong opposition, idle words

Window. Revealed, truth, prophecy, revelation, understanding, avenue of blessing, exposed, an unguarded opening for a thief to enter

Wine (strong drink). Intoxicant, strong emotion (such as joy, anger, hate, sorrow); Spirit of God or spirit of man, revelation, truth, witchcraft, delusion, mocker

Winter. Barren, death, dormant, waiting, cold, unfriendly

Wood. Life, temporary, flesh, humanity, carnal reasoning, lust, eternal, spiritual building material

Wrestling. Striving, deliverance, resistance, persistence, trial, tribulation, spirit attempting to gain control

Notes

Chapter 1: Hear Him!

1. For a more complete account of this story, see Chuck D. Pierce and Rebecca Wagner Sytsema, *Possessing Your Inheritance* (Ventura, Calif.: Regal Books, 1999).

Chapter 2: Speaking God's Words: Prophecy in Today's World

1. J.D. Douglas, ed., *New Bible Dictionary* (Wheaton, Ill.: Tyndale House Publishers, 1982), n.p.
2. Dutch Sheets, *Watchman Prayer* (Ventura, Calif.: Gospel Light Publications, 2000), 29.
3. Graham Cooke, *Developing Your Prophetic Gifting* (Kent, England: Sovereign World Ltd., 1994), 119.
4. Ibid., 30–31.
5. Ibid., 39–40.

Chapter 3: Receiving the Word of the Lord: Testing and Responding to a Prophetic Word

1. Cindy Jacobs, *The Voice of God* (Ventura, Calif.: Regal Books, 1995), 76.
2. Ibid., 181.
3. Bruce Yocum, *Prophecy* (Ann Arbor, Mich.: Servant Publications, 1976), 119.
4. Jacobs, *The Voice of God,* 83–84.

Chapter 4: Warring with a Prophetic Word

1. Some of the material in this section has been adapted from Chuck D. Pierce and Rebecca Wagner Sytsema, *Receiving the Word of the Lord* (Colorado Springs, Col.: Wagner Publications, 1999), 24–25.
2. Graham Cooke, *Developing Your Prophetic Gifting* (Kent, England: Sovereign World, Ltd., 1994), 119.
3. Ibid., 120.

4. Ibid., 123.

5. Cindy Jacobs, *The Voice of God* (Ventura, Calif.: Regal Books, 1995), 85.

6. Jim W. Goll, *Kneeling on the Promises* (Grand Rapids, Mich.: Chosen Books, 1999), 172.

7. Ibid., 173.

8. Chuck D. Pierce and Rebecca Wagner Sytsema, *Possessing Your Inheritance* (Ventura, Calif.: Regal Books, 1999), 134–135.

9. Ibid., 23.

10. Goll, *Kneeling on the Promises,* 173.

11. Cindy Jacobs, *Possessing the Gates of the Enemy* (Tarrytown, N.Y.: Chosen Books, 1991), 178.

Chapter 5: Walking in Revelation

1. Marilyn Willett Heavilin, *I'm Listening, Lord* (Nashville, Tenn.: Thomas Nelson Publishers, 1993), 33–37.

2. Ibid., 49–51.

3. Ibid., 54–57.

4. Chuck D. Pierce and Rebecca Wagner Sytsema, *Possessing Your Inheritance* (Ventura, Calif.: Regal Books, 1999), 100–101.

Chapter 6: Hearing God through Dreams and Visions

1. Ira Milligan, *Understanding the Dreams You Dream* (Shippensburg, Penn.: Treasure House, 1997), 3.

2. Fiona Starr and Jonny Zucker, *Dream Themes: A Guide to Understanding Your Dreams* (China: Barnes and Noble Books, 2001), 10.

3. "Praying Around the World," *The Prayer Track News,* vol. 8, no. 2 (April/June 1999), 8.

4. Jane Hamon, *Dreams and Visions* (Ventura, Calif.: Regal Books, 2000), 22–24.

5. Chuck D. Pierce and Rebecca Wagner Sytsema, *The Future War of the Church* (Ventura, Calif.: Regal Books, 2001), 28–35.

6. Milligan, *Understanding the Dreams You Dream,* 9–10.

7. Hamon, *Dreams and Visions,* 37.

8. Ibid., 60–63.

Chapter 7: Interpreting Dreams and Visions

1. Chuck D. Pierce and Rebecca Wagner Sytsema, *The Future War of the Church* (Ventura, Calif.: Regal Books, 2001), 22–23.

2. Some excellent resources for interpreting symbols include Ira Milligan, *Understanding the Dreams You Dream* (Shippensburg, Penn.: Treasure House, 1997) and *Every Dreamer's Handbook* (Shippensburg, Penn.: Treasure House, 2000); Jane Hamon, *Dreams and Visions* (Ventura, Calif.: Regal Books, 2000); Kevin J. Conner, *Interpreting the Symbols and Types* (Portland, Ore.: City Christian Publishing, 1999); and Ed F. Vallowe, *Biblical Mathematics: Keys to Scripture Numerics* (Columbia, S.C.: Olive Press, 1995).

3. Ira Milligan, *Understanding the Dreams You Dream*, 31–33.

4. Rabbi Shmuel Boteach, *Dreams* (Brooklyn, N.Y.: Bash Publications, 1991), 17.

5. For further insight into spiritual housecleaning, we highly recommend Chuck D. Pierce and Rebecca Wagner Sytsema, *Protecting Your Home from Spiritual Darkness* (Ventura, Calif.: Regal Books, 2004).

Appendix: Dream Symbol Interpretation

1. This list of dream symbol interpretations is compiled from the following references: Kevin J. Conner, *Interpreting the Symbols and Types* (Bible Temple Publishing, 1992); Jane Hamon, *Dreams and Visions* (Regal Books, 2000); Ira Milligan, *Understanding the Dreams You Dream* (Treasure House, 1997); Ed F. Vallowe, *Keys to Scripture Numerics* (Ed F. Vallowe Evangelistic Association, 1966). For further explanation or biblical references on any of the listed symbols, or for complete lists, please see these references.

Recommended Reading

Bickle, Mike. *Growing in the Prophetic*. Lake Mary, FL: Charisma House, 1996.

Cooke, Graham. *Developing Your Prophetic Gifting*. Grand Rapids, MI: Chosen Books, 2003.

Conner, Kevin J. *Interpreting the Symbols and Types*. Portland, OR: City Christian Publishing, 1999.

Deere, Jack. *Surprised by the Voice of God*. Grand Rapids, MI: Zondervan Publishing Company, 1996.

Hamon, Bill. *Prophets and Personal Prophecy*. Shippensburg, PA: Destiny Image Publishers, 1987.

Hamon, Jane. *Dreams and Visions*. Ventura, CA: Regal Books, 2000.

Jacobs, Cindy. *The Voice of God*. Ventura, CA: Regal Books, 1995.

Joyner, Rick. *The Prophetic Ministry*. Wilkesboro, NC: MorningStar Publications, 2003.

Lord, Peter. *Hearing God*. Grand Rapids, MI: Baker Books, 1988.

Milligan, Ira. *Every Dreamer's Handbook: A Simple Guide to Understanding Your Dreams*. Shippensburg, PA: Treasure House, 2000.

Milligan, Ira. *Understanding the Dreams You Dream*. Shippensburg, PA: Treasure House, 1997.

Vallowe, Ed F. *Biblical Mathematics: Keys to Scripture Numerics*. Columbia, SC: Olive Press, 1995.

Yocum, Bruce. *Prophecy*. Ann Arbor, MI: Servant Publications, 1976.

Prayers That Outwit the Enemy

Making God's Word Your
First Line of Defense

With much love,
we dedicate this book to our wonderful spouses,
Pam Pierce and Jack Sytsema,
who have consistently and strategically
outwitted the enemy in our lives and homes.

Foreword

by Dutch Sheets

Since Chuck Pierce first mentioned it to me, I have been fascinated by the title of this book, *Prayers That Outwit the Enemy*. I remember wishing I had thought of it first. Actually, I'm glad I didn't, because no one is as qualified to write this book as is Chuck. I do not hold this opinion based only on his theological excellence, intellectual brilliance or wise insights, but also because I have marveled as I've watched him live out the truths he now writes about.

When Chuck has faced spiritual challenges and opportunities, time and again I have observed him receive clear strategies from the Holy Spirit, process them through sound biblical truth and apply them with practical wisdom. Moreover, as predictably as the sunrise, I watch the resulting fruit. Chuck has developed a remarkable ability to know when to act and when to wait. He knows how to discern what to do and what not to do. Though at times it looks like a sixth sense, I have come to understand that actually his heart and his mind are well trained and acutely sensitized to the Holy Spirit. He really is a modern-day son of Issachar: "Men who understood the times, with knowledge of what Israel should do" (1 Chronicles 12:32 NASB). It is now our great opportunity to glean fruit once again from this Spirit-led man on a subject of paramount importance: prayers that outwit the enemy.

Genesis 3:1 says of Satan: "The serpent was more crafty than any beast" (NASB). The Hebrew word translated here as "crafty" has in its etymology the concept of being bare or smooth. We still use the concept today when we speak of someone as being cunning in a bad sense, saying of them that they are slick, or perhaps that they are a smooth operator.

This same Hebrew word is sometimes translated as "wily," or "wilily." The New Testament, no doubt picking up on this concept, says of Satan's perverted yet subtle abilities: "Put on the whole armour of God, that ye may be able to stand against the *wiles* of the devil" (Ephesians 6:11 KJV, emphasis added). The point is clear: Satan is far more dangerous to us as the wily serpent than as the roaring lion. He is far more effective with his slick craftiness than with his power or strength. The first verse of Martin Luther's hymn "A Mighty Fortress Is Our God" is very true:

> For still our ancient foe doth seek to work us woe;
> His craft and power are great, and, armed with cruel
>   hate,
> On earth is not his equal.

But as Chuck teaches us in this wonderful book, that isn't the end of the story. There is good news for us as we face our shrewd adversary: The wisdom of God infinitely supersedes the craftiness of the serpent. The Scriptures clearly state, "He captures the wise by their own shrewdness" (Job 5:13 NASB), and He "catches the wise in their craftiness" (1 Corinthians 3:19

NASB). Placed in the context of the cross in order to prove His point, God confidently declares in 1 Corinthians 1:19, "For it is written, 'I will destroy the wisdom of the wise, and the cleverness of the clever I will set aside'" (NASB). Yes, He outwitted Satan at the cross, and that is the ultimate proof that He will outwit him in every circumstance of our lives. Verses 2 and 3 of Luther's great hymn are equally true and poignant:

> Did we in our own strength confide, our striving would
>   be losing;
> Were not the right Man on our side, the Man of God's
>   own choosing:
> Dost ask who that may be? Christ Jesus, it is He;
> Lord Sabaoth, His Name, from age to age the same,
> And He must win the battle.

> And though this world, with devils filled, should
>   threaten to undo us,
> We will not fear, for God hath willed His truth to tri-
>   umph through us:
> The Prince of Darkness grim, we tremble not for him;
> His rage we can endure, for lo, his doom is sure,
> One little word shall fell him.

Luther would have liked this book. He knew, when facing the evil one, how dependent we humans are on God's supernatural aid. He was also very confident of its availability. He understood our foe but was impressed only by our God. So is Chuck, so am I, and so will you be after enjoying this great book.

A Note to Our Readers

We cowrote this book but write in a singular voice. Whenever a first-person pronoun is used (I, me, etc.), it is either Chuck speaking or both of us speaking. Whenever the illustration or point comes from Becky alone, we have identified it as such.

Checkmate

The painting was eerie and disturbing—the kind not easily erased from one's memory. It hung on a wall inside a farmhouse somewhere outside Richmond, Virginia. Dinner had just been served when the chess master noticed. He was the guest of honor that night—sometime in the mid-1800s—but he could not help but stare at the image, almost speechless.

This particular piece of art depicted a chess match well under way. On one side of the board sat a man whose slumped shoulders and panicked eyes showed utter defeat. The look on his face left the viewer with the impression that the stakes surrounding this duel had been high—his very soul had been waged on the outcome. On the other side of the board was an awful and terrifying image of Mephistopheles—the legend of Faust who represents the spirit of the devil, the soul stealer. Mephistopheles's large figure was rising from his chair in obvious victory, gloating over the spoils he was ready to seize from this pitiful opponent. He was ready to shout, "Checkmate."

The chess master's host was a preacher. No doubt on many occasions he had stood and looked intently into the hopeless and horrified eyes of the defeated man depicted in the painting and pondered how many people in his own town lived with their souls overtaken by the devil. The chess master, on the other hand, focused on the board, intently calculating how the game had been played. He stared for a long time. So intrigued was the chess master that he set up his own prized chessboard and meticulously re-created the game shown in the painting.

Satan will try to declare checkmate time and time again, seeking to convince us that he has won.

The preacher and the other dinner guests, no doubt, were intrigued. "What are you doing?" they likely asked. The chess master most surely looked up from the chessboard with a gleam in his eyes. As legend has it, he then challenged the others to a game of chess. He would start severely handicapped, with his pieces placed in the position held by the young man in the painting who was on the brink of defeat. Whichever dinner guest would take the devil's side would seem to have the upper hand. At least one guest could not resist the temptation to beat the master at his own game and chose to side with Mephistopheles.

One version of this popular tale has the legendary nineteenth-century chess champion Paul Morphy declaring, "This artist has made a mistake. There is no checkmate. Satan has not won. See here? Look." Pointing to the board, he drew a deep breath and loudly announced, "The king has one more move."[1]

How true it is in our lives, as well. Satan will try to declare checkmate time and time again, seeking to convince us that he has won and that there is no way out. But God, our King, has a destiny for each of our lives. Our destiny, our family's destiny and our territory's destiny are at the heart of any attack that the enemy launches against us. Satan knows that if our spirit ever comes alive to all God has, we will become a weapon in His hands, and we will have the authority to oppose evil with great force. When we know God's direction for our life, and allow Him to work out the gifting within us, we become a real and present threat to the enemy. That is why Satan will make strategic moves against us in order to stop us from accomplishing God's purposes.

But knowing that God has something greater and bigger planned for us is central to our gaining both the energy and the strategy to outwit our enemy. We can be assured that, even as Satan launches his assaults against us and all may seem lost, the King has one more move.

The Game of War

Many times we can learn a lot from games. In fact, I think that some games were inspired by God to teach us about the spiritual dynamic around us. Chess fits into this category. In his book *Chess: From First Moves to Checkmate*, Daniel King wrote,

> Chess is a game of war. You control one army and your opponent, the enemy, controls the other. The fate of your army depends entirely on your own skill. Most other games rely on chance—a move may be determined by a roll of the dice, or the turn of a card. But in chess there is no luck. You are entirely responsible for your own success or failure, and this is why chess can be one of the most satisfying of all games to win. . . . Before you make a move on the chessboard you must try to predict, as far as you can, how your opponent will react. In deciding what to play, you will need to use reason, memory, and logic combined with a dash of intuition and inspiration.[2]

Here is where I see that chess takes on a spiritual dimension. As we find ourselves engaged in war with the enemy, not only does God require us to yield our minds to His control, but He also gives us greater levels of spiritual intuition and inspiration. We will discuss both of these in greater detail throughout this book, but for now let's take a brief look at each aspect.

Within every one of us, men and women alike, there is a function called intuition. Once we have been saved and our spirit is connected back with its Maker and Creator, our intuition is then activated in new dimensions and becomes much sharper. Stimulated by the Holy Spirit within us, intuition includes God-given wisdom, knowledge, discernment and other similar supernatural understanding of what is going on around us. Our intuition, therefore, helps us to understand the moves the enemy makes against us, what he is likely to do next and how we can make strategic moves that both thwart his plans and advance us toward victory. Intuition, guided by the Holy Spirit, gives us the ability to overcome our enemy.

Inspiration is another issue. It is the very core of faith. When we have faith deep within our spirit, we are inspired. If we are inspired, we have been breathed upon or infused with life. This breath of life causes us to be guided, to be motivated and to seek out the communication with God that we need in order to bring divine influence into our lives and actions. In order to stay the course for the long haul without growing weary, we need to have divine inspiration that refreshes, renews and provides us with hope—especially in those times when the enemy tries to wrongly convince us that he has won. Inspiration is that which arises within us to shout, "The King has one more move."

The Role We Each Play

King writes further about chess, but he could be setting up my next point about the spiritual realm.

It has been claimed that there are more possible moves on the chessboard than there are atoms in the universe. This helps account for the game's popularity through the ages. Chess has never been "solved." Even in today's computer age, it remains as complex and fascinating as it must have been when it emerged in India, almost 1,500 years ago.[3]

We can apply the same concept to our spiritual life. It is very much like a chess game. There are an infinite number of possible moves that can turn the game in this or that direction. The Lord's leading in our lives is, therefore, essential. This applies both to individual believers and to the corporate Body of Christ.

Let's continue to use the analogy of the chess game as we see where each of us fits in the Body of Christ. When playing a game of chess, we need to know each piece and its function. Let's again turn to King for an explanation of how it works in chess.

The value of each piece is based on its power on the board. Remembering these values will help you decide which pieces to exchange, and which pieces to keep.[4]

We all have value in the eyes of the Lord. Each one of us has a different place to stand, different gifts and a different measure of faith, but we all have value.

O Lord, You have searched me and known me . . . For You formed my inward parts; You covered me in my mother's womb. I will praise You, for I am fearfully and wonderfully made. . . . My frame was not hidden from You, when I was made in secret. . . . Your eyes saw my substance, being yet unformed. And in Your book they all were written, the days fashioned for me, when as yet there were none of them.

Psalm 139:1, 13–16

In other words, God valued you enough to make you.

In chess, the queen, with its ability to move like a bishop and a rook, is by far the most powerful piece on the board. When the queen is in the center of the board, it exercises extraordinary power. The queen's influence stretches from one side of the board to the other. The queen can move to any square. If the queen is lost, the chances of winning the game become greatly reduced.

The rook (also known as the castle) is another strategic piece, although unable to utilize its full power at the beginning of a game. A rook can only move up and down or side to side; it cannot leap because it is hemmed in. The bishop and the knight are also important, but not as versatile. These pieces are all useful guides when we are making strategic decisions in a heated battle for the board.

Then, of course, there is the pawn. Even though the pawn seems lowly, it protects the other pieces. At times, it is sacrificed to gain valuable positioning for future moves. Ordinary and humble as it may seem, the pawn has incredible potential because, if it reaches the far side of the board, it can be exchanged for a queen, bishop, knight or rook. The pawn is like you. You were born with great potential. You might go through some hard times that seem very sacrificial, but you can cross over and make it to the other side. It is in the persevering and overcoming that the fullness of your potential can be recognized.

Each one of us has a different place to stand, different gifts and a different measure of faith, but we all have value.

The End of the Game

The king is the most important piece on the chessboard. The whole game revolves around the struggle to trap the king. This is called checkmate. Lose this piece and you lose the game, so it is vital to keep the king as secure as possible.[5]

Once we come into covenant with a holy God and He inhabits our life and dwells within us, our opponent, the devil, must devise strategies to stop the King from being recognized and established within us.

> Checkmating your opponent's king is the ultimate aim in a chess game. The term comes from the ancient Persian "Shah mat," meaning "the king is defeated." You have to threaten the enemy king with one of your pieces so that it is unable to move and escape capture. A checkmate usually occurs when one side's forces—or "army"—are overwhelmingly superior, or by a direct and unexpected assault on the king.[6]

The enemy of our soul will threaten us constantly. He will devise plans to trap us. Though our adversary at times seems overwhelmingly superior, God in us, the hope of glory, will always give us a way to escape.

King explains how checkmate is different from checking.

> [Checking] occurs when the king is attacked by a piece, but can still escape. In other words, it is not necessarily fatal. Don't panic if your opponent suddenly thumps down a piece and cries "check." It does not end the game, and it does not always benefit your opponent. So what exactly is the point of checking? A check can help you gain time. Checking can drive the enemy king to a weak square making it vulnerable to further attack.[7]

Many of us are thrown off when the enemy checks us. Be willing to keep going and know that, in reality, you have a way to escape. In Matthew 24:13 we find, "But he that shall endure unto the end, the same shall be saved" (KJV). When the enemy checks you or tries to convince you that the game is over, you can be the one to remind him that "the King has one more move."

And as you move forward and outwit the enemy, you will be the one who ultimately shouts, "Checkmate."

Revelation

In order to get to that place of declaring "Checkmate." we must learn to live in the revelation of the Lord. Why? Because Satan, the father of lies, works to keep us in darkness and tries to keep us believing his lies, much like the poor man in the painting who believed the chess game was over. He was ready to relinquish his soul to the enemy because he believed a well-disguised lie. Satan tries to blind our minds in many ways in order to deceive us. He tries to convince us with wrong thoughts about God. He attempts to develop prejudices of all kinds within us that build walls that darken our understanding. He attempts to infiltrate us with philosophies of this world that create wrong belief systems. He attempts to erect false reasoning in order to occupy our thoughts with earthly things. He tries to overwhelm us with the cares and pleasures of this world.

Though our adversary at times seems overwhelmingly superior, God in us, the hope of glory, will always give us a way to escape.

Satan loves to mix his lies with partial truth. That is what makes the lies seem so believable. It is also why we need revelation. I like what Paul Keith Davis wrote in *Engaging the Revelatory Realm of Heaven*.

> Currently the Lord is allowing many in the Church to see things taking place in the second Heaven as well as portions of His perfect plan in the third Heaven. The enemy would have people believe all is well, by calling good things as "evil" and base or foolish things as "good." Presently a deceptive voice seeks to

find an outlet to hinder the preparation of God's people for the end-time battle.[8]

"Revelation" means to manifest, to make clear, to show forth, to unfold, to explain by narration, to instruct, to admonish, to warn or to give an answer to a question. When God speaks to us, He brings one or more of these aspects of revelation so that the eyes of our minds may be enlightened to who He is. Throughout history, God has actively disclosed Himself to humanity. God has not wavered in His desire that we also understand Him. He continues to reveal His power, His glory, His nature, His character, His will, His ways, His plans and His strategies to His people today.

Revelation from God has three important functions in our lives.

1. **Revelation causes obscure things to become clear.** Jeremiah 33:3 in The Amplified Bible reads, "Call to Me and I will answer you and show you great and mighty things, fenced in and hidden, which you do not know (do not distinguish and recognize, have knowledge of and understand)."

2. **Revelation brings hidden things to light.** One important definition of "revelation" is *apocalypse*, which means to unveil or reveal something that is hidden so that it may be seen and known for what it is.

3. **Revelation gives us signs that point us to our path of destiny.** We need revelation in order to know God's will for our lives and, as we come into agreement with His will, how to walk it out. By this we see that revelation is not a onetime deal. We need fresh revelation on a continual basis to keep moving forward in God's plan and timing, and to keep our minds from the enemy's deceptions.

These three functions of revelation help us understand the why, but an even bigger question is, How? Let's look at Ephesians 1:20–23:

Which He worked in Christ when He raised Him from the dead and seated Him at His right hand in the heavenly places, far above all principality and power and might and dominion, and every name that is named, not only in this age but also in that which is to come. And He put all things under His feet, and gave Him to be head over all things to the church, which is His body, the fullness of Him who fills all in all.

This passage shows us that Jesus is able to defeat the enemy's structures in our lives from His position as Head because all things are under His feet. Because Jesus is Head, we need to think the way He thinks and put on the mind of Christ (see 1 Corinthians 2:16).

The problem is that our minds are naturally at enmity with God because of our flesh. We must put on the mind of Christ so that the Spirit of wisdom and revelation is activated in our lives. To do this, we need to believe that God will show us new revelation in a way that we, individually, can receive. The first important step in gaining revelation, therefore, is to trust that God has a way to communicate it to us. The next step is being open to and aware of what God is saying. The third step is to enter into a new dimension of faith, which we will discuss more in chapter 7.

We need to think the way Jesus thinks and put on the mind of Christ.

It is one thing to decide that we want to enter into this new dimension, but it is quite another to get there. We need the Holy Spirit to help us through this process. Because revelation does not come through our own strength, we have to stay in intimate contact with God in order to gain revelation from Him and eventually yell, "Checkmate," against the enemy. Revelation leads us to wisdom, and wisdom gives us strategy. Strategy overthrows Satan's plans. But if we don't stay close to God, we won't have clear revelation. We must continue our dialogue with Him. Once we're dialoging in intimacy with God, He will give us three important revelations.

1. **He reveals Himself to us.** Unless we truly know who God is, we will never have what we need to outwit the devil. Our foundation will be shaky, and we will not enter into the level of faith that we need to conquer our enemy. When we have faith we are saying that we know God will do what He has promised to do. But unless we have a glimpse of who He really is, our faith will not have an opportunity to arise with us. We need to know God and His faithfulness to His promises in order to see how committed He is to overthrowing the enemy in our personal situations.

2. **He will reveal who you are in Him.** As we draw close to God, we begin to understand why He has made us. That is what the hope of His calling is all about (see Ephesians 1:18). Hope is an important element for moving forward with confidence. As God reveals who we are and what our calling is, we gain hope for our future. The enemy loves to come against our hope, and usually does so with trauma and grief in our lives. Trauma and grief are diametrically opposed to hope, and can cause us to lose our insight into God's identity for us. Of course, there are events and seasons in our lives that will naturally bring us into feelings of trauma and grief. If, during such seasons, we are able to remain intimate with the Lord, these natural feelings will not be able to overtake our spirits and souls in such a way that they become instruments in the hands of the enemy who wants to destroy our future.

3. **He will reveal who our enemy is and how he is working against us.** If we are to outwit the devil, we need to know

the devil. This may be a very new thought for many who have somehow come to believe that paying any attention to the devil is the same as coming into agreement with him. That is not the case. Every successful war strategy that has ever been launched in history has included both reconnaissance and an understanding of how the enemy thinks and what he is likely to do. In this case, we need to allow the Lord to be our reconnaissance, and we need to actively seek both wisdom and strategy from Him. As we learn more about our enemy, we need to remember that there is great truth in 1 John 4:4: "You are of God, little children, and have overcome them, because He who is in you is greater than he who is in the world."

Prayer

We must rise up now and become intimate with God. The only way to do that is to spend time communing with Him in prayer. Prayer is dialogue. If we dialogue with God, we will overcome our enemy. The enemy cannot overcome God. That is why this book is called *Prayers That Outwit the Enemy*. As we utilize the different forms of prayer described in this book, we will become more intimate with God. Moreover, as we become more intimate with God, we'll also come to know the workings of the devil in our midst.

It is time for us to recover our losses. It is time for Satan to release our supply. It is time for a release of strength. It is time for God's people to invade Satan's territory and advance His Kingdom on earth.

Our prayer for you in days ahead is that you will become connected to God's Spirit of wisdom and revelation so that you will have all that you need to outwit and checkmate the devil in your life, your family and your territory.

Know the Enemy

One night I was at home watching a movie with my kids. It was a good movie about an unconventional musician who takes an assignment as a substitute teacher in a very conventional prep school. What caught my ear was when I heard the teacher defining "the man" to these kids. He defined "the man" as an individual who has such influence or authority in your life that your freedom becomes hindered and controlled.

How interesting. That sounds like Isaiah's definition of Lucifer. After describing Satan's boasting and his eventual fall, Isaiah 14 reads, "Those who see you will gaze at you, and consider you, saying: 'Is this *the man* who made the earth tremble, who shook kingdoms?'" (verse 16, emphasis added). We see in the Bible that there are many instances of "the man." Pharaoh was "the man." The Amalekites were "the man." Jezebel and Ahab formed a team to become "the man." In the New Testament, we find Jesus dealing with "the man" and calling him Satan.

Know the Enemy by Sight

I believe that it is very important to know the overall purpose of a thing. In other words, why do we do what we do? Why do we try to understand something? First John 3:8 clears up a lot about the enemy: "He who sins is of the devil, for the devil has sinned from the beginning. For this purpose the Son of God was manifested, that He might destroy the works of the devil."

Every time we sin, who is behind it? The devil. Some may question this statement, but we must remember that he is the father of all lies and the author of all sin. When our flesh aligns itself to do the will of the enemy, we have come into communion with "the man" in our life. He will eventually dominate us.

As a teenager, I strayed from the Lord. I had lived through several terrible years. My family was torn apart as my father sank deep into gambling and many other sinful patterns. This season culminated with my father's death. When I was eighteen, I became very ill and ended up in the hospital for some time. During that time I began to reconnect with God. I asked the Lord why I was drawn to do the things I hated to do. God showed me that even though I belonged to Him, the devil was superimposed over my body, and He said, "This is the controlling force in your life, not Me." I called upon the Lord, who was in me, and I said, "You are greater in me than that which is superimposed over me. If You will rise up over me, the devil will have to leave me." In those days I knew nothing about the Bible, much less deliverance. But when I called out, the Spirit of God came down in that hospital room and visited me for three days.

While there the Lord said to me, "It wasn't your father who ruined your family. It was the devil. Your father came into agreement with him. Therefore, all the prosperity that I had planned for you as a family, Satan seized through sin, and he is trying to keep it from coming to the next generation." I knew right then that I had a choice. I could rise up and begin to become a student of God and a student of the Holy Spirit, or I could go the way of my earthly father.

During this time, the Holy Spirit became tangible to me. There has to come a time when the Holy Spirit becomes real for each of us. Once that happens, we are propelled into warfare. If we have been taught that the Holy Spirit is released in us purely for our joy and comfort, we have only been taught part of the picture. He can keep us filled with joy. He can comfort us and He can teach us. But the Holy Spirit will also open our eyes to the dark world around us so that we are able to see how the enemy is working against us. We can't truly outwit the devil until we have an understanding of who he is and how he operates.

> *We can't truly outwit the devil until we have an understanding of who he is and how he operates.*

Know the Enemy by Name

In the Bible, particularly the New Testament, the devil is described in many ways. Here we also learn that he operates not only on earth as a whole, but also in the lives of individuals. He opposes God's purposes on earth and devises schemes to prevent God's people from entering into those purposes. He is not a creature in a red suit with horns; rather, he can be a deceiving angel of light. We know people by their names. Therefore, let's look at some of the names and terms the Bible uses to describe Satan.

1. **The dragon or the old serpent** (see Revelation 12:9; 20:2). The dragon or the serpent reveals a characteristic of the enemy that will war with the Church until the end. Jesus Christ defeated him fully at the cross, but because we

159

live in a time before the Second Coming of Christ, when Satan's defeat will be complete, we, too, must arise and face this creature who continues to wreak havoc on earth. We will be in enmity with the serpent until the end. He is clever, religious and filled with political strength and authority.

2. **A deceiver** (see Genesis 3). Satan came to Adam and Eve and deceived them. Basically he said to them, "God is holding back on you." Once Adam and Eve believed the lie, Satan was able to attach himself to their desires and manipulate them into sin. Satan will often deceive us in the same way by telling us that God is somehow holding back on us, and if we will do this or that, we will get whatever it is that God does not want us to have. If we buy in to the lie, Satan can then lure us into sin, which separates us from God's path for our life. The absolute truth is that God *doesn't* hold back on us. God loves us and wants the best for us. He has a path and a destiny that will add everything to us that we need (see Matthew 6:33). But we, just like Adam and Eve, can choose to be diverted from that path through sin and disobedience, and Satan knows it. Therefore, he will do whatever he can to deceive us into sinning.

3. **Our adversary** (see Numbers 22:22). An adversary is one who opposes us. Satan opposes the work of God's chosen ones (see 1 Thessalonians 2:18). He opposes our faith. He knows that our devotion to God can overthrow his power in the territory where we have been positioned on earth. The enemy is looking for ways to stop our faith from propelling us into God's full plan for our life. As more and more of God's servants arise, Satan's defeat becomes inevitable.

4. **A usurper** (see Genesis 3). When Satan disobeyed God, he moved in to usurp God's rightful place. Satan's downfall

was that, before he was expelled from heaven, he had an inordinate desire for the angels to admire him. He, therefore, sought to exalt himself higher than God by usurping and betraying his creator. Satan has worked in the same way throughout the ages. He seeks ways of dethroning God in individuals' hearts and in territories. His pride causes him to both beguile and seduce—traits that he has fully mastered.

5. **An accuser.** Notice that the moment God confronted Adam and Eve, they turned on each other (see Genesis 3:13). The sin that Satan drew them into caused an accusing spirit to rise up within them. Satan will always try to do the same with us by causing us to question our brothers and sisters in the Lord through false accusations spread by gossip; by causing us to accuse one another through our own anger or hurt; by causing false accusations to be launched against us; or by causing us to accuse ourselves

> *Satan is always seen as hostile to God and is working to overthrow God's purposes.*

with an ungodly spirit of condemnation. If God is bringing conviction to our heart, it will cause us to want to get right with God and move forward in His plan. But if an ungodly spirit of condemnation is coming against us, we will feel separated from God in a way that will seem irreparable, and we will turn aside from His path and go into various forms of self-destruction.

6. **A tempter** (see 1 Corinthians 7:5). Satan loves to find our weaknesses. He can and will tempt us to fall into sinful patterns. Satan's goal is to cause us to fail and then deviate from God's path for our life. When we give in to his temptations, he is able to divert us and clothe us in shame, disgrace and condemnation. But we need to remember

that even though he has the power to tempt us, he cannot force us to do his will. In fact, temptation offers us the possibility of choosing holiness over sin. James 1:2 shows us that we can even count such things as joy. If we do not allow the tempter to overtake us, we can use his temptations to produce overcoming faith in our lives, and we will be able to rejoice in his defeat.

7. **A legalist.** We see throughout the Bible that Satan tries to use the law to bind and restrict rather than bring the freedom of God. The Pharisees are a good example of how legalism can obscure God's true intent. Furthermore, as we will see a little further in this chapter, Satan works to change laws so that they align with sinful practices rather than with bringing God's righteousness to territories.

8. **Supremely evil Beelzebub, "The Lord of the Flies"** (see Matthew 12:24, 27). He is the prince of the devils (see 12:24). He controls elaborate and well-organized demonic structures that have been set up to exalt himself and further his purposes throughout the world.

9. **The prince of the power of the air** (see Ephesians 2:2). His power is very great on this planet. He is always seen as hostile to God and is working to overthrow God's purposes. He works to rule entire societies, and he attempts to fill the atmosphere (air) around us with his presence and influence.

10. **The prince of this world** (see John 12:31; 14:30). A prince is one who holds legal right to a kingdom. Satan exercises and maintains his legal right as prince through human sin and failures on earth. He manipulates the structures of the world.

The above characteristics enable us to better know our enemy. By knowing his names and descriptions, we can detect his presence whenever he is around us.

Know the Enemy by His Actions

Just as we can know the enemy by his name, we can also iden-tify him by his actions. Knowing how he acts helps us discern when he is in our midst.

1. **Satan has a discernible presence.** When we are walking with the Lord and are being guided by the Holy Spirit, we are able to discern the presence of evil. It is almost as if all the hair on our arms will stand up when Satan or his forces are around. When this happens, we have come to know his presence. We know what's going on. Our spirit tells us that something isn't right. This discernment is a function of the wisdom that comes through the Holy Spirit.

2. **Satan will bind us to doctrines.** Satan is very religious and legalistic. Therefore, he creates structures that hold us in place through religious legalism. But let's be clear about this point. Religious legalism is nothing more than superstition. Superstition says that if we do A, B and C, then we can expect D to occur. Or it says, if A occurs, then we need to do B, C and D in order to cancel out any bad effects of A. For instance, some may feel they have to leave their Bible open to a certain passage in their bedroom or else Satan will gain access. Others may think that they have to light a candle or burn incense to maintain the pres-ence of God. Some fear actually saying the name of the devil or coming against him because they think that such acts are invitations for him to operate in their lives. The truth is that Satan already plots against each of us. These superstitious rituals are legalistic and come with demonic snares. If the Lord has someone do a prophetic act for a particular reason, that's one thing. There is freedom in that. But if people blindly follow rituals that they do not

understand, there is no freedom in that because they are bound to that ritual instead of seeking a fresh strategy from God.

3. **Satan is continually opposed to the Gospel.** We see evidence of this throughout the Lord's ministry; Satan attempted to work through Jesus' followers. He hates those who carry the Good News, and he connives to confuse and hinder anyone who is communicating God's redemptive plan.

4. **Satan searches for men and women who can be "taken captive by him"** (2 Timothy 2:26). He longs to seduce us from God's path and to control our wills.

5. **He is "like a roaring lion, seeking whom he may devour"** (1 Peter 5:8). He lurks and lies in wait to ambush us on our path.

6. **He looks for opportune times.** When the period of testing in the wilderness had been completed for Jesus, the devil left Him "until an opportune time," which implies that the enemy would watch for his next opportunity (see Matthew 3:11). This is essential for us to understand. We defeat the enemy battle by battle. Even if we have won a victory against him, we need to remember that he will look for another opportunity to attack or oppose us.

7. **He changes laws.** Because he is a legalist, Satan must use laws and control entire political and social structures to benefit his plans. By doing so, he is able to obscure the absolute truth of God's righteousness and cause that which God abhors to seem almost benign. An example of this in the United States at the time of this writing is same-sex marriage. This is a huge debate in which Satan has diverted attention away from righteousness and toward the so-called rights of individuals to act in whatever way seems right to them. The push in many states to allow

such marriages will ultimately produce legally sanctioned unions that are diametrically opposed to an absolute truth that God has set forth in both the Old Testament and the New Testament.

Know the Enemy's Limitations

Despite looking at the power and intent of the enemy, we can't ever forget that he is a defeated enemy. Paul can say confidently, "The God of peace will crush Satan under your feet shortly" (Romans 16:20). Satan and the demonic forces have been defeated by the life, death and resurrection of Jesus Christ. In the end, Satan and his angels will be completely overcome. In fact, Jesus came into the world to "destroy the works of the devil" (1 John 3:8). The cross was a decisive victory over Satan and Satan's host (see Colossians 2:15). This victory ensured that countless numbers would be delivered from the dominion of darkness and transferred to the Kingdom of Christ (see Colossians 1:13). But this is not just an end-time promise for when the clouds part and we see the Lord descend. We have promises of Satan's defeat in our lives today. We are the only ones who can allow him to become "the man" in our lives, but we, through the leading of the Holy Spirit, also have the authority to outwit his schemes and dethrone him.

Satan and the demonic forces have been defeated by the life, death and resurrection of Jesus Christ.

Always Pray

Keep praying and seeking the Lord and you will overcome your enemy. The Lord began to move in me in the late 1970s to renew and energize my prayer life. I found myself staying up late and praying. God gave me actual prayer assignments. He had me pray for individuals, for my Sunday school class, for our church, for my pastor and for the church staff. I prayed for the company at which I worked. I prayed for my family. I simply was enjoying communicating with the Lord and watching Him work.

One night after I had my prayer time, I went to bed. At 2:00 a.m., I was awakened and our dog was growling and getting into the bed with us. My wife, Pam, was awakened and startled, as well. I felt a presence in our room. Pam described this presence as a slimy green vapor—it was at the end of our bed. I stood up on our bed and commanded this presence to leave our house. I knew that the enemy was angry over my prayer becoming active. This evil force was hoping to deter me from getting to know the Lord better. It was as if he was attempting to produce fear in me so I would stop praying. He knew that if I kept seeking the Lord with all my heart, I would eventually be free and able to recognize and confront him in new ways to defeat his purposes.

I want to encourage you not to let the enemy create fear in you. Do not be afraid to understand the enemy's schemes, character and ways. Go all the way with the Lord. Keep gaining victory over the enemy's plan to control and ruin your life. Remember, one small word fells him, this "man" who would rob you of your joy and life.

When contending with "the man," I am reminded that we have The Man contending for us. I am often encouraged by remembering the words of the classic hymn *A Mighty Fortress Is Our God*.

> Did we in our own strength confide, our striving would
> be losing,
> Were not the right man on our side, the man of God's
> own choosing.
> Dost ask who that may be? Christ Jesus, it is He—

Lord Sabaoth His name, from age to age the same,
And He must win the battle.

And though this world with devils filled, should
    threaten to undo us,
We will not fear, for God hath willed, His truth to tri-
    umph through us.
The prince of darkness grim, we tremble not for him—
His rage we can endure, for lo, his doom is sure:
One little word shall fell him.[1]

3

Passion along the Path

It must have been a beautiful spring that year, one in which David was particularly enjoying his reign as king. After all, it had only been a year since he had successfully restored his nation to peace after defeating the Syrians and had also made his army a great military power in the land. Ah, yes. How good the days were.

The rainy season of winter was behind, and many crops were now ready for harvesting—a spring tradition in Israel. Spring also meant that the roads were dry, making travel easier for wagons and chariots. Because of these good travel conditions and the plentiful supply of food, spring had become the traditional time to wage war on enemies, and the armies were usually led by their kings.

But this spring was different. David was ready to wage war against the Ammonites, but instead of leading the army himself, he stayed behind in Jerusalem and sent Joab. Because David abandoned his purpose by staying home from the battle, he was outwitted and encountered many needless struggles.

Four Questions

Satan seeks to outwit us, God's people, in ways that will divert us from God's path. By rerouting us, he can embroil us in problems and situations that keep us from God's destiny for our life. As we seek to be the outwitters rather than the outwitted, here are four key questions we should ask ourselves.

1. **Am I prepared for the warfare ahead?** We do not have to make a conscious decision to engage the enemy before we find ourselves in warfare. Our enemy is actively waging a battle against us whether or not we fight back. Nevertheless, a wise Christian will look at the warfare in which he or she is involved and ask whether he or she is truly prepared to move forward in the fight.

2. **In what area do I need the most training (e.g., finances, vision, family, etc.)?** As we take stock of our preparedness, we will need to seek out training in any areas in our own lives or in our families that are weak.

3. **What war am I in?** God has not called us to fight every battle. It is important to know our role and how the Lord is positioning each of us in the war.

4. **Is there an area in my life in which the enemy is outwitting me?** We will devote much of this chapter to looking at this question in some detail. How is it that we are so susceptible to becoming outwitted by the enemy?

The Two Types of Passion

The first type of passion is a driving or compelling force, a dominating emotion, a strong desire or a potent enthusiasm. This is the type of passion that is commonplace today. But in the King James Version, the word *passion* is only used once in the New Testament. It appears in Acts 1:3 to describe a different type of passion. Here the word means the suffering of Christ on the cross—hence the title of Mel Gibson's movie *The Passion of the Christ*. For us, then, this second type of passion is entering into the sufferings and endurance of our Lord against temptation; experiencing His death in our flesh; and receiving and experiencing His resurrection life.

A wise Christian will look at the warfare in which he or she is involved and ask whether he or she is truly prepared to move forward in the fight.

The Greek word used for *passion* in Acts 1:3 is from the root word *pathos,* which is defined as "path." From this we can see that our passion is linked to our path. If the enemy can cause us to become passive as we traverse our God-given path, then our passion for God will become misdirected. Passivity will cause us to quit resisting the enemy who is in our path; the enemy can then outwit us by misdirecting our passions and causing us to fall into sin.

That is exactly what happened to David. At the time when he was supposed to enter into war, he fell into passivity and chose to stay home. Because he stayed home, he was not in the place God wanted him to be and the enemy took advantage of him. There are times when we, like David, are called to war. We war against everything that is set against our destiny or our accomplishing the fullness of our path. If we do not go into battle when God calls us to war, then we will be in serious danger of being outwitted by the enemy—he can stir up our passivity into a passion that God never intended. Success means that you're at the right place at the right time, doing the right thing. God blesses that. When we are in this place, God's favor rests upon us and we can see the true, God-given desires and passions of our hearts fulfilled.

Ungodly Passions

David belonged on the battlefield, not looking out onto Bathsheba's roof, where she was bathing. As lust for this woman filled his heart, he further entertained temptation by inquiring about her. This demonstrates how our thoughts can be led astray by our emotions. Passion is a powerful, controlling sentiment that can overwhelm our state of mind and influence our actions. If we never bring our emotions under the control of the Holy Spirit, our emotions will tend to become hooked into ungodly passions that lead to sin. As David continued to give place in his mind to his misguided passions, those passions turned into the actions of committing adultery with Bathsheba and the murder of her husband, Uriah. Because of David's murderous scheme, many others were killed on that day.

If we do not go into battle when God calls us to war, then we will be in serious danger of being outwitted by the enemy.

David's passivity caused him to be diverted from his path; his passivity turned into ungodly passion and sin, and he suffered the consequences.

- Murder became a constant threat in his family (see 2 Samuel 13:29–30; 18:14–15; 1 Kings 2:23–24).
- His household rebelled against him (see 2 Samuel 15:13).
- Absalom disgraced David by sleeping with his wives in public view (see 2 Samuel 16:20–23).
- The child whom David had with Bathsheba died (see 2 Samuel 12:18).[1]

The enemy had outwitted him, and as a result David paid a great price.

There are demonic forces that work to tempt us in whatever way they can, and every time we fall into a particular sin, our passion becomes misdirected in some way. God wants us to be a passionate people. While walking in that passion, we have to stay on the right path.

Misdirected Paths

When our desire deviates from our true purpose, the enemy will give us opportunities to make wrong choices and sin. The enemy is after our will. If he can misdirect our desire, he can eventually capture our will; when he captures our will, we're not accomplishing the purpose of God and will suffer many needless consequences.

A great illustration of this is found in Proverbs 7, in which a young man gives in to the temptations of a seductress. Let's look carefully at the following passage to see how our path can become diverted.

> My son, keep my words, and treasure my commands within you. Keep my commands and live, and my law as the apple of your eye. Bind them on your fingers; write them on the tablet of your heart. Say to wisdom, "You are my sister," and call understanding your nearest kin, that they may keep you from the immoral woman, from the seductress who flatters with her words.
>
> Proverbs 7:1–5

In the opening statement of this proverb, God tells us that we need His commandments to take root down deep in our spirits so that when the seductress comes, we won't be drawn away from our path. It is important to note that the "seductress" here is not only a woman, but also represents a seducing spirit that will attempt to divert our passion away from God. That spirit says to us, "Wait a minute. Come here." If we even give her a second look, suddenly, instead of having the strength to resist, we feel a pulling away and a shift in our desire. Before long, instead of our spirit's being in communion with God, our spirit begins to come into communion with another spirit.

> For at the window of my house I looked through my lattice, and saw among the simple, I perceived among the youths, a young man devoid of understanding, passing along the street near her corner; and he took the path to her house.
>
> Proverbs 7:6–8

This young man's passion was not for God; instead, his affections put him on the path to the seductress's house, and she continued to entice him.

> Come, let us take our fill of love until morning; let us delight ourselves with love.
>
> Proverbs 7:18

The enemy is going to try to convince us that he can bring a delight in us, which is an emotional response. He's going to have to counterfeit the love of God in some way, now that he's moved us off the path of God's love. Often, this illustration is sexual in nature, but it can apply to any fulfillment of ungodly lust. When we aren't being directed by the Holy Spirit, our body will seek to fulfill its senses in ways that cause it to feel good.

> With her enticing speech she caused him to yield, with her flattering lips she seduced him. Immediately he went after her, as an ox goes to the slaughter, or as a fool to the correction of the stocks, till an arrow struck his liver. As a bird hastens to the snare, he did not know it would cost his life.
>
> Proverbs 7:21–23

Here we see that sin will affect us physically. It will affect even the organs of our body once we deviate from the path and align ourselves with the enemy. This is particularly true of sexual sins. This was very clearly illustrated to me once when I was ministering. I received a word of knowledge that a man present at the meeting had had sex with a witch and, as a result, was suffering from disease in his liver. Not wanting to publicly embarrass this suffering man, I said that I would be in my room for two hours that afternoon, and that whoever it was could come for private ministry. That afternoon I heard a knock on the door. When I opened it, there were eight men who had come for deliverance, all having had sex with witches and all suffering from some kind of liver disease. Sin defiles the body often in ways we do not understand.

The English Puritan preacher Richard Sibbes once said, "Satan gives an apple, but he looks to deprive us of a paradise."[2] Oh, how true this is. Therefore whenever the enemy makes us an offer, we should consider not what we would gain but what we would lose.

The Problem with Passivity

One of Satan's most effective ploys is to lure us into passivity. We saw this at the beginning of this chapter when David did not follow his path to war. When we lose our passion and zeal for God and for His purposes in our life, we are then at our most vulnerable for becoming diverted from our path and into ungodly passions.

One of Satan's most effective ploys is to lure us into passivity.

If the enemy can ever get us into passivity so we are not communing, we end up just wandering through life and are in danger of Satan's filling our mind with lies. This is one circumstance he will use to develop strongholds in our mind. Because of passivity, our thoughts are not connected to the mind of Christ, and we cannot see the full plan that God has for us. Think of a room in which stacks and stacks of materials have accumulated. Those stacks have not been dusted in years. It's hard to know what is in the stacks. Cobwebs have overtaken the room. That is what our mind looks like when the devil brings us into passivity. *Shake out those cobwebs. Get them out of your brain.* We periodically need deliverance in our lives, simply because we can so easily fall into places of passivity and end up in a position in which the enemy can start trying to convince us of lies about God and about our God-given destiny.

A Return to Passion

In order for us to be totally free, we must submit to death. We have to enter into the second type of passion and experience the death of the cross. To have this kind of passion is to experience His death in our flesh. We must not be afraid of this death—such a fear will prevent us from entering into the resurrection and crossing over into our next level of power and authority.

Part of this death in our flesh will entail suffering and trials. The truth is, whenever there is warfare in our lives that we will need to press through, there will also be an amount of suffering that we will encounter in overcoming. Yet it is through that process that our godly passion originates and is completed. Via this overcoming in the midst of great difficulties, we are able to move into new dimensions of God's best for our lives.

At the time of this writing, my coauthor, Rebecca Sytsema, and her husband, Jack, were undergoing a difficult type of suffering in that their oldest son, Nicholas, has autism. This has been a deeply painful and incredibly trying experience, affecting every area of their lives and draining them of resources. Yet as they have walked this situation out over the past several years and have remained faithful to the Lord, He has infused them with a tremendous new passion they could not otherwise have known.

Their hearts burn with a desire to minister to other children and families who are struggling with autism. As a result, the Lord has led them to Florida, where Jack is working full-time in the field of autism. They have also begun their own ministry called Children of Destiny, through which they minister to individuals and families who have been broken through autism. Their ministry reaches literally thousands each and every day, offering God's hope for the future. Could this passion have been birthed without the suffering they have experienced? They would be the first to tell you that the answer is no. Trials are difficult, and the fire can be intense, but godly passion birthed out of times of suffering and endurance has much greater depth and potential for changing the world than passion acquired by any other means.

When we don't sense the life of Christ flowing through us, we need to ask the Lord, *What has happened to my passion? In the midst of my circumstance, Lord, did I just get tired and quit withstanding?* In truth, we can pray until we are green. We can do all sorts of religious activities. But if we don't resist the enemy—the temptation toward passivity and all other temptations—in the midst of that trial, and if we do not let that trial bring the working of the cross into us, then we won't really enter into the passion and fullness of life that the Lord has for each of us. And having God's passion as we walk in wisdom and revelation is the key to protecting ourselves from becoming outwitted by the enemy.

The Mindset of War

Few of us equate God's revelation of peace in worship with a release to go to war. We want peace, but peace at what price? Some think that if we show ourselves to be peace-loving people, we will never have to war. In 1938, France just wanted to live in peace. So they ignored their neighbor Germany, which was preparing for war. But the desire for peace did not bring peace. Germany was able to take possession of France in a very short period of time. It is not our inclination for war that invites war; rather, it is our having possession of something that someone else wants. The enemy has declared war on us. He wants our worship, our loyalty and our souls. He is willing to war for these things. We are at war, whether we want to be or not.

Passivity does not bring peace, and it never has. History has shown us that as long as we are willing to give up what is ours, we will not have to face war. If we give up our possessions, war can be averted. If we give up our rights, war can be averted. If we give our children as slaves, war can be averted. But wait. How far are we willing to go here? That's a good question for the Church today. We've given up prayer in our schools. We've given up the rights of the unborn. We've allowed a small minority to determine what is acceptable in society, such as same-sex marriages and allowing those couples to adopt children.

We've allowed ourselves to be ridiculed for taking any kind of stand for righteousness. Wendell Phillips, in a speech before the Massachusetts Anti-Slavery Society in 1852, said, "Eternal vigilance is the price for liberty."[1] We haven't been vigilant and much has been lost. Now God wants back what is His, and He is looking to us to go get it.

> I beseech you therefore, brethren, by the mercies of God, that you present your bodies a living sacrifice, holy, acceptable to God, which is your reasonable service. And do not be conformed to this world, but be transformed by the renewing of your mind, that you may prove what is that good and acceptable and perfect will of God.
>
> Romans 12:1–2

It is time for a breakout. The word *conformity* means "to be formed to a blueprint of the world." The enemy longs to form us according to his blueprint, but God wants to transform our minds to the way that He thinks. Once that occurs, we can gain wisdom from God. Wisdom will dismantle any plan of the enemy and outwit him.

The Importance of Wisdom

In order to gain the revelation we need to war with the enemy and see him defeated, we need the wisdom of God. The devil is by no means stupid. He is crafty and deceitful, and he has been working against God's purposes much longer than any of us has been working for God. He knows what he is doing and how to divert us from God's perfect path. In order to overthrow his plans against us, we need access to the wisdom of the

Ancient of Days, not only to gain strategy for today but also to see what snares the devil is setting in days ahead. God will release ancient wisdom to us so that we can outwit the devil in our present-day battles. We, therefore, need to constantly seek the Lord for new and fresh wisdom for each new day and each new battle we face.

The devil has been working against God's purposes much longer than any of us has been working for God.

Proverbs 3:13–26 gives us a great list of the benefits of godly wisdom that should motivate anyone to seek Him for wisdom. The passage begins like this: "Happy is the person who finds wisdom and gains understanding. For the profit of wisdom is better than silver, and her wages are better than gold. Wisdom is more precious than rubies; nothing you desire can compare with her" (NLT). The passage goes on to list the following benefits of living in godly wisdom.

- "*Wisdom is a tree of life to those who embrace her; happy are those who hold her tightly*" (v. 18 NLT). Through concerns of this world and cares that overwhelm us, Satan will often try to thwart the abundant life God has promised to us. But when we have the wisdom of the Lord, we can see our way past the circumstances of the moment and not spiral into defeat. The ongoing strength and energy we need for life and happiness are products of living in the wisdom of God.

- "*By wisdom the LORD founded the earth; by understanding he established the heavens. By his knowledge the deep fountains of the earth burst forth, and the clouds poured down rain*" (vv. 19–20 NLT). Satan would love for us to forget the majesty and power of the God we serve. The wisdom of the Lord causes us to remember His awesome creative power, not only to form the earth and the heavens, but also to supply us with everything we need to sustain our lives. Wisdom will cause us to see our supply for days ahead, even when Satan has hidden it from us.

- *"Have two goals: wisdom—that is, knowing and doing right—and common sense. Don't let them slip away, for they fill you with living energy, and are a feather in your cap"* (vv. 21–22 TLB). God has a certain stature that He longs to bring to His people. He will establish them in places of honor and respect so that His will can be done on earth. Wisdom will cause us to walk in the place God intends for us, so that His purposes can be accomplished through us.

- *"[Wisdom will] keep you safe from defeat and disaster and from stumbling off the trail"* (v. 23 TLB). Satan has defeat and disaster planned for each of us. Wisdom is an indispensable tool to outwit his schemes.

- *"You can lie down without fear and enjoy pleasant dreams. You need not be afraid of disaster or the destruction that comes upon the wicked, for the LORD is your security. He will keep your foot from being caught in a trap"* (vv. 24–26 NLT). In wisdom we will find great peace. As we walk in the Lord's wisdom, we can rest in Him, knowing that our path is certain and that our footing is secure.

God's Surprise for the Devil

It is wonderfully true that as we seek the Ancient of Days for wisdom, we will see God surprise the devil. And why should that surprise us? There are many instances in Scripture in which God thwarted Satan's plans through wisdom that Satan did not have access to. The most significant of these occasions was the cross. Satan was so wrapped up in seeing that Jesus was humiliated, discredited and eliminated from the earth, that he did not see that the cross was the very instrument God would use to liberate the human race from death, hell and the grave. Satan thought he was gaining a huge victory as the tide of public sentiment turned against Jesus. Even though the Old Testament prophets had predicted what would occur, Satan did not have the ability to see God's wisdom—that through His death, Jesus would establish a path to freedom from Satan's grip over each of us. The cross completely surprised and defeated the devil.

The cross completely surprised and defeated the devil.

God can do the same for us. God can use even those things that look like defeat in our lives to establish His victory and authority. He does this by giving us wisdom to which the enemy does not have access.

> However, we speak wisdom among those who are mature, yet not the wisdom of this age, nor of the rulers of this age, who are coming to nothing. But we speak the wisdom of God in a mystery, the hidden wisdom which God ordained before the ages for our glory, which none of the rulers of this age knew; for had they known, they would not have crucified the Lord of glory. But as it is written: "Eye has not seen, nor ear heard, nor have entered into the heart of man the things which God has prepared for those who love Him." But God has revealed them to us through His Spirit. For the Spirit searches all things, yes, the deep things of God.
>
> 1 Corinthians 2:6–10

This passage reveals the following important keys for surprising the devil through wisdom:

- God has wisdom greater than any worldly wisdom.
- Powers and principalities do not have access to this wisdom.
- The authority of demonic forces is limited.
- There is wisdom that has been hidden since the beginning of time for His glory.

- Through the redemptive cross of Jesus Christ, we have access to this wisdom.
- God is prepared to release this wisdom to us as we get to know Him intimately through prayer.
- This wisdom will overthrow high places and release captives.
- Wisdom dismantles demonic structures and dethrones thrones of iniquity.[2]

How to Obtain Wisdom

Proverbs 4 shows us that we are to be seekers of wisdom. In fact, verse 7 in *The Living Bible* declares, "Getting wisdom is the most important thing you can do."

Intimacy with God

There is no way we can hear the voice of the Lord without drawing near to Him. The primary way of doing this is through worship and prayer. Without making a commitment to seek God in these ways, we will never be able to gain an understanding of His wisdom. It is from a place of intimacy that we can tap in to all of God's covenant promises to us. But as with any covenant, if we don't hold up our end of the deal, we will not reap the full benefits of the covenant. If we don't seek true and intimate relationship with God, we, like Satan, will not have access to His wisdom and strategy for moving forward, because we will not be positioned to hear His voice when He speaks to us.

Meditation on God's Word

For thirty days they had wept and mourned the death of their great leader—the one who had led them out of centuries of terrible slavery. They had followed him faithfully for forty years as they maneuvered the wilderness in search of God's Promised Land. Most of a generation had died, and now Moses was gone.

In his place rose Joshua, whose job it was to take possession of the land God had prepared for the Israelites. Joshua had received great promises from God. Every place the sole of his foot touched, God would give to Israel. None of his enemies would be able to stand up against him. God would never leave him nor forsake him. But in order for Joshua to gain the wisdom he needed to possess the land, God instructed him to meditate. Joshua 1:8 says, "Do not let this Book of the Law depart from your mouth; meditate on it day and night, so that you may be careful to do everything written in it. Then you will be prosperous and successful" (NIV).

If we will willingly take time to meditate on God's Word, He will bring success to our lives.

Why was meditation such a key to Joshua's success? Among other things, it was in his times of meditation that the Lord spoke to Joshua His strategy for moving forward. The strategy for conquering a particular enemy would not work against another.

Joshua needed a fresh, new revelation for every step he took. To understand the strategy he needed for the next move, he had to connect with God. And he did so through prayer and meditation.

If we will willingly take time to meditate on God's Word, He will bring success to our lives. Why is that? The Bible contains great wisdom and strategy for our lives that transcend time. But if we just read the Bible without taking the time to give it thought, we don't have the opportunity to really understand what we've just read. Without meditation, how can the words of truth provide refreshment to our soul and spirit? How can we understand the true wisdom lying beneath the words? And how can prayer flow out of a passage that has been read but not understood?

Pastor and author Donald S. Whitney put it this way: "Meditation is the missing link between Bible intake and prayer. . . . There should be a smooth, almost unnoticeable transition between Scripture input and prayer output so that we move even closer to God in those moments. This happens when there is the link of meditation in between."[3]

Sin and Iniquity Overthrown

Sin and iniquity in our lives will keep us separated from God in such a way that we will be unable to hear His voice. Satan's objective is to block the plans of God by gaining legal access to us through sin. From that position, he is then able to derail us. We need to understand the full impact of sin on our lives, especially those secret or besetting sins that we may be reluctant to fully vanquish. Sin is a powerful roadblock that keeps us from outwitting the devil. Few of the principles outlined in this book will have much of an effect unless we have dealt with our sin. But here, again, God will provide wisdom and insight to those who genuinely seek Him to overthrow sin in their lives.

Affections Guarded

After admonishing us to seek wisdom, Proverbs 4 goes on to declare, "Above all else, guard your affections. For they influence everything else in your life" (v. 23 TLB). This principle cannot be stated any better. As human beings, our affections (those things that we love or have a special attachment to) are linked with our desires. The word *affection* is defined as the emotional realm of love, a feeling, devotion or sentiment; a bent or disposition of mind able to sway reason. If the fire of God is not in our affections, we often lack the faith we need to move forward in

God's plan for our lives. If an affection has gained a hook in our hearts, it will have a hook in our lives because it will be able to sway our reason. If we have not guarded our affections and brought them under the Lordship of Christ, our reasoning will, therefore, not be able to accept the wisdom of God.

The Power of Lies Broken

Every lie we receive in our minds works like an anesthetic to deaden us. In the Bible this is described as a spirit of slumber. It attaches itself to an unbelieving, mocking, blasphemous spirit so that we can't capture the truth and be liberated. At a particular time, it'll make us go to sleep to prevent us from hearing truth. The enemy will whisper false arguments and philosophy to exalt himself above the knowledge of God in our minds. So we are to cast down these things.

We have another dynamic in that sinful acts are iniquitous. Iniquity forms a pattern and a deviation from God's plan in a bloodline. Once that iniquity is there, it is passed on to the next generation. If we don't guard our hearts (according to Proverbs 4:23), that iniquity becomes part of the DNA structure that we pass on to our children.

God-Given Authority Heeded

One of my favorite stories is found in Matthew 8:5–13—the story of the centurion. This man goes to Capernaum to find Jesus to plead with Him to heal his servant, who is dreadfully tormented and paralyzed. Because of this man's cry for help, Jesus said,

> "I will come and heal him." The centurion answered and said, "Lord, I am not worthy that You should come under my roof. But only speak a word, and my servant will be healed. For I also am a man under authority, having soldiers under me. And I say to this one, 'Go,' and he goes; and to another, 'Come,' and he comes; and to my servant, 'Do this,' and he does it" (vv. 7–9).

Jesus marveled at this man's faith. In fact, He called it great faith and exclaimed that He had not seen this type of faith in all of Israel (see v. 10). He then said to the centurion, "Go your way; and as you have believed, so let it be done for you," and the centurion's "servant was healed that same hour" (v. 13).

> One of the greatest lessons of faith is the relationship between faith and authority. My father died prematurely when I was 16. Even though I lived through some traumatic times, I was never left fatherless. God placed fathers and mothers in my life so that I would never be outside an authority structure. I believe this has been a key to my personal development of faith. . . . The understanding of authority is a key to unlock our destiny and enter into God's promises by faith.[4]

We must recognize the voice of authority in our lives, particularly the voice of the Holy Spirit, so that we can advance in the promises the Lord has for us.

The Human Spirit Filled with the Holy Spirit

The Holy Spirit inhabits our human spirit and connects us to the heavenly abiding place that God has prepared for us. It is in this abiding place that the Lord will reveal His wisdom to us. The Holy Spirit is also the One who reveals God's will to us and empowers us to accomplish it. He is our Helper. Thus, when we cry out for help, we are crying out for a manifestation of His presence—and in His presence, we will gain the wisdom and understanding needed to overthrow the enemy in our lives.

Wisdom and Discernment Linked

When God speaks His wisdom to us, it is often through our spiritual intuition, known as discernment. Through our spiritual discernment, God communicates to our spirits when something is not right or when the enemy has linked himself to a particular situation or place. "Discernment" is the act of distinguishing, recognizing, discriminating or perceiving by sight or other sense. God can use our senses to help us discern our spiritual surroundings. For example, the Bible speaks of the fragrance of His knowledge, or the fragrance of Christ (see 2 Corinthians 2:14–15). This can be an actual fragrance that we can perceive with our real sense of smell. People who discern in this way regularly report that they know when demonic forces are lingering because the forces have a particularly foul odor about them.

Throughout the Bible we read verses in which the Lord asks, "What do you see?" One such instance is recorded in Jeremiah 1:11. When the Lord asked Jeremiah what he saw, he replied, "I see a branch of an almond tree." Verse 12 shows the result: "Then the LORD said to me, 'You have seen well, for I am ready to perform My word.'" The almond was the first tree to bloom. It was also used as a breeding device to increase Jacob's herds. It was one of the best fruits of the land and was given as a gift. Aaron's rod produced ripe almonds, signifying the priesthood to come. The early-appearing white bloom of the almond is linked to the graying head that signifies wisdom. Jeremiah was called to watch, and when he saw the almond it meant that spring was coming. When the Lord asked Jeremiah what he saw, the almond branch that he saw with his physical eyes became a spiritual indicator of what was to come.

When God speaks His wisdom to us, it is often through our spiritual intuition, known as discernment.

Starting in verse 13, we read, "And the word of the LORD came to me the second time, saying, 'What do you see?' And I said, 'I see a boiling pot, and it is facing away from the north.' Then the LORD said to me: 'Out of the north calamity shall break forth on all the inhabitants of the land. For behold, I am calling all the families of the kingdoms of the north,' says the LORD" (vv. 13–15). Here again God was using one of Jeremiah's physical senses to bring spiritual insight and wisdom over what was going to occur.

The Lord can use any of our senses to communicate with us. Biblically some examples of this include "taste and see that the Lord is good" (Psalm 34:8), hear the sound calling us to war (see Joshua 6:5; 2 Samuel 5:24) and touch His garment to be made well (see Matthew 9:21). The use of our senses to discern also includes what might be described as intuitive sensing, or what some might call a sixth sense, which is when we know something within our spirit.

Hebrews 5:14 reads, "But solid food belongs to those who are of full age, that is, those who by reason of use have their senses exercised to discern both good and evil." As we spend time communing with God and maturing in Him, we will find that He will use even our senses to provide us with wisdom to outwit our enemy. According to this passage, wisdom comes through the use and exercise of our senses. Therefore, we should ask the Lord to help us discern His wisdom in all things, and to be open to seeing, hearing, tasting, smelling and touching Him in new ways.

We have used the first four chapters of this book to lay the groundwork for understanding both our authority and what we need to be successful in our warfare against Satan. Now let's look at the various types of prayers that, when prayed through the leading and wisdom of the Holy Spirit, will truly outwit the enemy.

Confrontation, Breakthrough and Rearguard Prayers

Many years ago I often found myself staying up late and spending time with the Lord. One night His presence was very strong. While praying, the Lord began to speak to me about the enemy. I was praying for several people, for our church, the city in which we lived and for my wife, Pam, who had already gone to bed. This was before we had any children. We had been talking about what to do about the results of medical tests that she had completed that diagnosed her as having a severe case of endometriosis. She had also been diagnosed as barren with a low possibility of ever conceiving. She went to bed with her emotions on a roller coaster.

As I questioned the Lord about this, He spoke a simple word to me: "You can turn the enemy into his own fire." I knew that He was saying that the enemy's plan of destruction could be turned back on him. I began to pray accordingly, not only for Pam but also for all the other burdens that were on my heart. That prayer time was one of the most incredible I have ever experienced because I was both praying and warring. I would worship and then I would war. It was 2 a.m. when I finally went to bed.

I was awakened about an hour later by a visible evil presence standing next to my bed. I said: "In the name of Jesus, who are you?" This presence identified itself as Ashtoreth. It looked like a woman, but it had a man's voice. The voice from the presence said: "I have come to take your children." I commanded the presence to leave in the name of Jesus and by His blood. By this time, Pam was awake. She could also feel the evil in the room.

When the presence left, light filled the room. Pam and I stood and began to shout and worship. The Lord then filled us with faith instead of fear. We had been told that we could not have children. This demon force was telling us that it had come to take our children. The attempt to intimidate us had not worked. Instead, the enemy had overplayed his hand and we came into great faith that the Lord would break barrenness in our lives. It was a strategic revelation in our lives that moved us forward.

The Confrontation Prayer

Once we have received strategic revelation from the Lord, we must then obey Him in what He is asking us to do, which includes warfare. There are times when God calls us to confront the powers of darkness at different levels. To confront is to face with hostility or defiance, or to come with opposition. The prayer of confrontation directly addresses a structure that has been set in place in opposition to God's will. The prayer of confrontation has become known in missiological terms as a power encounter. C. Peter Wagner defines a power encounter as "a visible, practical demonstration that Jesus Christ is more powerful than the spirits, powers or false gods worshiped or feared by the members of a given people group."[1]

This type of prayer not only outwits the devil but also humiliates him and decreases his level of power in the process. When Jesus was crucified, we saw a clear example of how this works. Referring to that terrible yet awesome day, Colossians 2:15 reads, "Having disarmed principalities and powers, He made a public spectacle of them, triumphing over them in it."

Once we have received strategic revelation from the Lord, we must then obey Him in what He is asking us to do.

God allows us to enter into this type of power encounter to show His power over territorial spirits to which a particular group of people has been in bondage. As God displays that His power is greater than that of a demonic structure, that structure begins to crumble and those who have been held captive by fear are then free to follow Christ. In his book *Confronting the Queen of Heaven*, C. Peter Wagner writes the following great exhortation on confrontation.

What level of spiritual warfare does Paul have in mind as he writes to the Ephesians? He says that Jesus is on the right hand of God and "far above all principality and power and might and dominion" (Eph. 1:21). Undoubtedly, Diana of the Ephesians and the daily sacrifices in her ornate temple are in Paul's mind. Jesus is superior to Diana and to all similar territorial spirits, no matter how long they have ruled people groups or cities. The armies of God are being called forth to enforce the rightful rule of the King of kings and Lord of lords on the highest spiritual levels.

There are at least three very important things that the head [Jesus] is telling the body about spiritual warfare:

1. **Stand against the wiles of the devil.** Paul tells the Ephesians to put on the whole armor of God "that you may be able to stand against the wiles of the devil" (Eph. 6:13). This is not a benign command. It is not something which is easy to do. The reason for this is that the devil is an awesome being. Paul, in the same epistle, calls him "the prince of the power of the air" (Eph. 2:2). It is hard for me to understand why some Christian leaders insist on trivializing Satan's power. Referring to him as a wimp or as a toothless lion only serves to embolden people to think they can get away with attacking the devil with a fly swatter. I suspect that by saying things like this, some well-intentioned believers are comparing the power of the devil to the power of God, and it is true that there is no contest between the two of them. But this is not the scenario at hand. We are not spectators watching a fight between God and demons. We are the ones whom God has designated to stand against the wiles of the devil. The head tells the body to do it, and, clearly, the head is not going to do it for us.

2. **Engage in proactive spiritual warfare.** In the letter to Ephesus Jesus says, "To him who overcomes, I will give to eat from the tree of life which is in the midst of the Paradise of God" (Rev. 2:7). The word "overcome," which Jesus repeats seven times, is *nikao* in the original Greek. It is a military word meaning "to conquer," in secular Greek, but, according to *The New International Dictionary of New Testament Theology*: "In the New Testament [*nikao*] almost always presupposes the conflict between God and opposing demonic powers" (Vol. 1, p. 650). In other words, it means to do spiritual warfare.

3. **Declare God's wisdom to the principalities.** Paul expresses to the Ephesians his burning desire that "the manifold

wisdom of God might be made known by the church to the principalities and powers in the heavenly places" (Eph. 3:10). This is another one of the commands from the head of the body, and it explicitly says that *the church* should make this declaration to the powers in the invisible world. There are many interpretations as to what exactly this might mean, but one of them would be that we declare the gospel of the kingdom of God. The church, by deed and also by word, should remind the territorial spirits over places like Ephesus that the kingdom of God has invaded the kingdom of darkness beginning with the life, death, and resurrection of Jesus Christ. And that the god of this age will no longer blind the minds of unbelievers to the glorious gospel of Christ in Ephesus, Turkey, Japan, Nepal, Calcutta, or in any other place. This kind of a declaration of war will predictably spark negative reactions and counterattacks from the forces of evil and the spiritual battle will be engaged. One of the major apostles of the extraordinary Argentine Revival, now in its seventeenth year, is evangelist Carlos Annacondia. In virtually every one of his meetings, he literally declares the wisdom of God to the devil and to any spiritual principalities that might be in the vicinity. Many times I have heard him do this in a very loud voice and with powerful anointing of the Holy Spirit. The title of his excellent book is: *Listen to Me, Satan*. (Creation House). When this war cry goes forth, night after night, things begin to happen. Demons manifest and are summarily dispatched, sick people are healed miraculously, and sinners literally run to the platform to get saved. More than two million have been born again in his campaigns so far.[2]

Of course, C. Peter Wagner is referring to strategic-level power encounters with demonic structures dealing with whole people groups or territories. There are examples of this throughout the Old Testament and the New Testament involving people such as Moses, David, Elijah, Jesus and Paul. God's heart remains the same today. We need to enter into a mentality that God will display His power greatly over earth and over demonic structures in order to see great throngs loosed from Satan's grip, and from that mentality pray the prayers of confrontation according to His will. There are times when God will also call us into a confrontational type of warfare over demonic structures on a personal or family level, in which case the three points that we quoted above also apply.

The Breakthrough Prayer

Have you ever felt stuck in life? Stuck in a narrow place from which you just couldn't get to the next place God had for you? You might have been mired in illness, debt, grief, a job situation, an unhealthy relationship, loss of faith in God or any number of other things; almost everyone has felt frustrated by not being able to break through a situation he or she has faced. Breaking through many life situations can often be a long process that may test our ability to persevere and to believe that God will get us to a new place. We may also feel as though the devil has outwitted us, instead of vice versa.

In her book *The Breaker Anointing*, Barbara Yoder wrote,

> God has a great deal for us to possess, but it will take great faith and perseverance. God is continually putting new conquests before us to develop our faith and perseverance at a higher level. We can decide we want to quit at some point because the gate seems too hard or too unconquerable. We may be tired and weary of the battle. We want to sit down, take a rest, and check out. We have the option of sitting down and living a life of ease. But by doing so we will never reach our potential because fear or weariness overtook us at the threshold. Some make this decision and fail to reach their destiny.

Paul said that he kept pressing on to attain that which he was intended to attain (see Phil. 3:12–14). God apprehended Paul not just to convert him but also to use Paul to accomplish a great ministry, to take the gospel to the Gentiles in many nations. Paul pressed through despite many trials.[3]

The enemy will often get us in a vicious cycle through adverse circumstances. Satan attempts to weaken our faith, disillusion us and keep us going around Mount Sinai until we are so weary that we may even forget that there is a Promised Land. We can even see such desperation come over a territory that Satan has held captive. We must use the power of breakthrough prayer to smash the vicious cycle of unbelief and declare a breaking in the enemy's scheme.

> *Satan attempts to keep us going around Mount Sinai until we are so weary that we may forget that there is a Promised Land.*

To *break* means "to cause to come apart by force, to separate into pieces by shattering, to burst and force a way through resulting in splitting a barrier, and to interrupt and bring about suspension of an operation." It is a term that means an offensive thrust that penetrates and carries beyond a defensive line in warfare, a sudden advance in knowledge or technique, a moving through an obstruction and a disrupting of the continuity or flow of an old system. There are times when God calls us to use prayer to break the power of the enemy.

One of the names and characteristics of God is the Breaker.

> The Breaker [the Messiah] will go up before them. They will break through, pass in through the gate and go out through it, and their King will pass on before them, the Lord at their head.
>
> Micah 2:13 AMP

The Lord is ready to establish Himself at the gates of our lives, families, relationships, churches, cities and nations. Here are some of the principles and accompanying results of breakthrough power:

1. **Our light will break forth (see Isaiah 58:8).** Light dispels the darkness. Therefore, in order for our light to break through, we need to ask Him to remove any darkness within us. As our light breaks forth, we are able to break through into a new place. Two excellent principles for breaking out of darkness into light include fasting and giving. We should ask the Lord if there is a particular fast He has called us to in order to break out of darkness. Also, if we are willing to give in places in which we have not been willing to give before, we may be surprised at how the Lord will break open new avenues of supply.

2. **Our healing will spring forth (see Isaiah 58:8).** The Lord is bringing His Body from grief to glory. Infirmities that have afflicted us for years will flee. We must declare that hidden places of grief will be exposed in us so that we will be made whole. Like Hannah (see 1 Samuel 1), we need to ask the Lord to look upon our afflictions and barrenness, and to make us fruitful.

3. **The new song will break forth (see Isaiah 52:9).** Many times when breakthrough occurred in the Word of God, the people would sing and rejoice. Moses and Miriam sang when they crossed out of Egypt. Deborah sang when God defeated the Midianites. When we break through, we should rejoice in song and fill the air with praises to God.

4. **A renewed joy will arise in our spirit.** "Do not sorrow, for the joy of the LORD is your strength" (Nehemiah 8:10). This is a great account of how God's people came to an understanding of their covenant blessings. Nehemiah then

told the people not to grieve over what they had missed, but to break into joy instead. The moment we break through and understand the truth that has been hidden from us, a new joy and hope arise.

5. **New joy causes waste places to be rebuilt.** The breaker anointing causes comfort to be loosed (see Isaiah 52:9). That comfort restores what has been desolate and barren and causes places that have laid in ruins to be rebuilt.

6. **New strength will arise in our spirit.** "But those who wait on the LORD shall renew their strength; they shall mount up [break through] with wings like eagles" (Isaiah 40:31). We will be able to gain the strength we need to overcome the mountain in our path.

As we are looking at prayers that outwit the devil, we need to allow God to break through for us in a new way. It is time for the Lord to break through, for the Church to break out and for the devil's strategies to break up.

Let God Read Your List

So many times when the enemy comes against us and we need breakthrough, we try to get everyone around us to listen to our problems. However, we should really present our case to the Lord. In 2 Kings 18 and 2 Kings 19, we find that Sennacherib, a type of enemy against God's covenant, was overtaking everyone in his path. This ruler then threatened to defeat Hezekiah and the city of Jerusalem. When Hezekiah faced the most trying time of his life, he inquired of the Lord.

Many times the enemy will draw our eyes to what he is doing and will then convince us that we are next in line. As Hezekiah received a threatening letter from Sennacherib, he presented this letter to the Lord as a prophetic act. We should write down the enemy's threat against us and hold it up to the Lord. This produces an order in our thinking, gives us a strategy and paves the way for the Lord Himself to send help to break through and overtake our enemy.

The Rearguard Prayer

Once we see breakthrough in a particular area, it is important for us to understand that the enemy may very well pursue us into our new place with a strategy of backlash against us. In order to secure our victory and outwit the devil in his attempts at backlash, we need to allow God's standard to rise up behind us in rearguard prayer. This is a tremendous prayer strategy that I believe the Lord is teaching His people at this time.

> Then your light shall break forth like the morning, your healing shall spring forth speedily, and your righteousness shall go before you; the glory of the LORD shall be your rear guard.
>
> Isaiah 58:8

A rearguard is a detachment of troops detailed to guard the rear of a moving column. The rearguard is generally used for security during a forward movement, but it is also a detachment concerned with delaying the pursuit of a main military body in retreat. In *The Art of War*, Sun Tzu wrote, "Ground that is of great advantage to either side is contentious ground. . . . On contentious ground, hurry up your rearguard."[4] We live in contentious times and the ground that the Body of Christ has taken is very important.

James Robison wrote:

> In our spiritual struggle, we must show the same resolve as we have shown in the war on terrorism. But we must rely on the promises and power of God, rather than on the might of our armed forces. When the enemy raves and rants, we must

remember that more than 60 times in the Old and New Testaments, God tells us to "fear not." In many other verses, like the one above, He assures us of His protection against anything Satan can deploy against us. He will drive out the enemy before us (Deut. 18:12). He will be our rearguard (Isa. 58:8).[5]

Remember Isaiah 52:12: "The Lord will go before you, and the God of Israel will be your rearguard." God promises not only to look out for us as we go into battle, but also to be our rearguard after the battle. Nevertheless, we need to bear in mind that when God has worked mightily, when God has used us significantly, when there has been great spiritual breakthrough, we cannot allow ourselves to be spiritually careless. After a successful battle, we must give ourselves that all-important order: "Shields up."

In order to secure our victory and outwit the devil in his attempts at backlash, we need to allow God's standard to rise up behind us in rearguard prayer.

The life of David is one of the best examples of rearguard praying. Once David had a breakthrough over the Philistines, God had to secure his victory, because David's enemy mounted up another attack against him. That is what I see happening in our lives and in our nation. The enemy has a strategy of backlash against us.

We must pray from God's covenant plan of protection. God had a covenant with David. When I pray for individuals or regions, and especially our nation, I approach it from the standpoint of covenant. Psalm 89:3–4 reads:

> I have made a covenant with My chosen, I have sworn to My servant David: "Your seed I will establish forever, and build up your throne to all generations."

Verses 20–23 show how our covenant with God positions us to outwit the schemes of our enemy:

199

I have found My servant David; with My holy oil I have anointed him, with whom My hand shall be established; also My arm shall strengthen him. The enemy shall not outwit him, nor the son of wickedness afflict him. I will beat down his foes before his face, and plague those who hate him.

In Appendix A of this book, we present a 32-day prayer guide that is helpful in securing our victory through rearguard praying.

The Prayer of Travail and Agony

We learn from Psalm 127:3 that "children are a heritage from the LORD, [and] the fruit of the womb is a reward." The psalm goes on: "Happy is the man who has his quiver full of them; they shall not be ashamed, but shall speak with their enemies in the gate" (v. 5). There is a desperate, agonizing pain of the soul that comes with barrenness.

My wife, Pam, and I understand the agony of barrenness, as it was ten years into our marriage before we were able to have children. There were times of desperation during those years and times we agonized before the Lord. But God heard the desperate cries of our heart for children and brought a miraculous healing to Pam's body that allowed her to conceive. Since that time she has become familiar with the travailing pain of birth, having given birth to six children.

Because what we experience in the natural often mirrors what we experience in the spiritual, we can see that there are times when agony and travail are appropriate precursors and responses to spiritual birth, just as they are to natural birth. We agonize when something God intends to be has not yet manifested, and we travail as we birth God's new thing.

Hannah's Agony

One of the most poignant biblical stories of agonizing before God is the story of Hannah. Israel was in its lowest moral condition as a nation, and the priesthood had fallen into total disarray. However, individuals kept coming to Shiloh to offer sacrifices and to worship the Lord. As required by the Law, Elkahan took his entire family to Shiloh to offer sacrifices.

We agonize when something God intends to be has not yet manifested, and we travail as we birth God's new thing.

Hannah, one of Elkahan's two wives, was barren and unfulfilled. She was a desperate woman because she knew that the destiny of her creation had not been fulfilled. This lack of fulfillment had led her into grief and affliction of spirit, which the Bible calls "bitterness of soul." In 1 Samuel 1:10–18, we see how Hannah agonized before the Lord to give her a child. Her agonizing gives us a great pattern to follow. Hannah . . .

- prayed to the Lord
- wept in anguish (travailed)
- lifted her affliction to the Lord
- said, "Remember me" (in other words, "Remember why I was created")
- pleaded for God to fulfill her request and promised to offer Him her firstfruits offering
- told the priest her problem and expressed her emotion

- asked for favor to come upon her
- got up in victory
- birthed the new thing in Israel

Through her prayer of agony to the Lord, Hannah conceived and gave birth to Samuel. She then fulfilled her vow to the Lord by giving this child to the priest. This act changed the course of Israel. Samuel began to prophesy and the nation began to shift, although not everything went well. As the story progresses, we see that Israel is defeated in war and, as a result, loses the Ark of the Covenant, which represents God's presence among them. This defeat, however, sets the nation of Israel on course to restore the presence of God in the land, which David does many years later when he returns the Ark to its resting place in Jerusalem.

Travailing That Produces Birth

"Be in pain, and labor to bring forth, O daughter of Zion, like a woman in birth pangs. For now you shall go forth from the city, you shall dwell in the field, and to Babylon you shall go. There you shall be delivered; there the LORD will redeem you from the hand of your enemies" (Micah 4:10).

A "travail" is defined as a painfully difficult or burdensome work, particularly the anguish or suffering associated with the labor of childbirth. What does this have to do with prayer? If we stop to consider the story of Hannah, we realize that when she approached the Lord, she was in anguish over her circumstances. Her plea to God came from the very depths of her being. Her agony before the Lord did not come purely from the emotion of an unmet need or desire in her life. It rose up out of her spirit because, as we previously noted, the destiny for which she had been created had gone unfulfilled. At the time, she did not know in the natural that she had been chosen to give birth to Samuel, a great prophet and judge of Israel. But she knew that she could not settle for barrenness. She knew that such a condition was not God's plan for her life.

Before Hannah gave physical birth to Samuel, she travailed for and birthed something spiritually that overcame the curse of barrenness, not only in her own body, but ultimately in the nation of Israel through Samuel. When we travail in prayer, what we are doing is allowing the Holy Spirit to birth something through us. In her book *Possessing the Gates of the Enemy*, Cindy Jacobs wrote:

> There are times when we are called by God to pray strong prayer and help to birth the will of God into [an] area. Usually there is a sense of wonder after the prayer, and a sense that God has done something through it. Here are four points to help you recognize the work of the Holy Spirit:
>
> 1. Travail is given by God and is not something we can make happen. Travail is often a deep groaning inside, which may be audible or which cannot be uttered, as described in Romans 8:26 . . .
> 2. Travail sometimes comes as a result of praying in an area that others have prayed about before you. God then chooses you to be one of the last prayers before the matter is accomplished. You are the one who gives birth to the answer.
> 3. Those with the gift of intercession will often pray more travailing prayers than those [without the gift].
> 4. The travail may be short or extended. Some prayers will be accomplished quickly and some will be like labor pangs at different times until the birth of the answer comes.[1]

The Power of Travailing

There is tremendous power in travailing prayer because, as Cindy Jacobs noted, it births the will of God onto earth. This type of prayer always outwits the devil because he is so strongly opposed by the new thing God is producing as a result of travail. We, therefore, need to have an understanding of what God is wanting to birth through us. We, like Hannah, need to be in tune with what God is ready to bring forth in any given hour. That can only be done through intimacy with God and through a willingness to allow Him to use us in travail.

Many times we have so much that God has put into our spirits, but we don't have the strength to bring it to birth. Isaiah 60:1 paints the picture: "Arise, shine; For your light has come. And the glory of the LORD is risen upon you." *The Amplified Bible* expands this to "ARISE [from the depression and prostration in which circumstances have kept you—rise to a new life]. Shine (be radiant with the glory of the Lord), for your light has come, and the glory of the Lord has risen upon you." The word *arise* means "to stand firm, to come from a lying down position to an upright position." When we begin to arise and allow God's glory to arise through us, we can take our stand against the powers and principalities that have resisted us. As we allow the Spirit of the Lord to arise within us, we will find that He gives us the expectation of new life and the strength to bring that life to birth.

> *As we allow the Spirit of the Lord to arise within us, we will find that He gives us the expectation of new life.*

Once we identify which burden God wants us to pray over, we begin to agonize and feel the urgency of seeing the burden birthed. The burden becomes our own "baby" as God's heart for seeing that thing brought forth begins to press down on our spirits. With the burden comes an oppression, but it's not the oppression of the devil. If our assignment, for instance, is a travail to break an oppression over certain people, we can actually begin to feel the oppression they are under. We must war until the oppression breaks—until, as in natural childbirth, the opening in the second heaven is large enough so that God's will can come forth on earth.

The Wisdom of Caution

Because travailing is such an intense and often misunderstood form of prayer, there are some cautions of which we must be aware.

1. **Premature timing.** We cannot enter into travailing prayer any more than a woman can enter into labor before her time. It is something the Holy Spirit chooses to do in His time and through whomever He chooses, as long as we are open to allowing Him to work through us in this way. If we try to bring something to birth before its season, like a baby born prematurely, it is much more susceptible to destruction and death than that which is born in the right season.

2. **Becoming overwhelmed.** Cindy Jacobs offers sound advice: "Many times travail can be so strong that it seems to overwhelm the intercessor. Those around need to intercede for the one in travail if this happens in a group situation. We need to help bear the burden in prayer. . . . We also need to bind the enemy from entering into the travail. One word of caution. The Holy Spirit will rule over our emotions in a time of travail. We must be sure that we don't let our emotions run wild. Intercessors need to walk in the fruit of self-control."[2]

3. **Bearing a false burden.** If someone enters travail but does not have God's burden, they will travail with the wind. Isaiah 26:18 warns, "We have been with child, we have been in pain; we have, as it were, brought forth wind;

we have not accomplished any deliverance in the earth, nor have the inhabitants of the world fallen." Many well-meaning Christians travail with the wind because they do not understand God's heart in a matter and move forward in presumption. They either do not know what God is doing or have not taken the time with Him to identify with what He is doing. Instead, they go straight into intercession and get lost in it.

4. **Not completing the assignment.** "This day is a day of trouble, and rebuke, and blasphemy; for the children have come to birth, but there is no strength to bring them forth" (2 Kings 19:3). There are instances in which the timing is right and the burden is right, but we have no strength to bring forth the new birth. We must not grow weary in the Spirit, but allow God to bring forth the strength we need to complete our travail, much as we noted earlier in this chapter.

5. **Discounting prayer as travailing because there is no physical manifestation.** Dutch Sheets gives us great perspective on this issue: "I don't believe [travailing prayer] is defined by groaning, wailing, weeping and hard work. Natural travail certainly is, and spiritual travail *can* include these things. I do not believe, however, it *must* include them, and I'm convinced it is not defined by them. In fact, I believe a person can travail while doing the dishes, mowing the lawn, driving a car—anything a person can do and still pray."[3]

Abigail's Prayer

In 1 Samuel 25, we find the story of a wonderful woman named Abigail. At the time the events of this story unfolded, Saul was still pursuing David, who was in hiding. David moved down to the Desert of Maon, where he asked some of his men to request hospitality and supply from a man named Nabal. Nabal was very wealthy, owned property at Carmel and had a wife named Abigail. She was intelligent and beautiful. He was surly, mean and conniving—a perfect representative of the enemy's characteristics.

Nabal rudely refused David's request for supply for his men. Please do not sympathize with Nabal. In the custom of that day, hospitality was offered to any traveler. Nabal was hostile and defied the custom of that day. He could have been fully blessed by giving. David had even offered payment. Moreover, David and his men had been protecting Nabal's workforce.

The greatest example of travail comes from the agony of Jesus in Gethsemane.

When David's men returned to David and communicated Nabal's refusal, David said, "Put on your swords" (see 1 Samuel 25:13). However, Nabal's wise wife interceded. Abigail understood the gravity of the situation. Through her quick response and skillful negotiation, she kept David from taking vengeance upon Nabal and his household. I love how she saw the big picture and left plenty of room for the Lord to intervene.

Abigail provided a perfect picture of intercession as travail. She stood in the gap and travailed. Because of her burden, she actually won the war. God judged her husband, Nabal, and she ended up marrying David. She looked beyond the travail process in her present crisis. She saw the big picture, pressed through and changed the course of history.

The Garden of Gethsemane

The greatest example of travail comes from the agony of Jesus in Gethsemane. Here I would like to borrow from the excellent explanation of this given by Dutch Sheets in his book *Intercessory Prayer*.

> Without any question Christ's redemption of humanity—the work of intercession—began with His travail in the Garden. Isaiah prophesied of Him: "He shall see of the *travail* of His soul and shall be satisfied" (Isa. 53:11 KJV, emphasis added).
>
> In fulfillment of this, Jesus cried out in Gethsemane saying, "My soul is exceedingly sorrowful, even unto death" (Matt. 26:38 KJV). It was in the Garden of Gethsemane that redemption began and the victory of the entire ordeal was won.
>
> We know that redemption was beginning in this travail for a couple of reasons. Luke tells us Jesus began to shed great drops of blood. Jesus was not simply sweating so profusely that it was like a person bleeding. He was literally bleeding through the pores of His skin, a medical condition known as hematidrosis. We must understand that when the blood of Christ began to flow, redemption was beginning, for it is through the shedding of His blood that we have the cleansing from sin (see Heb. 9:22).
>
> We also know that redemption was beginning in the Garden because when Jesus said, "My soul is exceedingly sorrowful even unto death," the word used for death is *thanatos*. This word is often used for death as the result and penalty of sin. This is the death Adam experienced when he fell.[4]

The Result of Agony

Understanding the suffering and love that Christ demonstrated for us in Gethsemane and at the Cross causes us to have a heart for others. This is the ultimate example of agony that overcomes the strongman and unlocks the prison doors that he has held shut. The prayer of agony causes us to identify with the burden that is on God's heart. Agony leads us to identify with situations. This can include personal issues over people, crisis situations, territorial or national dilemmas or any number of other things.

When travail comes upon us, we should let the Spirit of God lead us. Romans 8:26 reads, "Likewise the Spirit also helps in our weaknesses. For we do not know what we should pray for as we ought, but the Spirit Himself makes intercession for us with groanings which cannot be uttered." He knows ways to pray that we do not.

The Jubilee Season

"A woman, when she is in labor, has sorrow because her hour has come; but as soon as she has given birth to the child, she no longer remembers the anguish, for joy that a human being has been born into the world. Therefore you now have sorrow; but I will see you again and your heart will rejoice, and your joy no one will take from you" (John 16:21–22).

We have not been designed to stay in the place of travail, either physically or spiritually. We have been designed to bring forth new birth and then move into the new season of life that birth brings to us. After travail, release comes. God has a jubilee season over every issue. For instance, if the issue for which we have been travailing involves financial needs, when release comes God will give us or whomever we have been travailing for incredible strategies over how to break debt structures and see financial increase and supply begin to flow. This breakthrough usually includes two arenas: First, there is a financial arena in which God will give strategic insight over how to be released from debt and how to increase income for future advancement; second, there is a relationship arena. When we or the one for whom we have been travailing has relationships that are broken, another type of debt exists. God can find supernatural ways to heal those relationships and cause them to flourish.

During a year of jubilee, labor is suspended. The difficult things for which we have travailed in the past—those things that have been so hard and unyielding, and yet in which we have faithfully pressed through—suddenly come forth and we are released from our hard labor. It is then that we enter into a joy and a faith that we didn't have before, and many things start to fall into place as a new order begins to come. As we agonize, travail and labor for those things that God has laid on our hearts, we should remember there is a time when the birth comes and we are able to enter a season of jubilee, partly because our enemy has been outwitted.

The Prayer of Faith

One morning a few years back, as I did every day, I was having a cup of coffee. Imprinted on the surface of the mug I chose that day were these words: "Faith: The substance of things hoped for, the evidence of things not seen." When I tried to take a sip, I lost my grip and the mug fell, breaking the handle. Immediately the Lord said to me, "I want you to learn how to grasp faith and not lose your handle on it." It was a simple yet profound moment that got me to study faith in a new way.

Faith is amazing. How wonderful it is to know that we can hope and trust in a power that can actually produce results in our lives. I hope that this chapter will help us all grasp faith in such a way that we can outwit the enemy.

The biblical definition of faith is found in Hebrews 11:1–6.

Now faith is the substance of things hoped for, the evidence of things not seen. For by it the elders obtained a good testimony. By faith we understand that the worlds were framed by the word of God, so that the things which are seen were not made of things which are visible. By faith Abel offered to God a more excellent sacrifice than Cain, through which he obtained witness that he was righteous, God testifying of his gifts; and through it he being dead still speaks. By faith Enoch was taken away so that he did not see death, "and was not found, because God had taken him"; for before he was taken he had this testimony, that he pleased God. But without faith it is impossible to please Him, for he who comes to God must believe that He is, and that He is a rewarder of those who diligently seek Him.

Faith is that conviction, confidence, trust and belief that we have in an object or person. Everyone has faith to some degree. But what causes our faith as believers to be different is that our object is God Himself. Therefore, our entire mind must operate around His rulership.

Faith is the persuasion given to us by God, that the things we have not yet seen, we will see. Faith is the pause between what God has said He will do, and our seeing Him act upon His word. If God has said something to us and we have not seen it appear, we must ask Him if we heard Him right or ask Him to give us faith to believe that we will see that which He has said.

Having noted that, there are seven issues of faith that are important for us to understand.

1. **Faith is linked with covenant.** In Genesis 15 we see that God promised Abram an heir who would come from his own body, an heir who would link God's covenant to Abram with all future generations. It took faith on Abram's part to see this promise come to pass. Covenant is initiated by God, but we must respond to it with faith.

2. **Faith is linked with our vision and destiny.** Habakkuk 2:2–4 reads, "Write the vision and make it plain on tablets, that he may run who reads it. For the vision is yet for an appointed time; but at the end it will speak, and it will not lie. Though it tarries, wait for it; because it will

surely come, it will not tarry. Behold the proud, his soul is not upright in him; but the just shall live by his faith." We cannot move into God's fullness for us without faith. Therefore, if our vision is clouded, we have trouble operating in faith and need God to infuse us with fresh faith.

3. **Faith comes from listening to the God with whom we have relationship.** "So then faith comes by hearing, and hearing by the word of God" (Romans 10:17). It doesn't have to be a super-spiritual moment. Often God will pick something as simple and ordinary as dropping a cup of coffee and breaking the mug to speak a profound truth to us. As we listen for God's voice, our faith will continually grow.

4. **Faith works from our love.** "For in Christ Jesus neither circumcision nor uncircumcision avails anything, but faith working through love" (Galatians 5:6). If we do not allow God to work love in us, we cannot have true faith. It doesn't matter what we do. Without love, faith does not work.

5. **Faith is based on our understanding of authority.** If we have a resistant heart toward authority, faith cannot truly manifest. But when we understand authority, we can have great faith. We see this clearly in Matthew 8:9–10, in which the story is told about Jesus' encounter with the centurion who understood authority: "'For I also am a man under authority, having soldiers under me. And I say to this one, 'Go,' and he goes; and to another, 'Come,' and he comes; and to my servant, 'Do this,' and he does it.' When Jesus heard it, He marveled, and said to those who followed, 'Assuredly, I say to you, I have not found such great faith, not even in Israel.'"

6. **Faith is the element of our relationship that must be demonstrated.** James 2:18 reads, "But someone will say, 'You have faith, and I have works.' Show me your faith without

your works, and I will show you my faith by my works."
We can't live in passivity. If we are not demonstrating our
relationship with God, we are not operating in faith. It
may be easy to hide in a prayer closet endlessly, but without demonstrating faith to the world, we are not pleasing
God. It is something He requires of us.

7. **Faith can be increased.** Luke 17:5 reads, "And the apostles
   said to the Lord, 'Increase our faith.'" Where we are now
   in faith doesn't mean that's all we're to have. God gives
   each one of us a measure of faith, and that measure of
   faith can be increased.

The Contention over Faith

Faith is an essential element in outwitting the enemy. In fact, we
can't outwit him without faith—and he knows it. Therefore,
the enemy will contend with us viciously to
weaken our faith. There are some basic strategies he uses to undo our faith: (1) murmuring
and complaining, which perpetuate unbelief
within us; (2) self-pity, which causes us to become self-centered instead of God-centered;
and (3) anger and bitterness, which harden our
hearts before the Lord so we cannot approach Him in faith.

Faith is an essential element in outwitting the enemy.

There are five major strategies that the devil uses to cut off
our faith:

1. **Cutting off our vision.** Without a vision, we will be unable
   to move forward in God's redemptive gifting in our lives
   and will be stuck in the same place long after God would
   have moved us on.

2. **Causing us to doubt God's goodness for the present day.**
   Satan wants to rob us of any joy and faith we have for

seeing God's goodness *today*. If he succeeds, discouragement will overtake us.

3. **Deepening the root of unbelief.** This is where murmuring comes into the picture. Murmuring waters unbelief and allows its roots to grow within us. From those roots, we speak words of unbelief and can defile everything around us.

4. **Inviting greater adversity into our life.** Not all the warfare we experience is because God intended that we fight this or that battle. When we get off track in our faith, we can find ourselves walking right into the enemy's encampment and having to fight our way out of a place we were never supposed to visit.

5. **Causing us to release cursing rather than blessing.** When we fall out of faith, it is easy to lose sight of God's good gifts around us and to see all the negative circumstances instead. When we allow negativity to flow out of us, we enter into cursing instead of blessing that which is around us.

From the effects of these strategies, we can easily see why the enemy seeks to engage us in a battle for our faith. Furthermore, the enemy knows that, without faith, we cannot please God. We can pray all day long, but if we do not pray in faith, we really do not touch God's heart. I remember when the Lord spoke to me and said, *Above all, take up the shield of faith that quenches all the fiery darts of the enemy.* This statement was pretty clear—if I could get my shield of faith in place, then I could outwit the enemy.

The Prayer of Faith

The prayer of faith is the gift of faith the Holy Spirit gives us that activates and permeates our entire being, aligning us with the will of God as we agree with Him. When we voice this faith or make a decree of God's will on earth, we see things happen. In this type of prayer, we fully agree with God and His purposes on earth. Even a herd of wild horses and every legion of demons cannot move us from our alignment with God's plan.

The prayer of faith saves, heals, forgives and liberates. The prayer of faith is fervent, earnest and filled with energy. The prayer of faith goes beyond our passions and emotions. As we pray in faith, the Holy Spirit begins to pave the way for a miracle to occur in our natural environment. Elijah demonstrated this principle for us. Even though he had emotions just as we do, he prayed the prayer of faith and miracles followed. Elisha entered into this type of praying and received a double-portion anointing of the faith and miracles Elijah had displayed.

Good Grades

Many years ago, Pam and I were the administrators of a children's home. I was there as executive director, and she was there to be my wife and support. One night, the house parents of the cottage of older boys unexpectedly left the home for personal reasons. We had no choice but to take on this cottage of eight wild boys ourselves.

Joseph was staying in the cottage. He was a thirteen-year-old Hispanic boy whose mother had been imprisoned; he did not know his natural father. Joseph had seen and experienced more than many adults do in a lifetime. When it came time for Pam and me to leave the children's home, we took Joseph with us and adopted him. I can't say it was easy to raise him, because his past still had a grip that was holding his future captive. However, he was a precious kid, my wife loved him, God loved him, and I had been chosen to father him.

In Joseph's senior year of high school, I was at my wits' end and finally decided to send him back from whence he came.

One day I left work early and came home from my office to tell Pam of my decision. When I walked through the door, she said to me, "I was praying for Joseph today and the Lord told me that He was going to fill him with the Holy Spirit." She had been praying and was filled with faith. I thought, *Oh, great*. I was not filled with faith, and I knew the war would continue. But I also knew he needed to stay.

The prayer of faith saves, heals, forgives and liberates. The prayer of faith is fervent, earnest and filled with energy.

The only thing the Lord had ever spoken to me about Joseph was one sentence: *He is called to be an A and B student*. This was hard to grasp by faith since by sight I never saw As and Bs on his report cards. He did manage to make Cs since he needed that grade level to continue playing sports. He attended college after graduation and again, only made Cs. Next he enlisted in the Air Force. He married and has four beautiful children and a wife who graduated from college magna cum laude.

Sometimes it takes time to see a word manifest. When Joseph and his family were visiting one Christmas Eve twenty years later, he gave me a gift: He had finished his college degree. He said, "Dad, we do not have much money. Having four kids and trying to finish college is not easy. However, I want you to know that here are my grades for my final semester. All As and one B." He had made the dean's list at the college he was attending. He is now filled with the Spirit and serves in ministry with young people—directing their lives toward victory.

Supply and Provision

I share this story because there are usually three areas in our lives that require a faith breakthrough: family, provision and physical healing. The story of Joseph illustrates how the prayer of faith can work in our family, even though it may take many years to fully manifest. Let's first look at provision. Provision is a stock of needed materials or supplies. As we share in *Possessing Your Inheritance*, the word *provision* also means "to prepare to meet a need—to have it already stored up. God's vision and strategy carries with it the necessary provision; it is only a matter of bringing the revelation of release down on earth."[1] Provision is released when vision is fully defined.

Know that the Lord will provide for your vision.

I love the whole story about Elijah. In 1 Kings 17, we see his prayer lock up the heavens for three and a half years so that no rain fell. Elijah was fine for forty days after making this declaration. He stayed by the Brook Cherith and had provision there. One key to seeing our provision is to be at the right place at the right time. He had water and food. However, his declaration of faith that had affected the heavens also affected him. The brook dried up. How many of us have ever had our provision dry up? When this happens, like Elijah, we need to gain new revelation from the Lord so that we can move forward.

Another key to God's provision is to watch for God's signs and supernatural connections along our paths. He sent Elijah to Zarephath and told him to look for a widow at the gate. When Elijah arrived, there she was, picking up sticks. He requested water and bread or a cake from her. It is important for you to be bold and ask for what you need.

Now let's turn and look at the widow. Notice her response in 1 Kings 17:12:

> As the LORD your God lives, I do not have bread, only a handful of flour in a bin, and a little oil in a jar; and see, I am gathering a couple of sticks that I may go in and prepare it for myself and my son, that we may eat it, and die.

How was that for a faith response? Things did not look good for Elijah. But God.

For our provision to be released, many times we must see what we already have in our hand. Elijah was filled with faith, but the widow was so overwhelmed with her circumstances that she could not see how to take what she had and multiply that for her future use. She had flour, oil and sticks. What makes bread? Flour, oil and fire. Once we start using what we have, the Lord begins to multiply our resources. The prayer of faith causes multiplication. When we are being tested in provision, we need to rise up, pray the prayer of faith and open our eyes to see the same way God sees.

Healing

The blood of Jesus, infused with the power to heal, is still as active today as ever. In fact, His blood will be active forever. Psalm 107:20 reassures us: "He sent His word and healed them, and delivered them from their destructions." We are moving into a new dimension of healing. Each of us should ask him- or herself, *Do I know Him as Healer?* Anyone who does not should then ask, *How can I get to know Him as Healer?*

The blood of Jesus, infused with the power to heal, is still as active today as ever.

I have prayed for people and seen many instantly healed. I have prayed for others who have not been healed and some who have died. At times, I have been sick and then instantly healed. At other times, I have had to war for years to overcome certain infirmities. However, God is God. We should not get discouraged; rather, we must keep warring in faith and keep seeking Him for our next step of revelation.

And the prayer of faith will save the sick, and the Lord will raise him up. And if he has committed sins, he will be forgiven.

James 5:15

Whether we are healed instantly or have to pray for years, the bottom line is that the prayer of faith heals the sick.

A Supernatural Dimension

"Then the LORD spoke to Moses and Aaron, saying, 'When Pharaoh speaks to you, saying, "Show a miracle for yourselves," then you shall say to Aaron, "Take your rod and cast it before Pharaoh, and let it become a serpent"'" (Exodus 7:8–9).

These verses are very important. When God speaks to us, that gives us a reply to the enemy with whom we are contending.

A Self-Evaluation

Here are some questions and statements that can help you evaluate where you are in outwitting your enemy.

1. What is your communication level with the Father?

2. Does your prayer life take on a supernatural dimension? Do you believe in the supernatural? Do you consider yourself operating in a supernatural dimension? Here are some words that are linked with the supernatural to help you think this through:
   - miracles
   - power
   - pictures of the throne room
   - spirit realm
   - faith
   - suddenlies
   - open heaven
   - demonstrations

- angels
- ability to see into the unseen
- communications through dreams and visions
- discernment of spirits
- prophetic
- deliverance
- beyond human boundaries
- kingdom mentality

3. Write down five supernatural experiences you have had that you don't understand. Also ask yourself:
   - When was the first time God spoke to me?
   - How did He speak to me?
   - When was the first time I was confronted by the enemy?
   - How did he manifest himself?
   - How did I respond to these supernatural events?

4. Do you know and have an intimate relationship with the Holy Spirit? You need to know the Person who is linking you into the supernatural. You should have the following goals if you intend to live and walk in the supernatural dimension of prayer, faith and overcoming victory. You should seek to understand:
   - the Person of the Holy Spirit
   - the Kingdom that we live in
   - the apostolic government and authority
   - the anointing
   - the realm of faith
   - glory

5. Do you understand that the enemy and his agents are set against you? These agents intervene supernaturally to stop

you from entering into your abiding place and wearing a mantle of favor.

6. Do you believe in and attempt to discern and evaluate supernatural manifestations? Discernment will be key for you in evaluating:
   - miracles
   - signs and wonders
   - symbols
   - dreams
   - visions
   - faith

7. What will it take to move into this dimension?
   - Break every limitation the enemy has put in your mind about the Holy Spirit. He has tried to keep you from knowing the Person of the Holy Spirit.
   - Understand the times in which you are living. Learn to recognize what the Holy Spirit is doing on earth today.
   - Enter into a new level of faith. Go from faith to faith. Let your faith increase.
   - Understand the authority structure of which you are a part. What is the foundation on which you stand? With whom are you connected? How do you fit into the government around you? Faith works through authority (see Matthew 8).
   - Define your connections at this point in your life and ministry. Who is shielding you, and whom are you shielding? This is a major issue. Pray for those above and beneath you.
   - Your willingness to worship and sacrifice in new ways must change. Know that giving + worship + authority = increased faith.

- What ceiling has been placed on your life that is limiting your breakthrough? How is the enemy limiting you? If you come into agreement with anything the enemy does in any area of your life, the result is oppression or depression.

To help you further understand vibrant faith that equips us for outwitting the enemy, Robert Heidler and I wrote *Restoring Your Shield of Faith*. There are many more principles covered in that book than we have been able to touch on in this short chapter.

Moving Forward!

At the time I wrote this book, the Lord had His finger on my son Isaac. One week, Isaac went with the youth group at church down to Big Bend National Park in West Texas. On that trip, Pam was one of the leaders. When I asked her how it went, she said everything was outstanding—except for one thing, which Isaac could share with me himself. Isaac told me that the kids had gone into the river and he had forgotten to take out his wallet before going in. As a result, he lost his wallet in the river. "My Six Flags (amusement park) season pass was in there," he explained. "I'm supposed to go to Six Flags one more time this year, so you need to get me a new season pass along with the seventy-six dollars cash that was also in my wallet."

I could have replaced his wallet and its contents, but a good father knows that sometimes he must point his children to their heavenly Father. I told him that I would join him in praying for his wallet to be found and returned. Imagine that—someone finding and returning his river-soaked wallet that had been lost in the Big Bend National Park along with all its contents. If that didn't sound silly enough, I then said that his mom would also help. Pam offered to call the warden and let him know about Isaac's lost wallet.

My son and I got down on our knees in his bedroom to pray for the return of his wallet. He prayed, "Lord, I lost my wallet in the river at Big Bend National Park. It's black with red flames on it, and it has a Six Flags season pass in it along with seventy-six dollars. I know I'm supposed to go to Six Flags one more time this summer, so I need Your help to get it back since my dad won't help me." Talk about shifting the blame onto me! When he was done, he told me it was my turn to pray. All I could do was say, "Amen," and resist the urge to throttle him. But in saying "Amen," I did sincerely come into agreement that his wallet would be returned.

Several weeks later I was in Minnesota. While ministering on the platform, my cell phone rang with a call from my family. The game warden in Big Bend National Park had found Isaac's wallet and was returning it—with the money and the Six Flags season pass still in it! Needless to say, my son immediately began to make plans for one last trip to the amusement park. What a poignant reminder this was to me of the power of two coming together in the prayer of agreement.

> Again I say to you that if two of you agree on earth concerning anything that they ask, it will be done for them by My Father in heaven.
>
> Matthew 18:19

The Prayer of Agreement

The Greek word for "agree" in this verse is *sumphoneo*, which literally means "to sound together," to be harmonious.[1] Sounding together in prayer is very powerful and opens the windows of heaven. The Lord doesn't call us to stand alone in our struggle to outwit the enemy in our lives. We need others to come into agreement with us. Sometimes it is the only way we will see real breakthrough. In fact, we will not be able to fully overcome his schemes in our lives without the wisdom, counsel and intercessory prayer of those with whom God has connected us.

We must not be distracted by the many things for which we could pray; rather, God has certain assignments for each of us.

Furthermore, the Lord does not call us to focus only on that which concerns us. We are part of a Body, and there will be times when He calls upon us to agree with others over their struggles. Seeing the enemy outwitted applies to everything that opposes God and His purposes. That is what intercession is all about. Of course, we as individuals aren't called to pray over everything. In fact, we must not be distracted by the many things for which we *could* pray; rather, God has certain assignments for each of us. We also need to be very open to His Spirit and understand that He may ask us to stand in the gap for an individual, a territory, an important issue or something else that is on His heart.

In the Gap

One of my roles has been to let the Lord give me assignments to fill a gap. This has meant everything from having a certain prayer emphasis to serving in an administrative role for various building projects.

In *Seasons of Intercession*, Pastor Frank Damazio explains the concept of "gap-standing."

> The word "gap" in the Hebrew means a rupture or breach. This word is taken from a military context, and applies to besiegers who rush into a city through breaches in the wall. The besieging

army would attack one specific place in the wall until it was weakened. Then with united strength, the enemy would rush the wall, causing a break or breach. The gap standing soldier's responsibility was to risk his life by standing in the breach and single-handedly repelling the enemy. This was known to be one of the bravest acts of a soldier, since he risked severe injury and danger. Often these soldiers gave their lives to fill the gap and save the city. A gap standing soldier was a highly respected and sought out name among soldiers.[2]

A Fifty-State Tour

One gap-standing assignment in which I had the privilege to participate was the Fifty-State Tour. One morning in October 2002, I awoke with a sense of urgency from the Lord. I sensed that I was to travel to all fifty of the United States to help raise up the prayer army of God in each state. The next time I was ministering with Dutch Sheets, who also has a heart for revival in our nation, I brought this up, only to find that he had felt the same urgency the week before.

We could sense that the Lord was calling us to work to-gether on this project. We called meetings to identify and draw together the intercessors of each state, and then align strategic intercession with apostolic, prophetic and pastoral leadership. As we did this, we saw God raise up an army in each state. This gap-standing has produced amazing, miraculous results, many of which are recorded in *Releasing the Prophetic Destiny of a Nation* (Destiny Image, 2005). This prophetic history book of our nation has a history of each state, what happened prophetically at each state's gathering on our Fifty-State Tour, and includes the prophetic destiny of each state. We truly have seen God's prophetic anointing rise to new levels in ways that will move the Body of Christ forward to accomplish His purposes in each territory.

God has a way of seeing His will accomplished on earth. We each play a part in this process. We need to pray, as Jesus taught us, that His will would be done on earth as it is in heaven. This begins when He releases His burden from heaven. One of the phrases related to intercession is "burden bearing," which means to sustain, bear or hold up against a thing. Dutch Sheets wrote, "This is likened to when a person will tie a stake to a tomato plant to sustain it from the weight it carries. The strength of the stake is transferred to the plant, and thus, 'bears' it up."[3] Sheets also wrote that another definition for *burden* is "'to bear, lift or carry' something with the idea being to carry it *away* or *remove* it. . . . The intercessory work of Christ reached its fullest and most profound expression when our sins were 'laid on' Him and He bore 'them' away."[4] Similarly, the Lord will lay His burden on us for something He wants removed, and we are to stand in the gap and pray until we get rid of it.

> *We need to pray, as Jesus taught us, that His will would be done on earth as it is in heaven.*

The Building Plan

The Lord calls us not only to tear down but also to build up. Nehemiah was a great example of one who stood in the gap and sought to see the foundations of Jerusalem restored. He was one of the Jews of the dispersion, and in his youth, he was appointed to the important office of royal cupbearer at the palace of Shushan. Through his brother Hanani, and perhaps from other sources, he heard of the mournful and desolate condition of the Holy City, and was filled with sadness of heart (see Nehemiah 1:2; 2:3). The king observed his countenance and asked the reason for it. Nehemiah explained it all to the king and obtained his permission to go up to Jerusalem and act as the governor of Judea.

229

Upon his arrival, he set himself to survey the city and to form a plan for its restoration. However, the enemies of the Jews had no intention of allowing the walls of Jerusalem to be repaired. From the moment of Nehemiah's arrival in Judea, Sanballat, whose name means "bramble-bush" or "enemy-in-secret," set himself to oppose every measure for the restoration of Jerusalem's security. Sanballat was "the man" whom Nehemiah had to overcome. Sanballat's opposition was confined at first to scoffs and insults, and he circulated all sorts of disparaging reflections that might increase feelings of hatred and contempt among Nehemiah's colleagues. However, Nehemiah prayed to the Lord that the enemy's insults would be turned back on his head, and the rebuilding continued until the wall reached half its projected height.

When Sanballat and his coalition saw that Nehemiah had reached the halfway point in the reconstruction, Sanballat staged another attack. He formed a conspiracy to surprise the Jews, demolish their work and disperse or intimidate the builders. From this it is important for us to recognize that the enemy cannot afford to allow our building plan to succeed. And if his initial strategy to thwart our efforts fails, he will regroup and try again—just as Sanballat did. However, Sanballat's plot was discovered, and Nehemiah adopted measures for ensuring the common safety as well as the uninterrupted building of the walls. Now half of the laborers were withdrawn to be constantly in arms. The workmen labored with a trowel in one hand and a sword in the other. Nehemiah also kept a trumpeter by his side, so that when any intelligence of a surprise attack was brought to him, an alarm could immediately be sounded. This would allow assistance to go wherever it was needed. By these precautions, the plans of the enemy were defeated. By seeking the Lord, Nehemiah executed a building plan and saw that the wall was completed.

Get Past Your Halfway Point

"So we built the wall, and all [of it] was joined together to half its height, for the people had a heart and mind to work!" (Nehemiah 4:6 AMP).

When I read this, the Lord said, *Tell My people to get past the halfway mark*. What does it take to get past the *halfway mark* and move forward? Here are twelve steps to get us to the other side. Most of these issues have been discussed throughout this book.

1. **Overcome accusations.** The accuser tries to stop us. False judgments lead to delays.

2. **Understand the conspiracy set against us.** The enemy does not play fair. He tries to mobilize others to help him stop God's covenant blessing.

3. **Break a demeaning spirit against what we are building.** If accusations don't stop us, he will try to place worthlessness upon what we are accomplishing. Break the power of worthlessness.

4. **Enter into a new dimension of bold praying and define our gaps.** Nehemiah prayed differently. He said, "Lord, blot out the enemies!" Let's get bold in our praying.

5. **Break legalistic structures.** The enemy always tries to change laws and times. He will develop a legalistic structure to restrain our movement.

6. **Receive a new dimension of faith.** Decree that **GOD IS ABLE** for us to accomplish our goal and get to our destination.

7. **Evaluate those who are building with us.** Many times the Lord wants us to review who is with us and what supernatural connections we need to move forward.

8. **Get a new force of intercession in place.** We need to close the gaps. Therefore, we must be sure to have an intercessory force surrounding what we are doing.

9. **Review our war strategy.** We need a strategy or set of plans to overcome the conflicts set against us. We also have to have God's blueprint to build His way.

10. **Find prophetic input.** We always need to know the prophetic trumpet to which we are listening. Without a vision, or a prophetic revelation, a people perish—and so does a project.

11. **See how to become better connected and to communicate in a more efficient way.** Sometimes communication is our downfall. Let's ask the Lord to streamline our process and make all communication efficient.

12. **Go past our halfway point!** Declare that we are headed to the other side.

The Goal

Once we get past the halfway point, we need a strategy to complete the assignment. This can be likened to a project. Looking at our assignments from the Lord in that light, here is a plan to help us complete our projects:

- **Project background.** Always review what has already happened.
- **Project problem statement.** Just as Nehemiah did, define the problems related to the project.
- **Project opportunity statement.** Write out how this project will open windows of opportunity in the future.
- **Project resource availability.** Analyze all resources to see what is available.

- **Project resource need.** Analyze the project to determine what resources are needed. Without doing this properly and getting prayer in place, many times we cannot acquire the necessary resources to complete the project, and we become frustrated.
- **Project time constraints.** We must stay in God's perfect time plan. Look at the time constraints. By walking in God's time frame, we defeat the plan of the enemy.
- **Project benefits.** We should always keep an eye on the benefits of each project. This will help our faith move up a level.

God is ready and able to work on our behalf. Whether He calls us to stand and watch His salvation occur, or calls us to engage the enemy, wielding our swords, God has a victory plan for us, and it is He who will ultimately outwit and defeat our enemy. We must seek the Lord, gain strategic revelation for moving forward, be obedient to His commands and let Him handle the rest for us: "'Not by might nor by power, but by My Spirit,' says the LORD of hosts" (Zechariah 4:6). Let us always remember that when it looks as though we have been defeated, the King has one more move.

Appendix A

32-Day Prayer Focus to Establish a Rearguard

It is time to put into action the strategies outlined in this book. This appendix walks you through 32 days of prayer to establish your rearguard. Each day, start by reading the specific Scripture we have selected. Most days, we have provided the entire reading. On a few days, we ask you to read a whole chapter, so you will need your Bible. After the Scripture excerpt comes an action point for you to focus on or instill in your life. Finally, pray. This is not something to be done by rote. You cannot skip over it, because it is vital to establishing your rearguard. This is not a book just about prayer concepts; it is also an action plan. Pray through each Scripture. Take notes. In the space provided, record what you have prayed and what you hear from God. In 32 days you will have fully established your rearguard and will be constantly outwitting the enemy along the way.

Day 1

Then all the tribes of Israel came to David at Hebron and spoke, saying, "Indeed we are your bone and your flesh. Also, in time past, when Saul was king over us, you were the one who led Israel out and brought them in; and the LORD said to you, 'You shall shepherd My people Israel, and be ruler over Israel.'" Therefore all the elders of Israel came to the king at Hebron, and King David made a covenant with them at Hebron before the LORD. And they anointed David king over Israel. David was thirty years old when he began to reign, and he reigned forty years. In Hebron he reigned over Judah seven years and six months, and in Jerusalem he reigned thirty-three years over all Israel and Judah.

2 Samuel 5:1–5

Action Point

Receive a new anointing. The Lord is bringing a new anointing to His people. That anointing will cause prophetic words that have lain dormant to begin to be activated in the atmosphere. The anointing breaks the yoke. Go where the anointing is moving and have a receptive heart.

Prayer Notes

Day 2

And the king and his men went to Jerusalem against the Jebusites, the inhabitants of the land, who spoke to David, saying, "You shall not come in here; but the blind and the lame will repel you," thinking, "David cannot come in here." Nevertheless David took the stronghold of Zion (that is, the City of David).

2 Samuel 5:6–7

Action Point

Allow the Lord to show you iniquitous patterns that are hanging around in your life. God had wanted the Jebusites to be overthrown when Canaan was taken. This was written around four hundred years later and eight hundred years from the time that the Lord first covenanted with Abraham to bring down the Jebusites. The Lord does not forget an old, iniquitous pattern that would weaken you.

Prayer Notes

Day 3

Now David said on that day, "Whoever climbs up by way of the water shaft and defeats the Jebusites (the lame and the blind, who are hated by David's soul), he shall be chief and captain." Therefore they say, "The blind and the lame shall not come into the house."

Then David dwelt in the stronghold, and called it the City of David. And David built all around from the Millo and inward. So David went on and became great, and the LORD God of hosts was with him. Then Hiram king of Tyre sent messengers to David, and cedar trees, and carpenters and masons. And they built David a house. So David knew that the LORD had established him as king over Israel, and that He had exalted His kingdom for the sake of His people Israel. And David took more concubines and wives from Jerusalem, after he had come from Hebron. Also more sons and daughters were born to David. Now these are the names of those who were born to him in Jerusalem: Shammua, Shobab, Nathan, Solomon, Ibhar, Elishua, Nepheg, Japhia, Elishama, Eliada, and Eliphelet.

2 Samuel 5:8–16

Action Point

Open your eyes and you will see the path that leads to victory. If you come into a new place of intimacy and communion with God, your eyes will open to see new strategies to break the enemy's power. Don't be afraid to get your knees dirty. Crawl through that narrow place and surprise your enemy.

Prayer Notes

Day 4

Now when the Philistines heard that they had anointed David king over Israel, all the Philistines went up to search for David. So David inquired of the LORD, saying, "Shall I go up against the Philistines? Will You deliver them into my hand?" And the LORD said to David, "Go up, for I will doubtless deliver the Philistines into your hand."

2 Samuel 5:17, 19

Action Point

Don't allow the enemy's backlash to get you off course. Many of God's people begin to have victory and then fall short. The enemy sees your new anointing and then raises up new forces to come against you. When you sense this backlash or retaliation once you are experiencing the victory, don't let fear engulf you. Stop and pray. Just as David did, ask the Lord if you are to war or to wait. If you hear Him say, "War," then do it.

Prayer Notes

Day 4

Day 5

So David went to Baal Perazim, and David defeated them there; and he said, "The Lord has broken through my enemies before me, like a breakthrough of water." Therefore he called the name of that place Baal Perazim. And they left their images there, and David and his men carried them away.

2 Samuel 5:20–21

Action Point

Declare deliverance and breakthrough throughout this day. Outline your Baal Perazims. Declare that the Master of Breakthrough will rise up on your behalf. Ask for a new anointing of intercession.

Prayer Notes

Day 5

Day 6

Then the Philistines went up once again and deployed
themselves in the Valley of Rephaim. Therefore David
inquired of the LORD, and He said, "You shall not go up;
circle around behind them, and come upon them in front
of the mulberry trees."

2 Samuel 5:22–23

Action Point

*Don't drop your shield until you see your enemy completely
pushed back.* The Philistines returned with another counter-
attack. Even after victory occurs, stay alert to the enemy's lo-
cation. Any time you discern the enemy's presence, inquire of
the Lord. Much creativity is needed to utterly defeat the enemy.
Yesterday you had God's strategy and direction; today He has a
new path for you to take. God is faithful morning by morning.
Gain your direction daily. See your enemy, which has encroached
upon your territory, totally removed.

Prayer Notes

Day 7

And it shall be, when you hear the sound of marching in the tops of the mulberry trees, then you shall advance quickly. For then the LORD will go out before you to strike the camp of the Philistines.

2 Samuel 5:24

Action Point

Wait for the sound of the Holy Spirit in your midst. The Holy Spirit is breathing a new, fresh sound for victory. If you miss His sound, it will take you out of God's timing in facing off against the enemy. Hear the sound of the Spirit of God.

Prayer Notes

Day 7

Day 8

And David did so, as the Lord commanded him; and
he drove back the Philistines from Geba as far as Gezer.

2 Samuel 5:25

Action Point

*Declare everything in your land—life, home, church, city and
nation—to be secured*. David secured his covenant territory.
We need to do the same with ours.

Prayer Notes

Day 9

Again David gathered all the choice men of Israel, thirty thousand. And David arose and went with all the people who were with him from Baale Judah to bring up from there the ark of God, whose name is called by the Name, the LORD of Hosts, who dwells between the cherubim.

So they set the ark of God on a new cart, and brought it out of the house of Abinadab, which was on the hill; and Uzzah and Ahio, the sons of Abinadab, drove the new cart. And they brought it out of the house of Abinadab, which was on the hill, accompanying the ark of God; and Ahio went before the ark.

Then David and all the house of Israel played music before the LORD on all kinds of instruments of fir wood, on harps, on stringed instruments, on tambourines, on sistrums, and on cymbals.

And when they came to Nachon's threshing floor, Uzzah put out his hand to the ark of God and took hold of it, for the oxen stumbled. Then the anger of the LORD was aroused against Uzzah, and God struck him there for his error; and he died there by the ark of God. And David became angry because of the LORD's outbreak against Uzzah; and he called the name of the place Perez Uzzah to this day.

David was afraid of the LORD that day; and he said, "How can the ark of the LORD come to me?" So David would not move the ark of the LORD with him into the City of David; but David took it aside into the house of Obed-Edom the Gittite. The ark of the LORD remained in the house of Obed-Edom the Gittite three months. And the LORD blessed Obed-Edom and all his household.

Now it was told King David, saying, "The LORD has blessed the house of Obed-Edom and all that belongs to him, because of the ark of God." So David went and brought up the ark of God from the house of Obed-Edom to the City of David with gladness.

And so it was, when those bearing the ark of the LORD had gone six paces, that he sacrificed oxen and fatted sheep. Then David danced before the LORD with all his might; and David was wearing a linen ephod. So David and all the house of Israel brought up the ark of the LORD with shouting and with the sound of the trumpet.

Now as the ark of the LORD came into the City of David, Michal, Saul's daughter, looked through a window and saw King David leaping and whirling before the LORD; and she despised him in her heart. So they brought the ark of the LORD, and set it in its place in the midst of the tabernacle that David had erected for it. Then David offered burnt offerings and peace offerings before the LORD.

And when David had finished offering burnt offerings and peace offerings, he blessed the people in the name of the LORD of hosts. Then he distributed among all the people, among the whole multitude of Israel, both the women and the men, to everyone a loaf of bread, a piece of meat, and a cake of raisins.

So all the people departed, everyone to his house. Then David returned to bless his household. And Michal the daughter of Saul came out to meet David, and said, "How glorious was the king of Israel today, uncovering himself today in the eyes of the maids of his servants, as one of the base fellows shamelessly uncovers himself."

So David said to Michal, "It was before the LORD, who chose me instead of your father and all his house, to appoint me ruler over the people of the LORD, over Israel. Therefore I will play music before the LORD. And I will be even more undignified than this, and will be humble in my own sight. But as for the maidservants of whom you have spoken, by them I will be held in honor." Therefore

Michal the daughter of Saul had no children to the day of her death.

2 Samuel 6

Action Point

Worship and establish God's presence in your midst. After a false start, David brought the Ark back as the central force of all of Israel. We need to recognize any false starts we have made and abide in a place of worship before God.

Prayer Notes

_____

_____

_____

_____

_____

_____

_____

_____

_____

_____

_____

_____

Day 9

Day 10

Now, O LORD God, the word which You have spoken concerning Your servant and concerning his house, establish it forever and do as You have said. So let Your name be magnified forever, saying, "The LORD of hosts is the God over Israel." And let the house of Your servant David be established before You. For You, O LORD of hosts, God of Israel, have revealed this to Your servant, saying, "I will build you a house." Therefore Your servant has found it in his heart to pray this prayer to You. And now, O Lord GOD, You are God, and Your words are true, and You have promised this goodness to Your servant. Now therefore, let it please You to bless the house of Your servant, that it may continue before You forever; for You, O Lord GOD, have spoken it, and with Your blessing let the house of Your servant be blessed forever.

2 Samuel 7:25–29

Action Point

Declare: The Lord will establish my house. Pray for your house. Also pray for the church or ministry to which you are most connected.

Prayer Notes

Day 11

After this it came to pass that David attacked the Philistines and subdued them. And David took Metheg Ammah from the hand of the Philistines. Then he defeated Moab. Forcing them down to the ground, he measured them off with a line. With two lines he measured off those to be put to death, and with one full line those to be kept alive. So the Moabites became David's servants, and brought tribute. David also defeated Hadadezer the son of Rehob, king of Zobah, as he went to recover his territory at the River Euphrates. David took from him one thousand chariots, seven hundred horsemen, and twenty thousand foot soldiers. Also David hamstrung all the chariot horses, except that he spared enough of them for one hundred chariots. When the Syrians of Damascus came to help Hadadezer king of Zobah, David killed twenty-two thousand of the Syrians. Then David put garrisons in Syria of Damascus; and the Syrians became David's servants, and brought tribute. So the LORD preserved David wherever he went. And David took the shields of gold that had belonged to the servants of Hadadezer, and brought them to Jerusalem. Also from Betah and from Berothai, cities of Hadadezer, King David took a large amount of bronze. When Toi king of Hamath heard that David had defeated all the army of Hadadezer, then Toi sent Joram his son to King David, to greet him and bless him, because he had fought against Hadadezer and defeated him (for Hadadezer had been at war with Toi); and Joram brought with him articles of silver, articles of gold, and articles of bronze. King David also dedicated these to the LORD, along with the silver and gold that he had dedicated from all the nations which he had subdued—from Syria, from Moab, from the people of Ammon, from the Philistines, from Amalek, and from the spoil of Hadadezer the son of Rehob, king of Zobah. And David made himself a name when he returned from killing eighteen thousand Syrians in the Valley of Salt. He also put garrisons in Edom; throughout all Edom he put garrisons, and all the Edomites became David's servants. And the LORD preserved David wherever he went.

2 Samuel 8:1–14

Action Point

Declare that you will take hold of that which is leading you, and that instead of being led, you will lead forth in God's purposes. David took Metheg Ammah. This means the bridle of the mother city. Once the presence of God was established, David actually took the stronghold of the Philistines. What strongholds do we need to take?

Prayer Notes

Awake, awake.
Put on your strength, O Zion;
Put on your beautiful garments,
O Jerusalem, the holy city.
For the uncircumcised and the unclean
Shall no longer come to you.
Shake yourself from the dust, arise;
Sit down, O Jerusalem.
Loose yourself from the bonds of your neck,
O captive daughter of Zion.
For thus says the LORD:
"You have sold yourselves for nothing,
And you shall be redeemed without money."
For thus says the Lord GOD:
"My people went down at first
Into Egypt to dwell there;
Then the Assyrian oppressed them without cause.
Now therefore, what have I here," says the LORD,
"That My people are taken away for nothing?
Those who rule over them
Make them wail," says the LORD,
"And My name is blasphemed continually every day.
Therefore My people shall know My name;
Therefore they shall know in that day
That I am He who speaks: 'Behold, it is I.'"
How beautiful upon the mountains
Are the feet of him who brings good news,
Who proclaims peace,
Who brings glad tidings of good things,
Who proclaims salvation,
Who says to Zion, "Your God reigns."
Your watchmen shall lift up their voices,

With their voices they shall sing together;
For they shall see eye to eye
When the LORD brings back Zion.
Break forth into joy, sing together,
You waste places of Jerusalem.
For the LORD has comforted His people,
He has redeemed Jerusalem.
The LORD has made bare His holy arm
In the eyes of all the nations;
And all the ends of the earth shall see
The salvation of our God.
Depart. Depart. Go out from there,
Touch no unclean thing;
Go out from the midst of her,
Be clean, you who bear the vessels of the LORD.
For you shall not go out with haste,
Nor go by flight;
For the LORD will go before you,
And the God of Israel will be your rear guard.
Behold, My Servant shall deal prudently;
He shall be exalted and extolled and be very high.
Just as many were astonished at you,
So His visage was marred more than any man,
And His form more than the sons of men;
So shall He sprinkle many nations.
Kings shall shut their mouths at Him;
For what had not been told them they shall see,
And what they had not heard they shall consider.

Isaiah 52:1–15

Action Point

Receive a new strength. Your strength to withstand the attack of the enemy is something that you actually have to put on. You must review the condition of your armor and repair every place that has been weakened through apathy or a spirit of slumber. This can rob you of strength. You need to order your prayers, gain strategy and allow your steps to be ordered of the Lord. In doing so, you will gain the necessary strength for the war that lies ahead.

Prayer Notes

Appendix A

Day 13

With whom My hand shall be established; also My arm shall strengthen him.

Psalm 89:21

Action Point

There is a new strength. *Strength* means "to have power, vigor, might, energy and fervency." But another definition of *strength* is "to have power by reason of influence, authority or resources." Like anointing, our covenant with God positions us for strength over the enemy by the very influence, authority and resources available to us. *Strength* also means "power to withstand an attack."

Prayer Notes

The enemy shall not outwit him, nor the son of wickedness afflict him.

Psalm 89:22

Action Point

Declare that any plan the enemy has set against you will be found out and seen. Read all of Psalm 89. We will not be outwitted by the enemy. The literal meaning of this verse has to do with demanding a debt be paid without showing mercy. Because you have a covenant position with God, in this case standing clean and blameless before Him through the blood of Jesus, you are not indebted to the enemy, and therefore, you need not be outwitted nor afflicted by him.

Prayer Notes

Therefore Jesus said again, "I tell you the truth, I am the gate for the sheep. All who ever came before me were thieves and robbers, but the sheep did not listen to them. I am the gate; whoever enters through me will be saved. He will come in and go out, and find pasture. The thief comes only to steal and kill and destroy; I have come that they may have life, and have it to the full.

"I am the good shepherd. The good shepherd lays down his life for the sheep. The hired hand is not the shepherd who owns the sheep. So when he sees the wolf coming, he abandons the sheep and runs away. Then the wolf attacks the flock and scatters it. The man runs away because he is a hired hand and cares nothing for the sheep.

"I am the good shepherd; I know my sheep and my sheep know me—just as the Father knows me and I know the Father—and I lay down my life for the sheep. I have other sheep that are not of this sheep pen. I must bring them also. They too will listen to my voice, and there shall be one flock and one shepherd. The reason my Father loves me is that I lay down my life—only to take it up again. No one takes it from me, but I lay it down of my own accord. I have authority to lay it down and authority to take it up again. This command I received from my Father."

John 10:7–18 niv

Action Point

Declare that the thief will have no power over you. You have the power to outwit the enemy because of what he is attempting to steal from you. He is, therefore, in debt to you, and because of your covenant position you have a right to fight him from that position and demand back what is yours through strategic prayer.

Prayer Notes

Day 15

Day 16

I will beat down his foes before his face, and plague those who hate him.

Psalm 89:23

Action Point

Praise God that He will take a stand on your behalf. Read all of Psalm 89. Once you are in covenant with the Lord, He displays Himself to overthrow the power of the enemy on your behalf.

Prayer Notes

Day 17

So shall they fear the name of the LORD from the west, and His glory from the rising of the sun; when the enemy comes in like a flood, the Spirit of the LORD will lift up a standard against him.

Isaiah 59:19

Action Point

Let the Lord raise His standard against your enemies. A *standard* was considered, in Old Testament times, a token of protection and fidelity. According to the *New Unger's Bible Dictionary*, God's lifting or setting up a standard implies a peculiar presence, protection and aid in leading and directing His people in the execution of His righteous will and giving them comfort and peace in His service. This covenant with the Lord positions you under this powerful standard.

Prayer Notes

Day 18

Finally, be strong in the Lord and in his mighty power. Put on the full armor of God so that you can take your stand against the devil's schemes. For our struggle is not against flesh and blood, but against the rulers, against the authorities, against the powers of this dark world and against the spiritual forces of evil in the heavenly realms. Therefore put on the full armor of God, so that when the day of evil comes, you may be able to stand your ground, and after you have done everything, to stand.

Ephesians 6:10–13 NIV

Action Point

Put on the whole armor of God. Position yourself for faith against any evil that might surround you. Hold at bay or stand in front of and oppose in active battle the enemy that has been taunting you. Take your stand for the next battle.

Prayer Notes

Day 18

Day 19

Stand firm then, with the belt of truth buckled around your waist, with the breastplate of righteousness in place, and with your feet fitted with the readiness that comes from the gospel of peace. In addition to all this, take up the shield of faith, with which you can extinguish all the flaming arrows of the evil one. Take the helmet of salvation and the sword of the Spirit, which is the word of God. And pray in the Spirit on all occasions with all kinds of prayers and requests. With this in mind, be alert and always keep on praying for all the saints. Pray also for me, that whenever I open my mouth, words may be given me so that I will fearlessly make known the mystery of the gospel, for which I am an ambassador in chains. Pray that I may declare it fearlessly, as I should.

Ephesians 6:14–20 NIV

Action Point

Get your back side covered with the glory of God. The armor that God has supplied to His New Testament soldiers does not provide for the protection of the back of the warrior outside of the intercession of others. This is also consistent with the armies of Old Testament Israel, where the "glory of the LORD" was to be their rearguard (see Isaiah 58:8).

Prayer Notes

Day 20

Reread Ephesians 6:13 (see Day 18).

Action Point

Withstand any attempt of the enemy's plans against you. To "withstand" is to *anthistemi.* The word "withstand" comes from the same word as "antihistamine." It means to vigorously oppose, bravely resist, stand face-to-face against—just as an antihistamine puts a block on a histamine. Declare a new resistance to be built within you. Ask God to show you any place where your resistance has been torn down.

Prayer Notes

Day 21

And the captain of the guard charged Joseph with them,
and he served them; so they were in custody for a while.
Then the butler and the baker of the king of Egypt, who
were confined in the prison, had a dream, both of them,
each man's dream in one night and each man's dream with
its own interpretation. And Joseph came in to them in the
morning and looked at them, and saw that they were sad.

Genesis 40:4–6

Action Point

Declare vindication from your enemy. Read Genesis 49:16–17,
Exodus 30:6 and Numbers 2:25–31. The tribe of Dan served as
a rearguard to the north for all of Israel. *Dan* means "vindication": "[He] will be a serpent by the roadside, a viper along
the path, that bites the horse's heels so that its rider tumbles
backward" (Genesis 49:17 NIV). When operating in rearguard
prayer, we ambush our enemy and cause our enemy to stop
pursuit and actually lose strength.

Prayer Notes

Day 22

And Leah's maid Zilpah bore Jacob a second son. Then
Leah said, "I am happy, for the daughters will call me
blessed." So she called his name Asher.

Genesis 30:12–13

Action Point

Prepare a special offering for the King. Read Genesis 49:20
and Deuteronomy 33:24–25. May your feet be anointed and
shod with the preparation of the Gospel of Peace. May you
be ready to accomplish anything God tells you. Receive new
favor and anointing for your steps to move forward. The tribe
of Asher also served as the rearguard. *Asher* means "happy and
fortunate." Ask the Lord for new joy to move forward. Asher is
linked with favor and blessing. Asher fought with Gideon and
pursued Midian. Anna was of the tribe of Asher (see Luke 2:36).
Wait patiently until you see a manifestation of the promise. As
you give your offering, declare that you will hit a deep well of
financial release.

Prayer Notes

Day 22

Day 23

And Rachel's maid Bilhah conceived again and bore Jacob a second son. Then Rachel said, "With great wrestlings I have wrestled with my sister, and indeed I have prevailed." So she called his name Naphtali.

Genesis 30:7–8

Action Point

Gain strength to wrestle your enemies to the ground. Put your feet on the head of your enemies. Read Genesis 30:7–8, Genesis 49:21 and Deuteronomy 33:23. Naphtali was also a rearguard tribe. *Naphtali* means "to wrestle." Wrestle over your promises.

Prayer Notes

Day 23

Day 24

Now Deborah, a prophetess, the wife of Lapidoth, was judging Israel at that time. And she would sit under the palm tree of Deborah between Ramah and Bethel in the mountains of Ephraim. And the children of Israel came up to her for judgment. Then she sent and called for Barak the son of Abinoam from Kedesh in Naphtali, and said to him, "Has not the LORD God of Israel commanded, 'Go and deploy troops at Mount Tabor; take with you ten thousand men of the sons of Naphtali and of the sons of Zebulun; and against you I will deploy Sisera, the commander of Jabin's army, with his chariots and his multitude at the River Kishon; and I will deliver him into your hand'?"

Judges 4:4–7

Action Point

Align yourself with those in your area who are warring for their inheritance. War alongside them, that you might obtain your inheritance. Read Judges 4 and Judges 6. See the example of how Naphtali fought with Barak and Gideon.

Prayer Notes

Day 24

Day 25

And they helped David against the bands of raiders, for they were all mighty men of valor, and they were captains in the army. For at that time they came to David day by day to help him, until it was a great army, like the army of God.

1 Chronicles 12:21–22

Action Point

Declare that the army of God will begin to grow. Read 1 Chronicles 12. Declare that the armies of heaven and earth begin to agree. Ask for the Host of Heaven to be your rearguard. In 1 Chronicles 12:40, Naphtali brought food and provisions to the men of war at Hebron. Celebrate the King's coming into your territory, and declare abundant provision for the leadership of the Church to advance God's Kingdom at this time.

Prayer Notes

Day 26

Then David consulted with the captains of thousands and hundreds, and with every leader. And David said to all the assembly of Israel, "If it seems good to you, and if it is of the LORD our God, let us send out to our brethren everywhere who are left in all the land of Israel, and with them to the priests and Levites who are in their cities and their common-lands, that they may gather together to us; and let us bring the ark of our God back to us, for we have not inquired at it since the days of Saul." Then all the assembly said that they would do so, for the thing was right in the eyes of all the people. So David gathered all Israel together, from Shihor in Egypt to as far as the entrance of Hamath, to bring the ark of God from Kirjath Jearim.

1 Chronicles 13:1–5

Action Point

Pray that the presence of God be established anew and afresh in the nation. Read 1 Chronicles 13. The rearguard was positioned to protect the nation and the Ark.

Prayer Notes

Day 27

Now the LORD spoke to Moses, saying: "Speak to the children of Israel, that they turn and camp before Pi Hahiroth, between Migdol and the sea, opposite Baal Zephon; you shall camp before it by the sea. For Pharaoh will say of the children of Israel, 'They are bewildered by the land; the wilderness has closed them in.' Then I will harden Pharaoh's heart, so that he will pursue them; and I will gain honor over Pharaoh and over all his army, that the Egyptians may know that I am the LORD." And they did so.

Exodus 14:1–4

Action Point

Declare that every Pharaoh spirit you are aware of will let go. Read Exodus 14. Allow God to establish His glory. Press out of your bondage and allow God to establish His glory behind you. Set your heart to worship differently. God's people wanted Pharaoh to let them go so that they could worship in a new way. Find some new way to worship differently, and cast aside everything that would prevent you from it.

Prayer Notes

Day 28

"And now, O priests, this commandment is for you. If you will not hear, and if you will not take it to heart, to give glory to My name," says the LORD of hosts, "I will send a curse upon you, and I will curse your blessings. Yes, I have cursed them already, because you do not take it to heart."

Malachi 2:1–2

Action Point

Give God all the glory for what He has done in your life. Take the words from Malachi to heart to give God the glory for all He has done in your life so that you might advance into His covenant blessings.

Prayer Notes

Day 28

Day 29

The LORD said to Joshua: "See. I have given Jericho into your hand, its king, and the mighty men of valor. You shall march around the city, all you men of war; you shall go all around the city once. This you shall do six days."

Joshua 6:2–3

Action Point

Do a Jericho march, even if it's in your prayer closet. Read Joshua 6. Ask God for quietness and confidence against your enemy. Do not release a victory shout until His perfect time.

Prayer Notes

Day 30

Thus says the LORD of hosts, the God of Israel, to all who were carried away captive, whom I have caused to be carried away from Jerusalem to Babylon: Build houses and dwell in them; plant gardens and eat their fruit. Take wives and beget sons and daughters; and take wives for your sons and give your daughters to husbands, so that they may bear sons and daughters—that you may be increased there, and not diminished. And seek the peace of the city where I have caused you to be carried away captive, and pray to the LORD for it; for in its peace you will have peace.

Jeremiah 29:4–7

Action Point

Pray for the peace of your city. Read Joshua 6 again, along with Jeremiah 29. Declare that any invincible force in your city will fall. Declare wholeness over your city.

Prayer Notes

Day 31

For you shall not go out with haste, nor go by flight; For the LORD will go before you, and the God of Israel will be your rear guard.

Isaiah 52:12

Action Point

Declare God's perfect timing over your life. Memorize Isaiah 52:12. Declare that God's redemptive work through Jesus Christ will come in new fullness in your life. "For you shall not go out with haste, nor go by flight; for the LORD will go before you, and the God of Israel will be your rear guard." Wait on the Lord. Let your feet be put in His perfect timing. Order your prayers. Write them on a sheet of paper. Once you have ordered your prayers, let Him order your feet.

Prayer Notes

_____

_____

_____

_____

_____

_____

Day 31

Day 32

So it was, whenever the ark set out, that Moses said: "Rise up, O LORD. Let Your enemies be scattered, and let those who hate You flee before You."

Numbers 10:35

Action Point

Let the trumpet sound. Hear the sound coming forth for war. Read Numbers 10. Move forth in God's order of victory. Declare the leadership of your church or ministry connection freshly established. Declare the leadership of this nation fully in order. War is on the horizon. Depart from the place at which you have settled. Go forth and know that God already has the victory plan.

Prayer Notes

Day 32

Notes

Chapter 1: Checkmate

1. Through the years variations of this story have been told, and pastors often use it as an illustration. It appears to have at least some validity and, for our purposes, works to illustrate our point. The painting in the story is likely one created by master artist Friedrich Moritz Auguste Retzsch (1779–1857). It depicts a young man playing chess against Mephistopheles, who has the upper hand. Though some claim that Bobby Fischer was the chess champion who re-created the game, Paul Morphy was more likely the man. In the November/December issue of *Virginia Chess*, John T. Campbell recounts how he located the actual Retzsch lithograph that had hung in the home of a nineteenth-century pastor named A. A. Howison. The pastor's descendants still possess the painting and, though the account is somewhat different from what we have presented, they continue to pass down from generation to generation memories of the night the chess champion came to dinner.

2. Daniel King, *Chess: From First Moves to Checkmate* (New York: King-fisher, 2000), 6.

3. Ibid., 6.

4. Ibid., 21.

5. Ibid., 12.

6. Ibid., 20.

7. Ibid., 20–21.

8. Paul Keith Davis, *Engaging the Revelatory Realm of Heaven* (North Sutton, N.H.: Streams Publications, 2003), 75.

Chapter 2: Know the Enemy

1. Martin Luther, "A Mighty Fortress Is Our God," 1529.

Chapter 3: Passion Along the Path

1. *Life Application Bible* (Wheaton, Ill.: Tyndale House Publishers, Inc., 1988), 477.

2. Richard Sibbes, "The Rich Pearl," *Lamb Lion Net*. http://www.lamblion .net/Quotations/sibbes.htm (accessed May 20, 2004).

Chapter 4: The Mindset of War

1. Wendell Phillips, quoted in *The Home Book of Quotations*, 9th ed., Burton Stevenson, ed., (New York: Dodd Mead, 1964), 1106. Quote also attributed to Patrick Henry and Thomas Jefferson, although the Jefferson Library at Monticello classifies the attribution to Jefferson as "spurious." See http://www.monticello .org/library/famquote.html (accessed May 21, 2004).

2. Chuck D. Pierce and Rebecca Wagner Sytsema, *Future War of the Church* (Ventura, Calif.: Regal, 2001), 123.

3. Donald S. Whitney, *Spiritual Disciplines for the Christian Life* (Colorado Springs, Col.: NavPress, 1991), 67.

4. Chuck D. Pierce and Robert Heidler, *Restoring Your Shield of Faith* (Ventura, Calif.: Regal Books, 2002), 123.

Chapter 5: Confrontation, Breakthrough and Rearguard Prayers

1. C. Peter Wagner, *Confronting the Powers* (Ventura, Calif.: Regal Books, 1996), 102.

2. C. Peter Wagner, *Confronting the Queen of Heaven* (Colorado Springs, Col.: Wagner Publications, 2001), 31–35.

3. Barbara Yoder, *The Breaker Anointing* (Colorado Springs, Col.: Wagner Publications, 2001), 43.

4. Sun Tzu, *The Art of War.*

5. James Robison, "Know God As Your Protector," With the Word, December 2, 2001, http://workliferhythm.org/partner/Article_Display_Page/0,,PTID34418_ CHID776334_CIID1493076,00.html (accessed April 4, 2016).

Chapter 6: The Prayer of Travail and Agony

1. Cindy Jacobs, *Possessing the Gates of the Enemy* (Tarrytown, NY: Chosen Books, 1991), 115–116.

2. Ibid., 116.

3. Dutch Sheets, *Intercessory Prayer* (Ventura, Calif.: Regal Books, 1996), 113.

4. Ibid., 129.

Chapter 7: The Prayer of Faith

1. Chuck D. Pierce and Rebecca Wagner Sytsema, *Possessing Your Inheritance* (Ventura, Calif.: Regal Books, 1999), 130–131.

Chapter 8: Moving Forward!

1. *Biblesoft's New Exhaustive Strong's Numbers and Concordance with Expanded Greek-Hebrew Dictionary.* Copyright © 1994, 2003 Biblesoft, Inc. and International Bible Translators, Inc.

2. Frank Damazio, *Seasons of Intercession* (Portland, Ore.: City Bible Publishing, 1998), 113–114.

3. Dutch Sheets, *Intercessory Prayer* (Ventura, Calif.: Regal Books, 1996), 62.

4. Ibid., 62–63.

Protecting Your Home from Spiritual Darkness

10 Steps to Help You Clean House, Place Jesus in Authority and Make Your Home a Safe Place

Spiritual Life, Liberty and Freedom

The loud crash of thunder jerked Cathy from her troubled thoughts. Pulling the curtain aside, she peered out at the ominous clouds that had suddenly filled the Texas sky. The turbulent weather only served as a dark reminder of Cathy's own life, as a fresh wave of the all-too-familiar depression seemed to overcome her once again. She could barely move under the weight of her own cloud, which had nothing to do with the summer thunderstorm.

Cathy often suffered from bouts of deep, overwhelming depression. Despite counseling and prayer, we could not seem to discover the source of her constant gloom. As I was visiting with her one day, she asked me about a Greek statue that had been given to her by her former husband. She wondered if perhaps that statue had something to do with her depression. I agreed that the statue had to go, but I knew deep within my spirit that it was not linked to her suffering. Even so, I knew that something in her house was not right. I knew that some *thing* was connected to the dark shadow that hung over her emotions. I began walking through the house praying, "Lord, show me anything in this home that is representing Cathy's depression."

We looked at many antiques she had collected throughout the years. While antiques are often laden with demonic oppression, I knew that none of these objects was the problem. Then the Lord led me over to a glass bookcase. I knew in my spirit that there was something inside that needed to go. I reached up to the top shelf and pulled out a copy of the handbook for thirty-second-degree Masons. Cathy had no idea where the book had come from or that it was in her home. I knew that the book had to be destroyed, so we built a fire and burned it. That act was a turning point in Cathy's life. It set in motion a chain of events that led to the breaking of a Masonic curse in her bloodline. As the curse was broken, the gripping, overwhelming depression that had been Cathy's constant companion completely let go of her mind, and she has walked in freedom ever since. Finding that book was a key to exposing Satan's stronghold over her emotions. Destroying that book was an act of obedience that led to the eventual dismantling of that stronghold and to the liberty that Cathy enjoys today.

If we do not understand spiritual life, we will not be able to see where death has established itself in our homes.

What happened to Cathy? How did I know what object needed to go? Were any demonic forces attached to the book? What did Cathy's bloodline have to do with her suffering? We seek to answer these and many other questions concerning how demonic forces work within our own homes. It is our prayer that this book will help you determine any spiritual housecleaning you may need to do in order to protect your home from spiritual darkness.

Understanding Spiritual Life

> "The thief does not come except to steal, and to kill, and to destroy. I have come that they may have life, and that they may have it more abundantly."

> John 10:10

Jesus' words in this passage are not only a great comfort to His followers, but they are also a profound key to understanding the spiritual war in which we as Christians find ourselves. There is a thief who has come to steal, kill and destroy. He is the enemy of our souls, and it is important that we are wise to his schemes. The real issue in understanding how Satan works to bring death is to have an understanding of spiritual life. If we do not understand spiritual life, we will not be able to see where death has gained access and established itself in our homes.

The "life" that Jesus has come to give us is translated from the Greek word *zoe*, which means "to be possessed of vitality; to have life active and vigorous; to be devoted to God; to be blessed; to be among the living (not lifeless or dead); to enjoy real life, true life worthy of the name; to pass life on to others; to be fresh, strong, efficient, active, powerful; to be endless in the kingdom of God."[1] Furthermore, Jesus tells us that He has come to give us this rich existence in abundance, which means excessive, overflowing, surplus, over and above, more than enough, profuse, extraordinary, more than sufficient, superior, more remarkable, more excellent.[2] Life means movement. Anytime the "life" of Jesus or the Holy Spirit quits moving within our lives, death begins its process. Death is the opposite of life. Therefore, we must be aware of anything that produces death within us.

The abundant life that Christ brings is not a promise of a fairy tale in which, as we live happily ever after, we find continual joy in our perfect life. In fact, the Bible clearly states that the opposite is true: "In the world you will have tribulation" (John 16:33). However, that verse goes on to say, "but be of good cheer, I have overcome the world." The apostle Paul takes it one step further by saying, "We also glory in tribulations, knowing that tribulation produces perseverance; and perseverance, character; and character, hope" (Romans 5:3–4).

Because of our covenant relationship with God, even in times of tribulation, suffering or loss, we have the promise of abundant, *zoe* life. According to Isaiah 61, Jesus is anointed to heal the brokenhearted, proclaim liberty to the captives and give beauty for ashes, the oil of joy for mourning and a garment of praise for the spirit of heaviness. Such promises are the heritage of God's children. Our joy does not come from a perfect, pain-free life, but rather from a peace that surpasses all understanding—from an intimate relationship with the author of *zoe* life (see Philippians 4:7).

Defining Liberty and Freedom

Part of the *zoe* life that we as Christians enjoy includes liberty and freedom. *Liberty* is defined as "freedom from control, interference, obligation, restriction, external or foreign rule."[3] *Freedom* is defined as "immunity, exemption and the power to enjoy all the privileges or special rights of citizenship."[4] Jesus lived, died and rose again to bring us liberty from the bondages of death, hell and the grave—that is, freedom from control, interference, obligation, restriction or the rule of Satan. Additionally, Jesus' shed blood gives us freedom to come before God with immunity and exemption from sin, and the power to enjoy all the privileges and special rights of heavenly citizenship.

The Indwelling and Empowering Work
of the Holy Spirit

The very basis of experiencing *zoe* life is the ministry of the Holy Spirit to each and every one of us. As Robert Heidler, my own pastor for many years, writes in his book *Experiencing the Spirit*:

> The indwelling Spirit is the Spirit of Jesus living in the hearts of His people, sent to give them new hope, new love, new peace, new joy and new direction. This ministry is foundational to everything else in the Christian life. Through the indwelling Spirit we are *sealed* in Christ and given an inner assurance that we belong to Him (see 2 Cor. 1:22).
>
> Why would the Spirit of God want to live inside people like you and me? He lives in our hearts to enable us to live life on a new level. He is working to change us from the inside out, so that we may become more like Jesus.[5]

Every Christian, at the time he or she accepted Christ, received the indwelling of the Holy Spirit. We know this is true because we are called "the temple of the Holy Spirit" (1 Corinthians 6:19). It comes with Christianity. However, as Heidler goes on to point out, being empowered by the Holy Spirit is another matter.

> The *indwelling* ministry of the Spirit is automatic. . . . He came and took up residence within your heart at the moment of your salvation. In contrast, the *empowering* of the Spirit is seldom automatic, usually coming instead in response to prayer (emphasis added).[6]

Empowering of the Spirit is just as much a part of *zoe* life as the indwelling of the Spirit.

Why is this important to the subject at hand—protecting your home from spiritual darkness? It is because we need the empowering work of the Spirit in order to wage warfare against the enemy. No demonic force will ever comply with our commands to be gone without spiritual power backing us up. The empowering work of the Spirit gives us the authority we need to evict demons from our homes and lives.

Cooperating with the Holy Spirit

The empowering of the Holy Spirit is not automatic; rather, it is one that we must pursue. Therefore, we need to learn ways to cooperate with what the Holy Spirit is longing to do. Here are eight principles outlining how to live a life prepared to receive empowerment:

1. **Meditating on the Word of God.** Mary pondered (meditated on) what the Holy Spirit spoke to her about the birth of Jesus, and it became a part of her until she brought it to birth and watched it grow to maturity and into the fullness of God's plan. The book of Joshua instructs us to meditate on God's Word day and night (see 1:8). If we read the Word without giving it any thought, when does God have the opportunity to give us any revelation on what we have read or show us how to apply it to our lives? How can prayer flow out of a passage that we don't understand? We need to be like Mary and allow God's Word to become a part of us.

No demonic force will ever comply with our commands to be gone without spiritual power backing us up.

2. **Praying.** My life is prayer. I would rather commune with God than with anyone else. Prayer is simply communicating with God; He longs to communicate with us. It is when we pray that the channels to God are open—both ways. He commands us to devote ourselves to prayer (see Colossians 4:2). To neglect prayer is to neglect God Himself. When we fail to pray, we break

that all-important commandment of loving God with all our heart, soul and mind (see Matthew 22:37–38).

3. Fasting. For the Christian, fasting is essential, because many times we cannot gain the revelation we need for our next step without it. Fasting removes spiritual clutter and puts us in a better position to hear God. Through fasting, we give up something temporal to receive something eternal. Fasting is not a magical formula to manipulate God, yet even Jesus agreed that there are some things that simply cannot be accomplished without fasting (see Matthew 17:19–21; Mark 9:26–29).

Anything that God has ordained us to accomplish is going to be met with resistance from our enemy.

4. Giving. Giving is the very heart of God. We are called to multiply what God gives us, yet we cannot do this without becoming givers as well as receivers. Instead of receiving and giving, we often operate in a lack, or poverty, mentality. We must overcome our fear of not having enough or of not being worthy of what God has given us. Fear of such things can keep us from giving. Instead, we need to allow God to lead us into freedom as receivers and as givers.

5. Warring. Anything that God has ordained us to accomplish is going to be met with resistance from our enemy. In order to reach our full potential in God, we must learn warfare. Sometimes, however, it is not as aggressive as it sounds. For example, each of these eight disciplines is a form of warfare, because each thwarts the enemy's plans to steal God's best from us.

6. Worshiping. Worship is that place where we can enter into an intimacy with God. It is not just about singing songs, although music can be a catalyst for expressing deep worship to the Lord. Worship is a lifestyle of focusing our mind and heart on God and all He is. It is a response to all He has done for us. It is a fragrant, flowering offshoot of our covenant relationship with Him.

7. **Working.** I love to spend as much time as I can each day in prayer. But there is more than prayer. There is a time to get up off your knees and do something. We can pray all day, but eventually we have to realize that God will come to us and show us what He wants us to do. Many times we can speak to the mountain (see Matthew 17:20), but at other times we must dig through it to get to the other side. I call that spiritual work.

8. **Resting.** While God labored six days, He rested on the seventh. He commands us to do the same in the Ten Commandments (see Exodus 20:8–10). It must be a big issue since it made the Top Ten!

Becoming Aware
of Spiritual Darkness

If we are supposed to be partakers of *zoe* life and live in the liberty and freedom described in chapter 1, why do so many Christians (like Cathy) suffer from oppression, fear, low self-image, depression, uncontrollable sin patterns and other bondages that produce death rather than life?

The two main reasons why Christians do not enjoy the *zoe* life that God has promised are (1) sin and (2) Satan. We will deal more with the issues of sin—both personal and generational—in later chapters. Here, let's take a look at Satan and the forces he uses to steal the fullness out of our lives.

In *Warfare Prayer*, C. Peter Wagner writes:

Satan's central task and desire is to prevent God from being glorified. Whenever God is not glorified in a person's life, in a church, in a city or in the world as a whole, Satan has to that degree accomplished his objective. . . . Satan's primary objective is to prevent God from being glorified by keeping lost people from being saved. . . . Satan's secondary objective is to make human beings and human society as miserable as possible in this present life.[1]

How does Satan accomplish these goals? He does whatever it takes to veer us away from God's path. As C. S. Lewis so aptly shows in *The Screwtape Letters*, our enemy's number-one tactic is deception. He is a deceiver—the father of lies (see John 8:44). He prowls about looking for the right moment to pounce on us (see 1 Peter 5:8). He takes advantage of every opportunity we give to him, but he is not omnipresent. So, how is it that Satan manages to make so many of us miserable in this present life? He delegates.

At the enemy's disposal is a vast demonic host whose assignment is to see that Christians never reach their full potential while on earth. In so doing, they have not only succeeded in causing us distress and grief, but they also have succeeded in keeping us from fulfilling the destiny that God has for us in this lifetime. God has a purpose—a great destiny for each and every one of us. This destiny is purposed to cause us to live *zoe* life, as well as designed to advance the Kingdom of God on earth. Getting us off course is, therefore, well worth Satan's efforts. He can steal *zoe* life from us and thwart God's purpose for our lives simultaneously.

Clever Disguises?

While there are many ways that demonic forces can oppress God's people, this book is written to help us discover how these forces gain a foothold within our own homes. As a first step, we must understand that demons use clever disguises to keep us ignorant of their work in our lives. As Noel and Phyl Gibson write in *Evicting Demonic Intruders*, "Demons cover their existence by deception, so that people concentrate on what they see, or how they feel, and overlook spiritual causes."[2]

Noel and Phyl Gibson go on to list four reasons why Christians may be unaware of demonic activity (I have added a fifth):

1. Fear of demons causes people to deny their existence.
2. Lack of spiritual discernment.
3. Most modern preaching and teaching avoids the subject of demonic activity.
4. First-century faith has largely been replaced by twentieth-century rationalism.[3]
5. Our Western mindset keeps us from validating that which cannot be explained through scientific study.

Do objects have power? There is really nothing in an object itself. However, as believers, we must understand that there is often an invisible spiritual force behind a visible object. This is called the law of double reference. Many times in the Bible the Lord deals with a person or thing and asks us to look deeper into the spiritual force behind that person or thing. For instance, we find this in Isaiah 14, where the prophet Isaiah addresses the king of Babylon, and then we find references made to Lucifer. We find the same situation in Ezekiel 28. This is one way that demons operate. Paul writes, "We do not look at the things which are seen, but at the things which are not seen. For the things which are seen are temporary, but the things which are not seen are eternal" (2 Corinthians 4:18). Paul implies that there is more we need to be aware of than that which we can perceive with our five natural senses.

Demons are masters of disguise.

Demons are masters of disguise. They can inhabit people, objects, portions of land or whole territories, depending on their purpose. They do not care *what* they inhabit, as long as they can accomplish their assigned objectives. They can gain access through sin, trauma, victimization, witchcraft, occult practices or cursing. While we do not want to become fascinated with demons, we must become aware of what they are and how they operate in order to keep our own homes free from spiritual darkness.

Haunted Houses?

When my coauthor, Rebecca Sytsema, met her husband, Jack, he asked her to come over to the apartment he was renting from the seminary he attended in order to pray. He reported that there was always a heavy, oppressive feeling inside the apartment. He didn't like being there at all. He knew the problem was spiritual and needed prayer.

When they arrived at the apartment, Jack gave Rebecca a quick tour and they began praying. An ominous feeling descended on them both. It was as if a dark shroud draped itself over the room. Suddenly, the microwave (which had not been in use) began beeping, the answering machine began making strange noises—rewinding itself and playing old, erased messages—and the lights began to flicker on and off—all within a matter of seconds, and all without explanation. Jack and Rebecca began praying harder!

Within a few minutes, a neighbor (also a seminary student) stormed down the stairs, pounded on the door and yelled a string of obscenities at Jack for causing the mysterious electrical fluctuations that were apparently affecting the whole building. There had been no history of electrical problems in the building and certainly no way for that man to know that anything was going on in Jack's apartment. Without a doubt, Jack and Rebecca had stirred up demonic forces that would have preferred to remain incognito.

In the name of Jesus, Jack took authority as the legal tenant of that apartment and commanded the spirits to leave. By the leading of the Holy Spirit, he repented for any past sins that had been committed there. He anointed the doors and windows with oil and consecrated the apartment to the Lord. By the time they were done praying, great peace filled his home. Jack reported that he got his first good night's sleep since moving in several months earlier. A few weeks later, Jack sensed that the spirits were trying to regain residence. He and two other friends prayed through the apartment once again, and he had no further spiritual trouble for the remaining time he lived in that apartment.

Was the apartment "haunted"? In a manner of speaking, the answer is yes.

Was the apartment "haunted"? In a manner of speaking, the answer is yes. It was not haunted by ghosts of human beings, but rather by demonic forces whose job was to cloud the air with oppressive darkness. What better place to set up camp than in seminary housing, where tomorrow's Christian leaders are supposed to receive training for ministry?

Does Your Home Need Prayer?

There is always a great deal of benefit in praying through a home for the purpose of consecrating it or setting it apart for the Lord. By doing this, you may or may not encounter spiritual darkness that needs to be dealt with. Yet there are indicators as to whether a home needs to be cleansed of spiritual darkness. The following list might indicate symptoms of a spiritually polluted atmosphere that requires spiritual cleansing:

- Sudden chronic illness
- Recurrent bad dreams and nightmares

- Insomnia or unusual sleepiness
- Behavioral problems
- Relational problems—continual fighting, arguing and misinterpreted communication
- Lack of peace
- Restless, disturbed children
- Unexplained illnesses or bondage to sin
- Ghosts or demonic apparitions (to which young children are particularly susceptible)
- Poltergeists (the movement of physical objects by demons)
- Foul, unexplainable odors
- Atmospheric heaviness, making it hard to breathe
- Continual nausea and headaches[4]

If you are experiencing any of these things on an ongoing basis, ask the Lord to reveal any spiritual darkness that may be in your home. Remember that Jesus gives us authority over these beings; He is far greater than any force that might come against you. There is no need to fear. Becoming aware of the demonic and how it may be affecting you is the first step to protecting your home from spiritual darkness.

3

The Jewelry Box

My wife has to be crazy! What other explanation can there be for wanting to destroy a beautiful—and valuable—jewelry box? There is nothing wrong with that box. How ridiculous! How wasteful!

Such were my thoughts on the day my wife, Pam, came home from a prayer meeting and told me that her jewelry box had to go. Little did I know that the Lord would use that jewelry box to deliver me from a covetous, greedy spirit *and* teach me the truth about demonic forces' inhabiting objects.

It happened several years ago. Pam was enjoying a spiritual revival in her life. During that time, she and six other ladies decided to meet together for seven weeks to pray that their husbands would come into a deeper spiritual walk and to experience renewal in their own lives. In the sixth week, a friend who was a missionary to China came to the prayer meeting. She began to discuss how demonic forces could inhabit objects in order to bring spiritual darkness into a home. Having lived in China, this missionary had a different approach to spiritual issues than those of us with a Western mindset. Her perspective made sense to Pam.

When Pam came home after that meeting, she recounted what the missionary told them. She told me that she could not stop thinking about a large, beautiful jewelry box from Thailand that her father had given her. The jewelry box was decorated with dragons, pagodas and buddhas—all kinds of images that she knew did not bring glory to God. The more she thought about it, the more she felt the box had to go.

I was aware of spiritual darkness, but I had no idea that demons could attach themselves to objects.

I thought she was totally off the wall! I was aware of spiritual darkness, but I had no idea that demons could attach themselves to objects. I told her that she was crazy for thinking that anything spiritual was linked to that jewelry box. I also reminded her that the box was a gift, and it was worth a lot of money. Why would we want to destroy such a valuable object? My wife immediately submitted to me and did not mention it anymore.

Three weeks later, Pam and I were in some friends' home attending a prayer meeting. During that meeting, the Spirit of God spoke to me and said, "You have caused your wife to rebel against My will for her life, and I hold you accountable!" Immediately, I knew the Lord was talking about the jewelry box. He had revealed to Pam that she needed to destroy it, and I had stopped her from obeying Him! At that moment, a deep fear of the Lord came over me. I knew that as soon as we got home, I had to take full responsibility for what I had done and burn that jewelry box myself.

When we got home, I immediately set a fire in the fireplace. I did not know exactly what I was doing, but I knew I had to do it. When I placed the jewelry box in the fireplace, a strange, eerie wind began to blow and stir all around the living room. The wind was not coming from outside. Something was generating it from within our home. The inexplicable wind blew so hard that it knocked a lamp clear off the wall. Not knowing exactly what I was dealing with, I became frightened.

At that time, there was a woman in our church whom I knew understood spiritual things. So I called her, told her what was happening and asked her what to do. She began to pray for me over the phone. She told me to read some Scriptures and command any evil presence linked with that jewelry box to leave our home. When I did so, the Lord spoke to me and said, "I am delivering you from covetousness and the love of money!"

Once I was liberated from that particular demonic force in my life, it was as if my eyes were opened to many issues within our home that were linked with other evil forces. Freedom began to come to us in incredible ways—not only freedom, but spiritual revelation.

What Did the Jewelry Box Represent?

What did the jewelry box have to do with covetousness and the love of money? At first it had nothing to do with it. The engraved images of dragons, pagodas and buddhas on the jewelry box were not glorifying to God. They were carven images of gods and creatures worshiped in the Thai culture, which was why the Holy Spirit convicted Pam to get rid of it.

When I stood in the way of ridding our home of unclean images on the basis of the box's monetary value, my own covetousness and greed, and the demonic forces that had been in my family concerning those issues, became linked with the jewelry box. In other words, it was simply a matter of my unwillingness to obey God and destroy something of value that made the object a symbol of an evil force in my life. When the fear of the Lord came on me and I chose to destroy the box, regardless of its value, my act of burning the jewelry box broke the back of a demonically inspired love of money that had been passed down to me from my father (see chapter 6 for more on generational iniquity). God delivered my home of an unclean object, *and* He delivered me of a covetous spirit at the same time.

When I chose to obey God, the demonic force lost its grip in my life.

Objects that we may possess, although not inherently wrong, often represent a demonic stronghold in our lives. The jewelry box was just that kind of item in my life. It had images on it that needed to be cleansed from my house. Yet even if the box hadn't had those images, my unwillingness to give it up due to its value showed a much deeper problem that was, in fact, a demonic stronghold of covetousness and the love of money.

The love of money is a major issue, especially in American society. It is the only sin of the flesh that is "hard-core idolatry," a term coined by C. Peter Wagner. Referring to Luke 16:13, "You cannot serve both God and Money" (NIV), Wagner writes:

> Covetousness is allegiance to a false god named Mammon. . . . It is correct to capitalize "Money" or "Mammon" because it is a proper name. Mammon is a person, not a thing or an urge or an attitude. . . . When Jesus mentioned Mammon, it was in the context of not being able to serve two masters. Serving any supernatural master in the demonic world, like Mammon, is hard-core idolatry.[1]

This was the allegiance that the jewelry box came to represent in my life. When I chose to obey God and get rid of the jewelry box, the demonic force of Mammon lost its grip in my life, and I was delivered.

When Mammon Interferes with Obedience

Have you ever noticed your dollar bill? I once was ministering at a deliverance conference on the issue of objects and how many times evil characters are embedded in objects. The evil eye is right there on the dollar bill. I'll explain more about the evil eye in chapter 7. Does that mean we should burn all of our dollar bills? Well, of course not. But it does make us aware that there is a snare to money. When the Lord was ready to send the people of Israel into the Promised Land, He had many warnings for them. He knew they would be in spiritual war with the god Mammon. Mammon can rule the economic system, which allows demonic forces to be involved in the administration, transfer and distribution of wealth. When you study Canaanite history, you find that the ruling god of the Canaanites was Mammon. The assignment or mission that Joshua and the tribes of Israel had to accomplish was to transfer wealth from all of the inhabitants of that region into God's covenant, Kingdom plan. Therefore, Mammon had to be defeated, and the wealth held by its false worship transferred.

> No one can serve two masters; for either he will hate the one and love the other, or else he will be loyal to the one and despise the other. You cannot serve God and mammon.
>
> Matthew 6:24

When Provision Becomes a Golden Calf

Provision is necessary for our lives to be functional in our world. However, the Lord says to be in the world but not of the world (see 1 John 2:15–17). When the Israelites left Egypt, God prompted the Egyptians to give them all kinds of goods. Exodus 12:36 reads, "And the LORD had given the people favor in the sight of the Egyptians, so that they granted them what they requested. Thus they plundered the Egyptians." Imagine the masters of these slaves filling their hands with silver and gold. This is an example of what the Lord still wishes to do for His children as He breaks us out of the system in which we live and points us toward the covenant blessings He has throughout the earth. God gave Moses a detailed plan for the people. However, the people did not wait on Moses. Instead of waiting patiently, as instructed, they grew impatient. Therefore, they took all of the provision God had provided them and, in their discouragement, wandered back to the other gods from whom they had been liberated.

> And he [Aaron] received the gold from their hand, and he fashioned it with an engraving tool, and made a molded calf. Then they said, "This is your god, O Israel, that brought you out of the land of Egypt!"
>
> Exodus 32:4

Not only was this molded bull calf a familiar god that had been in Egypt, but it also was worshiped in Canaan through the religious system that had been erected in Canaanite worship. When we do not offer God His portion and make our provision holy before Him, we open ourselves up to the operation of the evil eye working over our finances. The evil eye aligns with our idolatry, and our idolatry aligns with Mammon. Thus, we find ourselves under the control of this false god.

While covetousness may be the only sin of the flesh that is hard-core idolatry, it is not the only thing that may represent a demonic stronghold in your life. Take lust, for example. Perhaps there is something in your home from a past romantic relationship (maybe a gift, some old love letters or hidden photos), and you are now married to another person. A demonic stronghold of lust or of inappropriate love can easily attach itself to that item. Destroying whatever it is will help you overcome the enemy's grip in that area of your life. It will help you leave the past behind and move forward into God's destiny for you and your family.

Knowing what might represent a demonic stronghold in our lives or what objects are not glorying to God often takes spiritual discernment. In chapter 4, we will look at what discernment is and how to use it to protect our homes from spiritual darkness.

Why Should We Take a Look at What We Own?

The jewelry box brings up two distinct instances of objects that need to be dispatched in order to protect our homes from spiritual darkness: (1) objects that do not bring glory to God; and (2) objects that represent demonic strongholds in our own lives. Let's look at each one of these instances.

There are several instances in the Bible when disaster occurred because of objects. One instance is when Rachel died while giving birth to Benjamin (see Genesis 35). What was the cause of her premature death? In Genesis 31, Jacob fled from Laban. When Laban caught up with him and accused him of stealing some household gods, Jacob said, "With whomever you find your gods, do not let him live. In the presence of our brethren, identify what I have of yours and take it with you" (v. 32). Jacob did not know that Rachel had stolen the household gods and put them in her camel's saddle. When Laban was searching for the objects linked with his idolatrous form of worship, Rachel pretended to be in her monthly period and actually sat on the household gods. She was not willing to let go of an old form of worship linked with her father. As a result, she died prematurely.

A similar story is told in Joshua 7. Israel experienced defeat in the battle of Ai, which occurred immediately after its great victory in Jericho. Achan, despite God's warning not to take any cursed things, took and hid several of the forbidden objects. As a result, Israel was defeated. In the end, Achan and his whole family were destroyed because of his sin.

On the other hand, freedom occurred when believers in Ephesus brought their idolatrous items and objects linked with magic and sorcery, and burned them in the middle of the city (see Acts 19). This was a key to one of the greatest revivals and awakenings recorded in the Bible.

The Problem with Objects

Once we become aware of spiritual darkness, we can begin looking around in our homes and see what we own that does not bring glory to God. What we mean by this phrase is something that, by its very nature, can attract or be inhabited by darkness. Here are five categories of such objects:

1. Foreign Gods. "You shall not make for yourself a carved image—any likeness of anything that is in heaven above, or that is in the earth beneath, or that is in the water under the earth" (Deuteronomy 5:8). In this passage, the second of the Ten Commandments, a "carved image" refers to any tangible object that represents an idol, god or demonic figure. Not only is this a welcome mat for demonic activity, but also God hates it. Though it may be out of ignorance, it is surprising to realize how many Christians have such items in their homes.

These objects include buddhas (as was on Pam's jewelry box); Hindu images; fertility gods or goddesses (or any type of god or goddess); Egyptian images; Greek gods; gargoyles; kachina dolls, totem poles or any other Native American figures that depict or glorify a spirit or demonic being; evil depictions of creatures such as lions, dogs, dragons or cats (or any other creature made with demonic distortions); or any other image of a person, idol, god or demonic figure that is considered an object of worship or spiritual power in any culture in the world.

On trips, many people collect these types of artifacts as souvenirs without truly understanding their significance—much like the jewelry box that came from Thailand.

2. False Religions. Objects or materials related to false religions, such as Mormonism, Islam, Jehovah's Witness, Hinduism, Eastern religions, Christian Science, Native religions, Baha'i and so forth need to be carefully evaluated. This includes instruction books on yoga, transcendental meditation, mantras and so on.

3. Occult Objects. Anything related to the occult must be destroyed completely. These objects include Ouija boards; good luck charms; amulets; astrology items (including horoscopes); tarot cards; crystals; fetishes; water witching sticks; voodoo dolls; pagan symbols; crystal balls; any ritual item, such as a mask, a pyramid or an obelisk; any item obtained from occult or voodoo shops; any item related to black magic, fortune-telling, palmistry,

> *Anything related to the occult must be destroyed completely.*

demon worship, spirit guides, witchcraft, Satanism or New Age. None of these items or any other such item should have any place in the Christian home.

4. Secret-Society Objects. Remember the story in chapter 1 about Cathy and the handbook for thirty-second-degree Masons? That book was connected to her depression. Secret societies, such as Freemasonry, Shriners, Eastern Star, Job's Daughters, Odd Fellows, Elks, Amaranth, DeMolay, Rainbow Girls or Daughters of the Nile, often require their members to take oaths and go through initiation rituals, including pledging allegiance to various deities, which are completely contrary to God's Word. Because that is the case, demons can easily attach themselves to items, such as books, rings, aprons, regalia and memorabilia that represent these societies. Additionally, because such items are often passed down through family lines, there is a generational issue that must be dealt with (see chapter 6).

5. Other Objects. Our homes may be filled with other items that do not bring glory to God and may attract demonic activity. These include games such as Masters of the Universe and Dungeons and Dragons, in addition to myriad demonic or violent video games; books and magazines devoted to fantasy; comic books, posters, movies or music with demonic, violent or sexual themes; pornography; illegal drugs; sensual art, books or "toys"; or a number of other things that are demonic, illegal, immoral or contrary to God's Word.

By allowing any of these types of things into our homes, we give the enemy a legal right to invade our lives in ways that he would otherwise not have access. As Cindy Jacobs would say, we have holes in our armor. In order to bring clarity into the process of deciding what might need to go, C. Peter Wagner encourages us to ask the following questions:

- Might this open me to direct demonic influence?
- Does this give any appearance of evil?
- Does this glorify God?[2]

Ethnic Culture versus Kingdom Culture

A culture is the totality of socially transmitted behavior patterns, arts, beliefs, institutions and all other products of human work and thought. Culture is also the predominating attitudes and behavior that characterize the functioning of a group or organization.[3]

There are many objects in our lives that define the culture from which we come. Some objects are unique to a particular culture. Some things are just objects and do not represent any evil. Some objects are used in evil ways in one culture but are very harmless in another culture. Some objects are plain evil and irredeemable.

As Christians, we are part of the culture in which we are born, yet we also are part of God's Kingdom culture that transcends racial, national and physical boundaries. We can appreciate much about our natural culture, such as food, holidays and some traditions, but we cannot ignorantly embrace everything. We must consider the cultural object, practice or whatever it may be and weigh it against the standards God sets in His Kingdom culture.

A kingdom has a king. We must always represent our King in all that we do on earth. Anything in our culture that is contrary to or falsely represents the King in our Kingdom, we must be willing to let go of or remove from our sphere of authority or home.

Because every kingdom has a culture, we want to be sure the culture of God's Kingdom is overriding or sanctifying anything that is from our worldly culture. This does not require us to get rid of all the objects of our culture, but it does give us the responsibility to see that those objects are brought under the sanctifying blood of the Lord Jesus Christ. If we do not do this, our conscience will be hindered and our vision will be blurred over God's plan for our lives. We should never let an object in our culture become a stumbling block to entering into a new dimension of God's Kingdom.

We work very closely with Native Americans, or the host people of this land. Without the host people of a nation (any nation, not just the United States) coming unto their destined inheritance in God, the nation itself can never fully experience the plan of God.

There has been much discussion about Native artifacts, feathers, drums, dream catchers, jewelry and so on. Possessing such items usually becomes a matter of conscience. However, there are certain objects that were dedicated and used for occult purposes in our host culture. These objects were made solely for the purposes of evil or to gain illegal revelation from dark sources. These types of items will be a hindrance in a Christian walk. We must very carefully deal with objects that may be a stumbling block to our spiritual development, as well as to the spiritual development of new believers.

The Problem with Garments

In any culture, there are customs, traditions, values, laws, rules of supply, garments and dress. Some of these items are used in worship in different cultures. Therefore, we need to review very carefully all that we own when moving into the Kingdom of God—especially items of worship and dress.

Your wardrobe can represent a season in your life. Zechariah 3 talks about how Satan accuses Joshua the high priest over his past. The Lord rebukes Satan, but then He does something else. He changes Joshua's clothing. He removes the filthy garments linked with his past and puts on new garments—"rich robes" (v. 4). He also puts a new turban on Joshua's head, which represents the new thought process of his mind for a new season.

I periodically clean out my closet. I find clothes that have emotional ties or inordinate affections with which I associate them. I may have clothes that do not represent the expression of my personality any longer or outdated garments. I also may find clothes that are linked with a season of grief in my life.

Remember in Ruth 3, Naomi made Ruth change her clothes. She was still wearing the clothes linked with Moab. These garments were filled with grief because of the loss of her husband. In other words, Naomi said, "Take off that widow's garment. We have to make a move to shift into our inheritance!"

> Put off, concerning your former conduct, the old man which
> grows corrupt according to the deceitful lusts, and be renewed

in the spirit of your mind, and that you put on the new man which was created according to God, in true righteousness and holiness.

Ephesians 4:22–24

Clean out your closets! Change your clothes to reflect God and His Kingdom in this season of your life!

Spiritual Discernment

"How do we know when we've prayed enough?" she asked me. The woman and her husband sat across from me, describing their situation in some detail. There was a piece of property that they owned. They regularly prayed over it, hoping to plant a church there someday. But they knew that something was wrong.

"Every time we set foot on that property, the hair on my arms stands up!" she explained. "We've prayed and prayed. How do we know when we've prayed enough?"

"It's very simple," I told her. "Pray until the hair on your arms goes down!"

The Meaning of Spiritual Discernment

Spiritual discernment is the grace to see into the unseen. It is a gift *of the Spirit* to perceive what is *in the spirit*. Its purpose is to see into the nature of that which is veiled (emphasis added).[1]

This quote from Francis Frangipane is helpful in understanding what discernment is. It is something that we know by seeing with our spiritual eyes rather than with our physical eyes.

Gary Kinnaman defines it this way:

> There are three kinds of spirits: evil spirits, human spirits, and heavenly spirits, including angels and the Spirit of God. The discerning of spirits is the ability to identify the kind of spirit that is the driving force behind a particular event, circumstance or thought. If it is determined that the spirit is an evil one, the discerning of spirits operating with precision can also identify the specific kind of evil spirit.[2]

There are some in the Body of Christ who have a gift of discernment. Those with a developed, mature gift are able to discern what the spiritual atmosphere of a place or around a person is more often and with more accuracy than most Christians. But the ability to discern spirits is not limited to those with "the gift." God can speak to any Christian through the Holy Spirit and give spiritual insight into any given situation. Spiritual discernment may seem like a complicated or a difficult thing, but the fact is that discernment can be as simple as praying until the hair on your arms goes down. It's a matter of learning how to use the discernment God gives.

A Lamp unto My Feet

How do we learn how to have spiritual discernment? Discernment comes through knowing God. There are two main keys to knowing God: (1) God's Word; and (2) hearing by the Spirit through prayer (see Hebrews 5:14). They are both important factors to spiritual discernment.

Through Your precepts I get understanding; therefore I hate every false way. Your word is a lamp to my feet and a light to my path.

Psalm 119:104–105

As we read and digest the Word of God, we develop important spiritual principles within us. These principles help illuminate the path that God sets before us; they act as a lamp unto our feet. For instance, by knowing the Word of God, we understand that we are not to have any carven images of idols in our homes (see chapter 3). That understanding helps us become sensitive to seeing carven images of idols all around us, whether in our homes, in our places of work or wherever we may be.

God wants to give us the discernment we need to protect our homes from spiritual darkness.

I have developed a real aversion to any images of idols, false gods or the demonic, because I know how much God hates them. Just as Psalm 119 says, I gained understanding about such images through God's precepts (His Word), which helped me become aware of these kinds of images all around me. My understanding also has helped me set a rule about what I will not own, namely images of idols. God's Word has become a lamp unto my feet. From knowing God's Word, I can look at objects within my home and see what does not line up with the Bible. This is part of discernment.

The Voice of God

There are certain things we must discern, however, that are not as apparent as the image of an idol. These are spiritual issues; they must be discerned spiritually. We must hear from God in order to know what is going on, and the key to hearing God is

342

prayer—two-way communication in which you speak to Him and He speaks to you.

Hearing the voice of God is not as difficult as some might think. I have found that many of God's people hear Him, but they have not perceived it as His voice. To *perceive* means "to take hold of, feel, comprehend, grasp mentally, recognize, observe or become aware of something."[3] We must learn how to perceive God's voice and the prompting of the Holy Spirit.

God may speak to us through spiritual dreams (unusually vivid and detailed dreams that stick in our spirit), visions, visitations, a prophetic word, a conversation with a friend that brings revelation, a message we've heard or a feeling—like the woman whose hair stood up on her arms. When we hear from God, we suddenly know that we know something—a revelation takes place in our spirit. Our challenge is to sharpen our spiritual ears to hear God and not to write off what we hear as mere imagination. God *wants* to communicate with us. We must believe that. Furthermore, God does not want us to be ignorant of how the enemy tries to ensnare us. He wants to give us the discernment we need to protect our homes from spiritual darkness.

Spiritual Boundaries

When we discern something that we believe is from the Lord, we must allow the Lord to show us what to do with the discernment. This fact became apparent in my own life not long after the jewelry box incident. From that time on, the Lord began to open my eyes to other objects in my home that were linked with demonic forces. My discernment was sharpening all the time.

One day, I was walking by our fireplace and saw a large ceramic cat that I had purchased some time before. It was a beautiful object with piercing blue eyes. The cat was worth a lot of money, but money was no longer an issue since my deliverance from the love of money when I destroyed the jewelry box. As I looked at the cat, I immediately discerned that witchcraft was linked to it. I then remembered that, out of my ignorance, I had purchased the cat in a voodoo shop in New Orleans when I was on a business trip. I began to see that this cat was linked with spiritism in my bloodline, which was why I was drawn into the voodoo shop in the first place and felt compelled to buy the cat (see chapter 6 for more information about this phenomenon). I knew the cat had to go. Because it was ceramic, I knew that it would not burn like the jewelry box. Nonetheless, I passed it through the fire and then smashed it (see Deuteronomy 5:7).

In my zeal, I began to look around the house for other such objects. I found many ceramic cats that my wife had collected through the years. Because of my spiritual immaturity, I assumed that if the ceramic cat I bought was evil, all the other cats were evil, so I smashed them all. When Pam came home later that day, she asked what had happened to her cats. I explained to her what I had done. She just looked at me and said, "There was nothing wrong with my cats. It was *your* cat that had the problem. You have a choice. You can either replace the cats yourself or give me money to buy new ones."

She was absolutely right. My good discernment had run amok! The problem was not ceramic cats in general; rather, the problem was one particular ceramic cat that I had purchased ignorantly in a voodoo shop. I did not heed the spiritual boundaries that should have been obvious. As a result, I got in a lot of trouble with my wife!

Along these same lines, I have seen some people get rid of everything that has feathers on it. Even though feathers can be used in occult activities, it does not mean that all feathers are wrong. We have birds that have feathers. As long as those birds are for our enjoyment, their feathers pose no problem. Yet if I use their feathers as objects in occult worship, then those particular feathers become a problem. The same is true of many Native American artifacts (see chapter 3).

Spiritual Authority

Spiritual boundaries are linked with authority. Each of us is given a sphere of authority in which we are free to operate (see 2 Corinthians 10:13). When we move beyond that sphere of authority is when we run into real problems. Take the cats, for example. Even if there had been demons attached to my wife's ceramic cats, I did not have the authority to destroy them without her permission, because they simply did not belong to me.

I know many people who, upon learning the principles outlined in this book, made major mistakes because they did not understand their spiritual authority. Armed with discernment and the name of Jesus, they felt they could rid the world of demonic forces. That is just not so. We may begin to discern all kinds of problems, but we must understand that we are not free to deal with every problem we see—nor is it wise.

If you visit your mother's house, for example, and see that she has a statue of Buddha, and she is unwilling to get rid of it, you do not have the right either legally or spiritually to take her statue. It is beyond your spiritual authority. What you can do is pray and ask the Lord to reveal the principles outlined in this book to her. Maybe she would be willing to read this book. There may be other things you can do to help her understand, but taking what is not yours definitely crosses the line of authority, not to mention it breaks one of the Ten Commandments—"You shall not steal" (Exodus 20:15). Any spirit attached to the statue can actually gain greater power because of the sin of stealing.

If your mother, on the other hand, asks you to get rid of the statue and pray for her, then she has given you the authority not only to destroy the statue but also to command any spirits attached to that statue to leave. In this case, she has extended spiritual authority for you to act on her behalf, and you are free to deal with the situation.

Ask the Lord to show you what your sphere of authority is before moving out in presumption and thereby making things worse than they were before!

A Gargoyle in the Attic

Some years ago, I was asked to pray over a building owned by some friends. Their business was located on the bottom floor, and some apartments occupied the top floor. The building had been plagued with many continual problems, including flooding. My friends had come to believe that there was a spiritual problem, so they called me. When I entered the building, I immediately knew something was very wrong. The evil was so strong that I couldn't breathe! Through discernment, I knew that there was some object within the building that had demonic forces attached to it, and I knew it was somewhere above us.

The Lord revealed that the gargoyle had been planted as a fetish in order to curse the building.

My friends trusted my discernment, and they spent $30,000 to tear out the ceiling in order to see what might be there. They found nothing. I knew that, despite their great efforts, something had been missed. Some months later, as they were renovating the building and having electrical work done, they discovered a cement gargoyle hidden in one corner of the attic. I knew that was what we had been looking for! The Lord revealed that the gargoyle had been planted as a fetish in order to curse the building. We destroyed the gargoyle and prayed through the building, dedicating it to the Lord. Since that time my friends have not encountered any trouble with the building.

Planted Fetishes

A fetish is an object believed to have magical or spiritual powers, or is an object linked with an abnormally obsessive preoccupation or attachment or fixation.[4] These objects represent or are connected with some supernatural being. By possessing these objects or having someone plant them in what we possess, they can give place to demonic beings to operate through them. Many times in past generations, fetishes were planted in the ground.

Some people will discern that there is something wrong in their land or house or even a car, but they can't see where the problem is coming from. Items such as the gargoyle in the attic are fetishes. Until these objects are removed, demonic forces have the right to hinder God's plan in that place. We rented a house once that really had a problem in one room. My wife and daughter could both sense there was something wrong in that room. I freaked out every time I walked in it. I finally walked into the closet and looked up and saw an entry into the ceiling. When we got up into the ceiling, we found evil magazines and paraphernalia. Once we removed the material, we anointed the room and the portion of the attic above the room. The room was cleansed from that day forward.

A Demonic Foothold
in the Land

Elaine awakened suddenly to the anguished screams of her son. *Not again!* she thought as she pulled on her bathrobe and wearily shuffled down the hall to Joey's room. She pushed the door open to find the familiar sight of her three-year-old son sobbing on his bed. She dropped onto the bed, gathered the small boy into her arms and stroked his head, which was soaked with tears and sweat.

"It's okay, Joey," she whispered in his ear. "Mommy's here. No one will hurt you." She began to rock him back and forth as she had so many nights before, trying to calm him down. A full hour later, Elaine finally crawled into her own bed, but she could not fall asleep. She wondered why her son had not slept one full night since they had moved into this house, almost six months ago. He had slept well before, but something here was different.

Enough was enough. The next day Elaine called Joan, the pastor's wife, for counsel and prayer. Joan suggested that perhaps they needed to pray through Joey's room. She agreed to come over that afternoon. As the women began praying, Joan had a strong sense that something in the room was truly wrong—that there was an evil presence there.

As Joan prayed further, she began to see a picture of a young child being beaten in that room. She knew that the Lord was showing her why the evil presence lingered in Joey's room. Looking at Elaine, she said, "I believe that there may have been some kind of child abuse that took place in this room."

Stunned, Elaine began to explain to Joan that Joey's night terrors were often brought on by dreams of someone beating him. She had never understood this since neither she nor her husband had ever struck him with that kind of force. "What can we do?" Elaine asked.

Grabbing Elaine's hand, Joan kneeled by the bed and began asking God to forgive the sin of child abuse that had taken place in the room. Tears came to their eyes as they identified with the young child who had suffered in this place. After a few minutes of dealing with these revelations and asking God to cleanse the room, Joan rose to her feet, and with authority in her voice, she commanded the evil presence to leave the property and never return. At that moment, a great peace descended on the house. The room looked brighter. Elaine realized that for the first time since moving in, she felt totally at peace herself.

That night Joey slept well. Since praying through his room, the terror that plagued him never recurred. About a month after the incident, Elaine was visiting with her next-door neighbor who had lived there for several years. She asked about the family who had lived there before. Elaine's neighbor told her that she often heard yelling coming from the house and that on three occasions the police had to come break up the fights. Although the neighbor was not sure, she heard through the neighborhood grapevine that the authorities had removed the son from the home due to abuse suffered at the hands of his parents.

Understanding Land and Property

Up to this point, we have discussed the objects we own; however, part of protecting our homes from spiritual darkness also has to do with the land on which we live. In Elaine's story, we see that her young son was tormented by spiritual darkness unrelated to any object, or even to any sin in which Elaine had been involved. The land on which they lived, however, had been defiled through sin, which left an opening for demonic invasion that, until it was dealt with through prayer, continued to torment.

How can this be? Just as dark forces can inhabit an object, they also can inhabit land or places. In fact, some high-ranking principalities and powers can inhabit whole cities or territories. But if the earth is the Lord's (see Psalm 24:1), where do demons get the right to stake a claim to a particular part of the earth? The answer is through sin. Sin has a direct effect on land. We see this evidenced numerous times throughout the Bible.

In the story of Cain and Abel, for instance, God said to Cain, "What have you done? The voice of your brother's blood cries out to Me from the ground. So now you are cursed from the earth, which has opened its mouth to receive your brother's blood from your hand" (Genesis 4:10–11). Sin produces a curse in the land—in the physical ground where it occurs—and where there are curses, evil abounds.

Gaining a Foothold

The word *foothold* means "a secure position that provides a base for further progress or advancement."[1] When the enemy gains a foothold, he has firmly established himself in a position from which he can progress with his evil schemes to kill, steal and destroy (see John 10:10). Let's look at Ephesians 4:25–27:

> Therefore, putting away lying, "Let each one of you speak truth with his neighbor," for we are members of one another. "Be angry, and do not sin": do not let the sun go down on your wrath, nor give place to the devil.

First, we must understand how Satan can gain a foothold in our own lives. If we allow sin into our lives and do not confess it, we leave a door open, giving the enemy an opportunity to attack what is ours and to attack us. This verse in Ephesians talks about anger. Even though anger is an emotion and can be righteous, we see here that if we do not operate in a godly manner when we are angry, it can embed in our emotions and open the door to the enemy to gain a foothold. The same is true of any sin that has not been cleansed by the blood of Jesus. Sin that is not dealt with gives Satan a legal right into a situation, even in the life of a believer.

If we allow sin into our lives and do not confess it, we leave a door open.

A great doctrinal debate throughout the history of Christendom has been the issue of demonic influence in the lives of true, born-again believers. Most theologians do not have a problem with the concept of Satan's right to tempt a Christian. But if Satan cannot gain some benefit into the lives of believers through that sin, why does he bother? Anyone with experience in the field of deliverance knows that Christians are prime targets for demonization, or a demonic foothold. This does not mean that the person is demon possessed, which means a demonic entity has full control; rather, the person is demonically influenced or tormented in a particular area of life. The opening for demonization is often sin—either personal or generational.[2]

Just as the enemy can gain a foothold into our lives through sin, he also can gain a foothold into land through sin that has been committed there. Back to Ephesians 4:26–27, the phrase, "do not . . . give place to the devil" means do not give him a foothold or opportunity. *Topos* is the Greek word for "place" in this verse. From *topos* we get the word "topographical," which means a literal place, locality or piece of land.[3] Sin gives the enemy a foothold—a secure position that provides a base for further progress or advancement—to *topos*—a literal place, locality or piece of land. From the physical place where Satan has a foothold, he seeks to do his three favorite things: steal, kill and destroy (see John 10:10).

Therefore, the issue with our homes is not just what we own, but also what has occurred in our homes or on the land on which our homes were built. Has any sin occurred that gives the enemy a place there—a foothold? Remember the woman in chapter 4 whose hair stood up on her arms? She was discerning a problem on the land. She had found evidence of occult rituals having been performed there. The land was undoubtedly full of demonic forces that had gained a foothold as a result of the ungodly worship. No wonder her hair stood up!

Defiling the Land

While any sin can be an opening for demonic activity, there are certain sins that can defile (i.e., bring a foul, dirty uncleanness to) the land. These sins leave the land cursed and particularly susceptible to demonic footholds:

1. **Idolatry.** God hates idolatry (see chapter 3). Just as the worship of God brings blessing upon the land, the worship of false gods brings curses.

2. **Bloodshed.** Earlier we mentioned the story of Cain and Abel. From this story, we see that bloodshed affected the very land on which the violence occurred. As the blood of violence

penetrates the ground, "the prince of the power of the air" (Ephesians 2:2) gains right into the land through the cursing caused by violence and bloodshed.

3. Immorality. This issue is one that we here in America must take seriously. "Immorality" has become a vague term and a nonissue for those in power. Our society has come to believe that anyone can do whatever is right in his or her own sight. But Satan knows that every immoral act opens up a greater legal right for him to infiltrate land and homes. With the advent of the Internet, there is even greater access to things like pornography and adult chat rooms. None of these things is benign. What is done in secret can bring serious consequences through defilement of those involved, as well as of the land on which their sin occurred.

4. Covenant Breaking. During the reign of King David, a great famine came on the land. When David inquired of the Lord concerning this famine, God said to him: "It is because of Saul and his bloodthirsty house, because he killed the Gibeonites" (2 Samuel 21:1). The Gibeonites were a group of people who had entered into covenant with Israel in the days of Joshua. This covenant guaranteed their safety. However, Saul broke the covenant with the Gibeonites by murdering many of them and planning for the massacre of the rest. As a result, famine came on the land as God removed His blessing and Satan was allowed access. The famine did not strike immediately but came when the new king came to power. Many of our homes in the United States have been built on land that was taken through broken treaties with Native Americans. Those broken treaties from years ago can defile and give the enemy a foothold on the land where we live today!

Wondering about the Cause

You may be wondering why demonic forces can torment a Christian in a place if the Christian did not do the sinning that gave those forces the legal right to establish a foothold in that place. Here is where you must understand the spiritual principle of remitting sin:

> And according to the law almost all things are purified with blood, and without shedding of blood there is no remission [of sin].
>
> Hebrews 9:22

The principle is this: No sin is atoned for without the shedding of blood. It was a principle in the Old Testament; it was a principle in the New Testament; and it is still a principle today. The difference between the Old and New Testaments is Jesus. The blood that Jesus shed on the cross is what we can appropriate to remit or atone for sin, but we must appropriate it in order for the sin to be remitted. Until repentance has occurred and the blood of Jesus is applied, the sin—and thus Satan's legal right to a foothold—remains intact.

Land that has been defiled through sin is like a soul that has been defiled through sin.

Land that has been defiled through sin is like a soul that has been defiled through sin. Without repentance and the appropriation of Jesus' blood, a place remains defiled and Satan has a right there. A Christian's taking control of a piece of property is *not* enough to rid it of spiritual darkness! Any demonic force that has a foothold in that place will continue to operate from that foothold until it is expelled through the remitting of whatever sin gave it the right in the first place.

Discovering Prayer Needs

First, you must know what to pray for. The very first step is, of course, to repent of any known sin you or someone else participated in—in your home or on your land. Beyond that, there are two ways of figuring out what needs prayer: (1) spiritual discernment and (2) research. We already discussed spiritual discernment. Remember the little boy, Joey, who was tormented by dreams of child abuse? There are many instances when you will not know the history of a place and must rely on the Lord to show you how to pray. One important question to ask while praying is, What is the fruit of the problem? In Joey's case, his dreams of child abuse were a major clue. The fruit was connected to the root. Allow the Lord to fill in the blanks.

The other way of knowing what needs prayer is to be familiar, to the extent possible, with the history of the home or property. Go as far back as you can through research. Who originally owned the land? Was it part of a broken treaty with Native Americans? Who has owned it since, and what is their reputation? Has any illegal activity ever been recorded there? A trip to your local library and talking to a few neighbors often reveal some very pertinent information. Remember, it does not matter if you own a home or if you rent an apartment. If you have a legal right to inhabit a place, then you have the spiritual authority to pray cleansing over that place.

Praying over Land

When you get an idea about any sin that may have given the enemy a foothold in your home, the first step is to pray a prayer of repentance, like Joan did for Joey's situation. Even though you may not have been the one who committed the sin, you can go to God on behalf of whoever committed the sin and ask Him to forgive that sin and apply the blood of Jesus to the land. This is called identificational repentance.

Doing this does not mean that people who actually commit sin will not have to answer to God for their actions. They will. What identificational repentance does, however, is bring the blood of Jesus into the situation in order to cut off the sin's ongoing effects. It shuts the door to demonic occupancy in that place. Any demonic force that has been there because of a particular sin issue can, at that point, be commanded to leave in Jesus' name. They must do so because their legal right (which was linked with unremitted sin) has been removed. We can then pray and invite the Holy Spirit into the land and dedicate it for God's use. By doing these things, we actually have the power to bring cleansing to land that has been defiled and to protect our homes from spiritual darkness.

We can pray and invite the Holy Spirit into the land and dedicate it for God's use.

Sometimes it is good to *stake your land.* In other words, go to the boundaries of your land, take Communion and declare to the powers and principalities that you are now in authority over that land. Many people write on stakes Scripture verses that are very dear to their hearts and actually drive the stakes into the corner intersection points of their land. Therefore, the Word of God forms the boundary of that land. You then have the legal right and authority to declare the manifold wisdom of God to any evil force that crosses those boundaries.

Returning to the Land

The actual land can grieve once a sin is committed upon the ground. Because of this, once we are filled with the Spirit of God, He may require us to return and stand upon the place where the defilement occurred. One of the hardest things I had to do was to return to a place in Galveston, Texas, where my family fell apart. The wound and trauma in that particular place was linked deeply to the emotions of my soul. The only way my emotions could be cleansed was for me to go back and stand on the place where the trauma actually occurred. The first time I attempted to do this, I was overwhelmed with sickness. Many of our infirmities are linked with trauma.

My mother, my sister and I had gone down to visit my dad, who was working and overseeing a project offshore in the Gulf of Mexico. While we were there, a terrible situation occurred that became violent. This was one of the defining times of my life. The domestic violence situation was so intense that I wondered if we would escape alive. We were staying in a hotel room when this occurred. Years later the Lord made me revisit the hotel room in order to break the defilement of the situation. I was spiritually mature enough the second time I attempted to do this.

I stood there with my wife and thanked God for our wonderful relationship in the actual hotel room where the horrible situation had occurred 25 years earlier. I then asked forgiveness for my bloodline, which had produced such a horrid atmosphere in that hotel room. I asked forgiveness for the blood that was shed there. I asked the Lord to heal the trauma in my heart and emotions, as well as the land I was standing on. I asked the Lord to disconnect the spirit of infirmity that was linked to the trauma of that situation. As a result, God was faithful to cleanse the land and produce a new level of healing in my life.

Staying in Hotel Rooms

An interesting side note to the discussion of defiled land is hotel rooms. A great deal of immorality and who knows what else takes place in hotels—many times in the very rooms in which we stay and on the beds in which we sleep. Many good Christians have been inadvertently exposed to pornography through the television or through magazines left by others. Such things can hook otherwise innocent people into a lasting sin problem. How can we protect ourselves from a cheap shot by the enemy when we're on the road?

When we rent a room for a period of time, we have legal spiritual authority over the atmosphere while we are there. *A simple prayer can expel the demons and keep them from attacking us.* A simple prayer can expel the demons and keep them from attacking us while we occupy that room. Whenever you enter a hotel room, stop and pray, asking God to forgive any sins of abuse, idolatry, bloodshed, immorality, covenant breaking, occult activity or whatever else may be impressing you at the time. Then pray a prayer binding any forces linked with those sins from operating while you are there.

Also pay special attention to the artwork and pictures. If anything looks strange, unnatural or demonic, pray cleansing from evil spirits, and pray that any curses attached to those objects would be broken. Taking the time to pray this way can make a tremendous difference in your trip!

Walking the Land

The Lord told Joshua: "Every place that the sole of your foot will tread upon I have given you" (Joshua 1:3). From the soles of our feet, we emit life or death, very much like our tongues. If the glory of God permeates through our bodies, then wherever we walk experiences that glory and light. Light dispels darkness. Therefore, if we are filled with light, then wherever we walk darkness has to flee. When trauma has occurred on a piece of property or land and we are walking on that land, we bring change. Either we will discern where the trauma is and ask God how to bring healing, or else we will have authority to heal the land. The earth and the fullness thereof is the Lord's.

We are representatives in causing the earth to reflect the fullness of God's plan:

> Then the LORD will be zealous for His land, and pity His people. The LORD will answer and say to His people, "Behold, I will send you grain and new wine and oil, and you will be satisfied by them; I will no longer make you a reproach among the nations." Fear not, O land; be glad and rejoice, for the LORD has done marvelous things! Do not be afraid, you beasts of the field; for the open pastures are springing up, and the tree bears its fruit; the fig tree and the vine yield their strength.
>
> Joel 2:18–19, 21–22

This is such an incredible promise! It is given in the midst of a call to repentance. Once there has been defilement, if we change our minds and operate in the opposite spirit upon the land that was defiled, we will see the land become fruitful.

Your land can rejoice!

Overthrowing Generational Curses

With the day's business behind me, I decided to take a walk and explore New Orleans. As I ventured out of my hotel, I took in the sights of a place where the excitement never seemed to end. Crowds of visitors, tourists and locals lined both sides of Bourbon Street as they streamed in and out of shops, bars, restaurants and establishments that offered live sex shows. Small groups gathered around jazz bands, many dancing to the music. I heard an occasional roar of laughter, along with an argument in what sounded like French.

As I walked along taking in all of the activity, I found myself stopping in front of one particular shop. In the window was a beautiful ceramic cat with riveting blue eyes. The noise of the street seemed to fade as my concentration turned to the cat. I seemed drawn to it. I decided to take a closer look. The shop was filled with oddities, many of which were used in voodoo rituals. I thought little of it as I picked up the ceramic cat and gave it a closer inspection. Even though it was quite expensive, I had to have it. This beautiful cat would look great by the fireplace.

Generational Influences

In chapter 4, I tell the rest of the story of this ceramic cat. One day the Lord revealed to me that witchcraft was linked to the cat. After all, it was purchased in a shop with voodoo items. I should have known better, but at the time I was ignorant of the principles outlined in this book. Even so, many Christians would have shied away from the shop based on the weird feel of the place alone. I did not. In fact, I felt drawn to the shop. Why? Because of generational influences in my bloodline.

Occult practices were not unusual in previous generations of my family. I had seen occult power at work. I remember one instance in particular when my grandfather and I were working and we encountered a wasps' nest in the middle of a doorway we were trying to get through. He looked at his palm, spoke something to it and held it up, resulting in every one of the wasps dropping dead right before our eyes. He had used occult power to kill the wasps!

How is it that the actions of my grandfather and others in my ancestry had anything to do with my entering a questionable shop years later? Because I had inherited a weakness toward sins of occult and witchcraft that had been passed down through my family's bloodline. That weakness, known as iniquity, was operating in my life when I visited New Orleans and bought the cat. How can this be? Exodus 20:5 offers the answer: "For I, the Lord your God, am a jealous God, visiting the iniquity of the fathers upon the children to the third and fourth generations." Sin not only affects the land (see chapter 5), but it also affects bloodlines for generations.

In *The Voice of God*, Cindy Jacobs helps us understand sin and iniquity as it relates to the generations:

> The Bible speaks of them as two different things. Sin is basically the cause, and iniquity includes the effect. Generational iniquity works like this: A parent can commit a sin such as occultic involvement or sexual sin and that produces a curse. The curse then causes a generational iniquity or weakness to pass down in the family line.
>
> Here is an example that might clarify this process. A pregnant woman is X-rayed and the unborn child becomes deformed by the X ray. The unborn child didn't order the X ray and is entirely a victim but, nonetheless, is affected by the X ray. Sin, like the X ray, damages the generations. This is an awesome thought and should put the fear of the Lord in us before we enter into sin.[1]

Iniquitous Patterns

Have you ever noticed how, for example, alcoholism, divorce, laziness or greed tends to run in families? These aren't just learned behaviors. They are manifestations of iniquity that have been passed down in the generations—in other words, iniquitous patterns. Of course, there are isolated instances of sin that seem to have nothing to do with previous generations. In that case, a new iniquitous pattern may be beginning in a family if that sin is not made right before God. If you start looking around you with this in mind, you may be surprised at how many iniquitous patterns of sin you can find in family lines.[2]

Familial Spirits

Through the sin and iniquitous pattern, a familial spirit controls a certain person in a family. Sin is an opening for demonic forces to work in subsequent generations of a family through the iniquity produced. They know the family weaknesses and, therefore, entice, tempt or lure family members with that weakness into the same or related sin. Spirits that are assigned to a family are called familial spirits. Some have been in families for generations on end.[3]

Generational Curses

"Curse" is defined as the cause of evil, misfortune or trouble.[4] John Eckhardt of Crusaders Ministries defines it this way:

> A curse is God's recompense in the life of a person and his or her descendants as a result of iniquity. The curse causes sorrow of heart and gives demonic spirits legal entry into a family whereby they can carry out and perpetuate their wicked devices.[5]

Eckhardt goes on to quote Derek Prince's seven common indications of a curse: chronic financial problems, chronic sickness and disease, female problems (I would add barrenness, whether brought on by the husband or the wife), prone to have accidents, marital problems, premature death and mental illness. Eckhardt adds mistreatment and abuse by others, and wandering or vagabond tendencies to the list.[6]

Sin is an opening for demonic forces to work in subsequent generations.

Such curses are produced because of the law of reaping and sowing. When a particular sin takes hold in the generations, a family curse is part of the effects of that sin.[7]

Generational Sin and Iniquity Susceptibility

There are certain things we can see in our family history that can help us identify what problems may be affecting us today. In *The Voice of God*, Cindy Jacobs identifies four things that make us particularly susceptible to generational sin and iniquity:

363

1. **Occultic Involvement and Witchcraft.** Anything that draws its power from a source other than God is demonic in nature and can produce problems in the generations.

2. **Secret Societies.** This category includes Freemasonry, Eastern Star and the Shriners. Members are often required to take oaths that actually curse themselves and their families.[8] If you or an ancestor has been involved in Freemasonry, see appendix A of this book.

3. **Robbing and Defrauding God.** If you withhold your tithe (10 percent) from God, the Bible says that you are actually robbing Him and that a curse can come into your household as a result (see Malachi 3:8–9). This curse often manifests itself as financial trouble, including poverty, and can be passed from generation to generation.

4. **Bondages.** Bondages are often passed down through family lines. Dean Sherman defines "bondages" this way: "If we continue in a habit of sin, we can develop a bondage. Bondage means that there is a supernatural element to our problem. The enemy now has a grip on a function of our personality."[9]

The Problem of Objects

What do these generational influences have to do with protecting your home from spiritual darkness? As we discussed in chapter 3, objects that you own can often represent demonic strongholds in your life. They also can represent iniquitous patterns or generational curses, and they may be the hiding place for familial spirits. That was the case with my ceramic cat. It represented a weakness in my family of being drawn to things linked with the occult (as we explained in chapter 3, ceramic cats in general are not linked with demonic forces, but this particular one was). Ask the Lord to begin to show you what generational iniquities run in your family and what objects you own that might be linked with those iniquities.

The Problem of Heirlooms

Does everything passed down to you from a grandparent have to go? Of course not! The issue is determining what items are linked with iniquitous patterns, generational curses or ungodliness and then removing those objects from your home. It may be helpful to review the list of suspect objects in chapter 3.

Getting rid of something you have purchased is one thing, but destroying something that has been passed on to you may be another matter. Many people are often unwilling to give up something that may have belonged to an ancestor, either out of a sense of sentimentality or family pride, or a need to honor the ancestor, which is especially prevalent in Asian cultures that believe in spiritism.

Spiritism is communicating with demonic forces that are linked with the dead. Spiritualism is the belief that the dead survive as spirits and can communicate with the living. Many people hold on to an object because they feel it links them with someone who has died. In that case, the object has become more than a memento of a loved one. It has become a means of keeping spiritual contact with the dead person. In reality, the heirloom is not maintaining a link to their dead loved one but rather to a familial spirit who enjoys access to their homes through deception.

What dark forces are we allowing into our homes by owning certain heirlooms?

We must ask ourselves what dark forces we may be allowing into our homes by owning certain heirlooms. Do those objects honor God? Do they keep us in bondage to a generational curse or a familial spirit? Can we reach the destiny God has for us

Protecting Your Home from Spiritual Darkness

while continuing to allow openings to the demonic in our own homes? What effect do those objects have on our children? Do we have a greater responsibility to honor past generations or to mold new ones? Some things may be difficult to let go of, but we must honestly measure what we own against these kinds of questions, not only in our own minds, but also prayerfully before God.

If you remain unconvinced or have further questions about the cause and effect of generational sin and iniquity, you may want to read our book *Possessing Your Inheritance* (Regal Books, 1999), which offers an in-depth treatment of the subject.

A Locket with Hair

Our family has a friend named Penny Jackson, who lives in Houston. She had decided to come up for a weekend visit. Knowing that our church has a deliverance ministry, she had chosen to use this time to also pursue and review any spiritual issues in her life that could hinder her future. Here is Penny's testimony of her deliverance:

> Recently before I was planning to go in for a ministry time in Denton, I was filling out the questionnaire that asked about family ties, past dabbling in the occult, and so on. As I filled out the questionnaire, the Lord strongly quickened to me a piece of jewelry that my father had gotten for me years ago—in fact, 30 or more years ago. My father knew I loved antique jewelry and had given me an opal ring from an antique shop in downtown Dallas. Probably a man's pinky ring, it had a beautiful opal in the middle surrounded by black enamel. On the inside of the ring was inscribed March 25. I had felt prompted to get rid of this ring after hearing a specific teaching concerning objects. (I can't even remember now what the teaching was.)

The other piece of jewelry he gave me was a locket from that same shop. This gold locket was engraved with flowery designs and birds on the front as well as some initials. What stood out to me, though, was that this locket had "A birthday present, March 25/60" engraved in it as well as a lock of hair preserved under a piece of heavy glass. Because this store dealt with antiques from England in the 1800s, the consensus was that the "/60" was 1860.

Not knowing then what I do now about spiritual things, I thought that March 25 must surely be a special date to me. The fact that I caught a bridal bouquet soon after that at a March 25 wedding did nothing to change my opinion. Fortunately as years passed, I learned more about the things of the Spirit and realized that "lucky days" didn't have a place where the Lord was concerned. I repented for that mindset.

I really haven't worn the locket much or even given it much thought until this night recently when it was so clearly brought to my attention by the Lord. When I located the locket and picked it up, a strange feeling came all over me. I felt the Lord was clearly leading me to deal with this object. So I packed it up to come to the ministry appointment. When I showed it to Chuck, he immediately felt what I had felt when I picked it up. It was just creepy. I don't know how else to say it.

When I went to the ministry time, I brought the locket. We placed it on the table but didn't do anything with it right away. The two women ministering to me felt something strange about it also. I had felt the night before that I wanted to break it open and see if there was anything behind the fabric the lock of hair lay on. When we finally got it open and I took the hair out with tweezers, there was just the most powerful presence that invaded the room. There was nothing behind the lock of hair, but the hair itself brought a strong supernatural feeling—so bad, in fact, that we had to take it totally out of the church building.

Chuck reminded me of the significance of hair. Hair contains the DNA of an individual. Many times in witchcraft or magic rituals, people place a curse upon hair and then plant that hair on the person of the individual being cursed. One of the women felt that there was a curse linked with an inordinate affection that had been placed upon the locket. Regardless of what all it meant, we knew that the hair certainly was not of God.

There is some reason why my father was drawn to those two pieces of jewelry. He didn't even know, if memory serves, that the two had the same dates on them. Those in the deliverance session discussed how this type of knowledge about an object could cause a certain course of action to be set in the spiritual realm. Chuck suggested that I hang on to the locket until I had heard everything the Lord had to say about it. The locket definitely felt better since the hair was gone—not great, but better. When I returned to Houston, I began to do research on the date March 25. I checked family records and could find no instances of March 25. I then went to the Internet, where I found that March 25 is a day called Lady Day that used to be when Christmas was celebrated until it was moved to December. However, March 25 remained a day that some goddess worshipers celebrated because it was nine months before the birth of Christ and, therefore, conception day. And it was a time of spring when pagan cultures worshiped because of the return of spring, also goddess-related, I believe. So this was a date and time period that had spiritual significance. There was also a pagan rite, which occurred in March in which a representative couple had sexual intercourse while others looked on and celebrated to represent the sacred union between the male and female and their equal importance in religion.

I am still asking God about this piece of jewelry. I feel at the right time when a full revelation comes to me, I will then remove this from being a part of my life. And the cycle of whatever this ring represents will be broken and a new dimension of destiny will be released for me.[10]

After you read this chapter, the Lord may open your eyes to many objects that need to be dealt with in your home. Just as

Penny took her time with this one object, take your time. Let God reveal to you the real issue behind the object He has put His finger on. Only deal with what God is dealing with in your life and home. The Lord Jesus Christ has already paid the price for your total freedom. Take your time and allow the redemptive plan He has for you to fully mature.

Protecting Our Children from Spiritual Darkness

> He who fears the LORD has a secure fortress, and for his children it will be a refuge.
>
> Proverbs 14:26 NIV

We have looked at many issues that allow spiritual darkness into a home. The goal of this chapter is to help parents understand some issues that are specific to their children. Securing your children's spiritual freedom is an important step to protecting your home from spiritual darkness.

The Importance of Order

Now that we have briefly discussed generational sin, let's look at God's order in the family, primarily focusing on children.

In *The Christian Family*, Larry Christenson writes:

The secret of good family life is disarmingly simple: *cultivate the family's relationship with Jesus Christ*. There is no phase of family life left outside this relationship. There is no problem a family might face which does not find its solution within the scope of this objective.[1]

The most important way to cultivate your family's relationship with the Lord is to establish God's divine order in your home. God's divine order has to do with relationship and authority.

In both the Old Testament and New Testament, we find one key statement for children's relationships, which is to obey their parents, for this is pleasing to the Lord and will create long life for them (see Exodus 20:12; Colossians 3:20). A child's relationship to the Father, Jesus and the Holy Spirit usually thrives and prospers in direct proportion to his or her obedience in the home and to his or her parents. If you can teach your children obedience as prescribed in Hebrews 12, they will not only become children filled with joy and freedom, but they also will mature into adults filled with faith.

The word *order* means "to command or give orders in sequence to produce a specific result." *Order* also means "the arrangement of position and rank, resulting in the ultimate accomplishment so that peace occurs in one's person or environment."[2] The word, therefore, includes both relationship and authority—the very things we need to cultivate the family's relationship to Jesus Christ. Order also brings boundaries. I believe the real key for children's lives is to show them the boundaries that have been established for their prosperity. These boundaries include being aware that owning certain things could give place to the enemy, who longs to steal their peace and prosperity from an early age. Therefore, it is very important that we teach children to remove anything that enters their boundaries that would cause their peace to be lost or their prosperity to dwindle.

God's purpose is for us to be whole. The quicker we can teach this to our children, the better off they will be. First Thessalonians 5:23 reads: "Now may the God of peace Himself sanctify you completely; and may your whole spirit, soul, and body be preserved blameless at the coming of our Lord Jesus Christ." I believe this should be every parent's goal for his or her child.

Generational Issues in a Child's Life

With the basis we established for generational issues in chapter 6, let's take another look at those issues in relationship to the order of a child's life. Because a generational iniquity can be passed from generation to generation to generation (see Exodus 20:5), I believe it is important to look for the patterns of generational iniquity in a child's life.

We can do this by observing a child's outward actions and by watching what kinds of items draw the child's attention. One key symptom is if a child forms an addiction at an early age. Sometimes children's appetites are totally out of control. Sometimes they show signs of behavioral extremes and compulsive patterns. Often parents have been delivered totally of generational curses after a similar pattern began appearing in their children. For instance, a parent might be a deceitful person, but through the blood of Jesus and spiritual discipline, the parent overcomes the problem in his or her own life only to find that his or her child still becomes deceitful. Any time we overcome a generational iniquity, it weakens that iniquitous pattern in the bloodline. I believe sometimes we can do away with it, but sometimes it appears in a weakened form.

Often parents have been delivered of generational curses after a similar pattern began appearing in their children.

My wife, Pam, and I have five children. Pam and I had difficult childhoods that were mixed with both good and evil inheritances from the generations. Even though we have broken many generational iniquities and curses in our own lives, I do not assume the patterns have been annihilated completely. We always watch our children for signs of recurring patterns of what we know existed in the generations before us.

This principle appears throughout the Word of God. When Joshua, for instance, entered into the Promised Land, he defeated many but not all of the enemies. Some still remained in the land. Then we see David, four generations later, ridding the land of the Jebusites. We need to be aware of this principle in light of our children.

Sharing Experiences from the Children's Home

In the early 1980s, Pam and I had the privilege of becoming the administrators of one of the largest children's homes in Texas. This home was for children from broken families. Many of the kids were on the verge of becoming juvenile delinquents because the order of their lives had become so disrupted through a dysfunctional family unit. We learned many valuable lessons concerning the restoration of a child's innocence, resulting in a reestablishment of his or her future. I believe that sharing some of these experiences will help you better detect demonic behavior in children.

One thirteen-year-old boy whom we loved dearly and were responsible for had real problems with pornography and sexual addiction. His problem went far beyond any normal sexual curiosity. We had authority over the cottage he lived in, as well as when he came into our personal home. Therefore, we knew that God had given us authority and influence to restore the godly order of his life.

We set boundaries over this child. We explained the evils of pornography to him. Whenever he stayed within those boundaries, he was fine. However, every time he got out from under our authority, he fell into the same patterns of sin—gaining access to pornographic materials. Pam and I began to cry out to God for his deliverance. We needed to find the entry point in his life that gave this demonic force the right to influence him and keep him bound with pornographic materials.

Sometimes we need to see how the objects to which our children are drawn are linked with iniquitous patterns in their bloodline.

We eventually learned that he was conceived out of wedlock and was born into a perverted situation. The environment he lived in was fatherless, and the male figures who came into his life had only presented a perverse example of masculinity. These facts helped us pray for his deliverance with great success. He is now a young man with a family who remains delivered to this day. The point is that sometimes we need to see how the objects to which our children are drawn are linked with iniquitous patterns in their bloodline.

Infiltrating Boundaries

As was the case with this boy, it is important that we know how demons enter so that we can gain authority over their eviction. Consider, for example, the story about the woman with the spirit of infirmity that caused her back to be bent over (see Luke 13:10–13). The Bible says she had been bound for eighteen years, which means prior to that she had been free and at some point Satan afflicted her. You can always look back to the time when there was freedom to see where the enemy gained access. If there never has been freedom, we have authority through Jesus to establish it now.

I believe that every generation should excel beyond the one before. I want my children to establish a greater glory within their boundaries than I have. However, I also know that the enemy wants to infiltrate their boundaries and not only bring them into captivity but also cause the ground we have gained to be lost. Because this is the case, I always want to be protective of the order in my children's lives until they have fully established God's authority for themselves. I always review my children's boundaries and the order of their lives by the following:

1. **The Generational Bloodline.**

2. **Their Own Personal Sin.** Remember, kids are kids—they are born degenerate and with free will. I, of course, try to steer them away from sinning. Yet whenever I see my children choosing to sin, I look for the consequences of that sin in their lives. Then I explain why they are suffering those consequences so that they can develop within them a hatred of that sin.

3. **Occultic Activity.** I look for any power of the occult that has an influence in my children's lives. The word *occult* simply means "hidden."[3] I find that Satan tries to create deception and hide the truth of sin to a child. My job is to expose sin for what it is.

4. **Roots of Bitterness and Unforgiveness.** One of the children for whom Pam and I were responsible in the children's home had tremendous potential. I believe every child has potential, but this child was unique. However, he had been flunking out of school and had been truant for two months. He had big problems. The Lord often revealed to me what this boy had in his possession. Sometimes it was drugs; other times it was weapons. He was eventually caught at school with drugs, and when I told him of the punishment the authorities at school had set for him, he rebelled violently.

The Lord showed me a root of hatred and murder within him. He had been a part of a very good family that had fallen apart because of his dad's infidelity. The bitterness from the loss was very deeply rooted. I remember the night that the root of bitterness was finally dealt with. When that occurred, he immediately accepted the Lord as his Savior and his life and countenance changed suddenly and dramatically. He brought many, many things to me that represented his past nature and the bitterness that had been in him.

Dealing with a Younger Child

When dealing with younger children, demonic forces often torment them through fear. In their excellent book *A Manual for Children's Deliverance*, Frank and Ida Mae Hammond say, "Night troublers are common: fear of the dark, fear of being left alone, or fear 'something is going to get you.' We have found such fears rooted in television programs, terrifying experiences, abusive treatment, and in toys and objects in the child's bedroom."[4]

When a child exhibits fear of something in his or her room, trace the fear to the source. It may be as simple as a shadow cast by a stuffed animal. In this case, eliminate the shadow by moving the toy. At other times, the fear may be there as a result of some hidden item that needs to be uncovered. Enlist the child's assistance. Spend time "talking out" his or her fears. Because a child is more aware of what bothers him or her than we are, the child can often pinpoint the item. Allow the child to sift through his or her toys, games, music, pictures and books to show you what is bothersome.

However, children cannot always determine the source of their problems, and that's where they need your help. Here is a list of some items to watch for:

1. Video games with occult or martial arts themes
2. Posters or pictures with occult or frightening images
3. Books with scary pictures inside or on the cover
4. Books of an occult or questionable origin
5. Toys or other items of a frightening or occult nature[5]

Caution: Many parents worry about their children's imaginations. There is a difference between creative, God-given imagination and occult fantasies. I have seen many parents harm the development of their children's godly imaginations and creativity by "throwing out the baby with the bathwater." Do not become legalistic with your child. This only causes the creativity of God not to manifest in the child. Many times this also results in a poverty mentality.

You can learn the difference by seeing how your child's imagination is affecting his or her behavior. Is your child obsessed by his or her fantasies? Are the fantasies rooted in violence or anger? Here is where we can all use some parental common sense. As you deal with your child, remember that the forming of a child's conscience is important. You want to instill moral character, but not religious legalism. I have found it best to present my children with the right choice, instead of forcing a choice upon them.

As for teaching a child about spiritual discernment, here is some good advice from Graham and Shirley Powell:

Children can easily grasp the realities of spiritual conflict, and should be taught how they can do their part to keep themselves walking closely with Jesus. But it is imperative that these truths be shared in wisdom so that there is no ground given for fear of the enemy. The reality of Jesus being Lord and Satan being defeated must be imparted. Continually center their attention on the love, power, and glory of the Lord Jesus Christ. Let them grow up Christ-conscious.[6]

Extending Boundaries

As children become older and more mature, parents have to extend boundaries. Every time you extend boundaries, you have to allow the child to establish new authority and responsibility within his or her new boundaries. You, therefore, have to watch for what new influences come into the child's life. This can be very difficult for parents who would like their children to remain innocent and do not train them to discern the evils they will encounter.

Music is a great example. One of our sons went to the movie *Godzilla* and used his own money to buy the soundtrack. About a week later, I just happened to be talking to him about the movie (which I would not have gone to see to start with) as he was playing the soundtrack. I heard a song that I thought was terrible, so I tried to approach him to discuss the song and look at the words together. He resisted, so I asked the Lord to show him. A few nights later, he was visited by an evil, tangible presence. The force was the same color as that on the soundtrack. Because of the color, he knew that the evil presence was linked with the soundtrack he had bought. He immediately confessed the sin to his mother and me and destroyed the CD. With that act of obedience, the evil presence left. Even though he still experiments with some music, he now understands that evil power can reside in it and exercises a level of discernment he did not previously exhibit.

The Magic 8 Ball

My son Isaac once took his allowance and bought what is known as the Magic 8 Ball. This is an object that you ask a question to, shake it and then an answer pops up in the eye of the ball. It is just another form of the evil eye that seduces children.

I went into his room and began telling him that he had purchased an occult object. Of course, he retorted, "Dad, you think everything is evil!" I asked the Lord how to handle the situation. I left the room and prayed that Isaac would see the demonic force behind this object. Within a couple of days, an unknown fear began to grab hold of him. With our older children, he had watched part of a movie that had really affected him. However, the fear he was experiencing was beyond anything that was natural. His sister asked forgiveness for allowing him to watch part of the movie. He asked forgiveness for watching it.

Yet his fear continued. He told me that he felt like something was watching him in the middle of the night. I knew it was that eight ball. However, I was waiting for God to deal with him over this issue. Three days later, he came to me with a totally different attitude. He asked me to destroy the eight ball with him, which I did. He slept fine that night.

Hidden Things Revealed

As children grow older, they may become involved in activities that they choose to hide from their parents. The Holy Spirit, however, has the power to reveal hidden things to parents. This was another lesson I learned while working at the children's home. There was one particular boy who reminded me of Eddie Haskell on *Leave It to Beaver*. He could be real sweet, but he had a side we needed to watch out for.

The Holy Spirit can reveal hidden things that may cause danger for your children.

Once a month, the kids had the choice to go back and visit whatever home life they came from. These visits often caused a lot of problems, because the children got away from the influence of a godly environment and were immersed in situations that had caused their troubles in the first place. One weekend, our "Eddie Haskell" decided to go home. Pam and I went to church that Sunday as usual. During the service, there was an altar call. When I went up to the altar, the Lord revealed to me that our Eddie was coming back with a duffel bag. The Lord also showed me everything inside this bag.

When the boy returned that afternoon, I explained to him what the Lord had showed me at the altar. I then listed everything inside his duffel bag, including rock music, snuff and marijuana. Our Eddie turned white as a sheet. I was right on every count. He quickly repented. But more important, he saw the power of God to reveal the unknown.

The Holy Spirit can reveal hidden things that may cause danger for your children. This is sometimes necessary when raising children. Therefore, listen and respond to the Holy Spirit.

In Closing

Raising kids is one of the more difficult assignments in a world today filled with enticing, seducing forces. I wish we had more insight and a 1-2-3 method to help you. However, one thing we have learned with our children is not to major on minors. Many times we can get so caught up in wanting everything to be perfect that we miss the overall issue of what God is trying to do in a child. Children must be molded. They also must experiment. Therefore, in the midst of their maturing and experimenting, we must find creative ways to discipline and mold them.

It is important that we as parents have a heart to see our children's wholeness. We must help them understand the order that God has established for their lives. We must make them aware that God wants them to prosper within the boundaries He has established for them. We must show them how to detect for themselves when anything detrimental enters or disrupts God's order in their lives. We must trust God daily to rid our children's lives of spiritual darkness.

Let me caution you not to provoke your children. Talk to them. Let them help set boundaries. Let them explain to you why they are doing certain things. In the same way, express your heart and conscience to them, and let them know that you have set certain limitations on their freedom as long as they live within your home. Never let the devil create a situation that cuts off your communication. Find creative ways to communicate with your children and include them in decisions that affect them personally, as well as the whole family.

Let me end with this simple story. When Rebekah, our only daughter, was a child, she came to me and asked me to watch a movie with her. I resisted and protested at first. The movie was Disney's *The Little Mermaid*. I knew about the story and really saw all sorts of issues, because there was a witch in the movie and so on and so on. However, I felt the Holy Spirit check me. When we sat down and together watched the movie about this rebellious mermaid who went against everything her father said, something very interesting happened. My daughter began to weep and say, "Dad, I never want to be like that toward you." The Lord used this movie greatly in our lives.

The real issue in God's heart is that fathers' hearts turn toward their children, and children's hearts turn toward their fathers, so that no curse can come in and wreak havoc against God's destined plan in our generations.

Ten Steps
to Protecting Your Home
from Spiritual Darkness

Now that we have discussed a number of principles you need to know in order to do spiritual housecleaning, let's look at the whole process step-by-step. As you read through this chapter, please remember that this might take some time. Do not try to rush the process along. For instance, you may find that you need more time to do personal repentance than you thought or to look through your house for objects that need to go. Allow the Holy Spirit to set the pace for you.

Also remember that you do not have to own a home or property to follow this list. If you rent a house or apartment, you have the spiritual legal right to evict Satan's cohorts.

Step 1: Accept Jesus as Your Lord and Savior

Most of you probably have already taken this step, but for those of you who have not, the very first step to protecting your home from spiritual darkness is to secure your relationship to God by accepting Jesus as your Lord and Savior. It is through Jesus' name that we have the authority to expel demonic forces, and we cannot avail ourselves of using His name unless we have relationship with Him.

There is something much more important at stake—your eternal home. Living with spiritual darkness on earth is one thing, but living in utter and complete darkness with no hope of life for all eternity is another. Only the blood of Jesus can save you from such an awful fate. If you have not already secured your salvation, you must turn away from sin, believe in the death and resurrection of Jesus and receive Him as Lord and Savior of your life. To do this you must do the following:

1. Consider your life and then turn away from everything that is contrary to what God wants (see Matthew 3:7–10; Acts 3:19).

2. Acknowledge that Jesus Christ died on the cross to forgive you of sin and that you take Him as your Savior to cleanse you from sin. Jesus paid the price due for your sin (see Romans 5:9–10; Titus 2:14).

3. Ask Him to be the Lord of your life, acknowledging openly and verbally that Jesus is not only your Savior but also your Lord (see 1 John 2:23).[1]

Step 2: Take a Spiritual Inventory of Your Life

In order to remove demonic forces from our homes and keep them out, we must be willing to deal with sin issues in our lives. As Charles Kraft, professor at Fuller Theological Seminary, would describe it, demons are like rats and sin is like garbage. "If we get rid of the rats and keep the garbage, the person is in great danger still. But if we get rid of the garbage, what we have done automatically affects the rats."[2] In other words, you must get rid of the garbage in order to get rid of the rats.

When we rid our lives of sin, demonic forces do not have the legal right they once had to occupy our lives and our homes. However, if we go through these steps to protect our homes from demonic forces without making our lives right before God, we may actually make our situation worse!

Jesus taught that if we cast out a demon and it does not find rest elsewhere, the demon comes back to check out the situation. If the demon finds the house is still suitable for occupation, then it goes and finds seven other demons—even more wicked than itself—and they all set up shop right back where they started. If we expel one demon but do not remove its legal right, we get eight in return. And our final condition is worse than the first (see Matthew 12:43–45).

Ask the Lord to reveal any sin issues in your life that must be dealt with before continuing in this process. Because unforgiveness is a big bag of garbage on which demons love to feed, ask God to show you any places of unforgiveness toward others that you need to correct.

Step 3: Dedicate Your Home to the Lord

The next step in protecting your home from spiritual darkness is to dedicate it to the Lord. Simply pray and invite the presence of the Lord into your home. Ask the Lord to use your home for His purposes. Declare that as for you and your house, you will serve the Lord (see Joshua 24:15). Declare that your home will not be a haven for dark forces; rather, it will be a beacon of light for your family and to the world. It is best to pray these things in an audible voice, which affirms your intentions not only to God and to yourself but also to any forces of darkness that are about to lose their dwelling place.

Step 4: Prepare for Battle

What we are engaged in is spiritual warfare. We are warring in the heavenlies to establish our homes for the Lord and declare them off-limits to the powers of darkness. Here are the preparations we should make as we go into battle:

- Ask the Lord for the strategy of your war. He may lead you to play praise music throughout your home for a period of time, or He may lead you to read specific Scriptures in each room. Expect that He will answer your prayer and show you how to proceed.
- Plead the blood of Jesus over yourself, your family, your animals and your property.
- Pray Psalm 91 out loud.
- In Jesus' name, bind any demonic forces from manifesting in your home during this process.

Step 5: Take a Spiritual Inventory of Your Home

Ask the Lord to give you the discernment you will need as you look at what you own. Go through your home, room by room, and let the Holy Spirit show you any object that should not be in your home. Review the list of problem objects in chapter 3. Examine your heirlooms as outlined in chapter 6.

Step 6: Cleanse Your Home of Ungodly Objects

Whatever needs to go should not be considered an item for your next garage sale! Once you know something must go, be careful to destroy it. Deuteronomy 7:25 provides us an example to follow:

You shall burn the carved images of their gods with fire; you shall not covet the silver or gold that is on them, nor take it for yourselves, lest you be snared by it; for it is an abomination to the LORD your God.

Take what can be burned and burn it. If it cannot be burned, pass it through the fire (as a symbolic act of obedience) and then destroy it by whatever other means are available to you, such as smashing or even flushing. (I have known people to do this with jewelry that cannot be destroyed in other ways.)

Once you have destroyed the object, renounce any participation you or your family have had with that object (whether knowingly or unknowingly) and ask the Lord to forgive you. If the object is linked with Freemasonry, Eastern Star, Job's Daughters, Rainbow Girls or DeMolay, pray the prayer of release for Freemasons and their descendants (see appendix A).

Because the legal right for demonic forces linked with that object has been removed through these acts, you can now command any demonic forces linked with that object to leave in the name of Jesus.

Repeat these steps for every object that needs to go.

Step 7: Cleanse Each Room and Cleanse the Land

After cleansing your home of ungodly objects, the next step is to cleanse the spiritual atmosphere of each room. Demonic forces not attached to an object but in the home because of sin or trauma that occurred there need to be dealt with. Go through each room in your house and repent for any known sin that has been committed.

If someone else occupied your home before you, ask the Lord to show you what needs to be prayed for in each room. Trust the impressions you get during this process. Also, if you have noticed a major change in behavior or circumstances since moving into your home that cannot be explained any other way (e.g., fighting, financial troubles, violence, nightmares, accidents), this might serve as a clue as to what went on in your home before you moved in. Do identificational repentance in each room and over the land (see chapter 5).

Pray that the Lord would heal any trauma from the torment of demonic forces in your home. For instance, in chapter 5 we told the story of a three-year-old boy who had been plagued with nightmares of child abuse. In a case like that, you should ask the Lord to touch the boy's mind with His healing balm

> *Ask the Lord to restore to you and your family whatever blessings were stolen by the enemy through demonic forces in your home.*

so that he does not suffer lingering effects of the demonically induced nightmares.

Also, ask the Lord to restore to you and your family whatever blessings were stolen by the enemy through demonic forces in your home.

Step 8: Consecrate Your Home and Your Property

Once you have completed the first seven steps, now it is time to go through your home, room by room, and consecrate each one to the Lord. Speak specific blessings into each room. In the living room, for example, you may want to bless the time that your family spends together and ask the Lord to strengthen those relationships. In each bedroom, bless the plans and purposes that God has for each family member who occupies that room. In the bedroom of a married couple, bless the sexual relationship and the union between husband and wife. Bless the work that goes on in an office or den and declare that all work done will be done as unto the Lord. Think of why each room was designed and then bless that purpose. You can even bless the cleansing that goes on in the bathroom and ask the Lord to use it as a reminder of the cleansing He has brought in your own life!

Many people who consecrate their home room by room use oil to anoint the doors, windows and furnishings. Oil is used as a symbol of Jesus' blood—a reminder of both the cleansing and protecting power in His blood. If you feel so led, use oil. It is certainly appropriate for this type of praying.

Now take a moment to review chapter 5. Once you have completed the process outlined in that chapter, you can consecrate the land to the Lord. One way of doing this is to walk your property's perimeters and declare that the land is consecrated, or set apart, for the Lord. This physical act helps to establish spiritual perimeters.

Another popular way to consecrate land is to stake the land and raise a canopy of praise. Do this by taking wooden stakes and driving one stake in each corner of the property while praying for the Lord's blessing. Then from the center of the property, raise an imaginary canopy of praise to God by worshiping Him, singing songs and declaring Scriptures. Neither of these methods (whether used together or individually) is a magic formula, but rather a symbolic or "prophetic" act that declares to the Lord, to the powers of darkness and to yourself that this property is set apart (i.e., consecrated) for the Lord.

When I moved my family from Denton, Texas, to Colorado Springs, Colorado, we had a housewarming, consecration party in our new home. Along with about thirty friends, we took four oak stakes (about two inches thick) and with a heavy black marker wrote Scripture references on each stake, one on each side of each stake. We used Scriptures such as Psalm 91, Isaiah 54:2–3, Jeremiah 29:7, Luke 1:37 and Joshua 24:15. Teams of about four or five then went to each corner of the property, read the Scriptures listed on their stakes, prayed a prayer of blessing and consecration, and then drove their stake into the ground using a sledgehammer. We then met back in the house and began raising a canopy of praise by worshiping the Lord together.

If you choose to drive stakes into your property, ask the Lord what Scriptures you should use to consecrate the property to Him. You may come up with a whole different list than I did. You don't necessarily need to throw a party, either. Do whatever is right for you and your situation.[3]

You can be as creative as you want in finding ways to consecrate your property. I have had friends who placed Bibles in the concrete foundation of the homes they built to act as a symbol that Christ is the foundation of their lives and property.

Step 9: Fill Your Home with Glory

You are to fill your home with objects and activities that bring glory to God. Jack Hayford offers this list of six practices that promote healthy, happy, holy homes:

1. Take Communion with your family at home. Be sure to include the children.

2. Sing at home, both alone and together. Let your home be filled with the song of the Lord.

3. Pray at home. Pray as a family. Make table prayer meaningful, even though it is brief. Scheduled times of prayer are great, but so is prayer that rises naturally, and it helps the kids enter in as genuine participants instead of being forced.

4. Testify about the good things God has done for you at home. Dinnertime is a great time to talk about what Jesus did to help you today.

5. Speak the Word in your house. Besides your own devotional Bible reading, how about standing in the center of your living room periodically and reading a psalm aloud?

6. Keep your house bright. Cultivate a genuine mood of hope in your home. Refuse whatever influences (moodiness, sharp speech, unworthy music, activities or videos) that would extinguish the brightness of God's glory light in your home.[4]

Step 10: Maintain Spiritual Victory

Keep on your toes! The enemy loves to find new and creative ways of infiltrating your home with spiritual darkness. It is a good idea to go through your home periodically and check for any new objects that should not be in your home, or pray through any new sin issues that have come up. In addition, plan on consecrating the rooms of your house and walking the perimeters of your property at least once a year. You might want to pick a day (such as Good Friday) that will remind you each year that the time has come to do a spiritual checkup and to rededicate your house to the Lord.

May the Lord richly bless you as you seek to protect your home from spiritual darkness and to live the glory of His presence!

Appendix A

Delivered to Worship— Reversing the Effects of Freemasonry

As I stated earlier in this book, there are many objects linked with demonic activity. Let me just remind you that the Lord said, "Be in the world, but not of the world" (see John 17:14–16). One of these objects is the dollar bill, with the Eye of Horus embedded within its makeup. We would be foolish to burn each dollar bill we receive, but we must deal with the Evil Eye of Horus.

The Evil Eye

Satan is always watching for that opportune time to vex and blind us from seeing the best that God has for us. We are called to see, but many times we must unveil the evil eye to see clearly. The term *evil eye* is found in the Bible. The New King James Version of the Old Testament usually uses a literal translation of the Hebrew words for "evil" and "eye" ("your eye be evil," Deuteronomy 15:9; "an evil eye," Proverbs 28:22), whereas the New International Version uses a figurative translation ("ill will" and "stingy"). These Bible versions translate the New Testament Greek words in a similar manner. The New King James Version uses "is your eye evil" in Matthew 20:15 and "an evil eye" in Mark 7:22, whereas the New International Version uses "envious" and "envy" in these verses.

The Bible warns that God will judge people who have an evil eye: "Woe to those who call evil good, and good evil; who put darkness for light, and light for darkness; who put bitter for sweet, and sweet for bitter!" (Isaiah 5:20) From the Bible we also learn that our heart can be subverted by the evil eye. In Mark 7:20–23, Jesus explains, "What comes out of a man, that defiles a man. For from within, out of the heart of men, proceed evil thoughts, adulteries, fornications, murders, thefts, covetousness, wickedness, deceit, lewdness, an evil eye, blasphemy, pride, foolishness. . . . These evil things," Jesus says, "come from within and defile a man." In these verses, we see that covetousness is linked to an evil eye, as are evil thoughts.

The Evil Eye Defined

As we have seen, having an evil eye can cloud our spiritual perception and cause us to look at things from a perverse, ungodly perspective. That leads us to the definition for "*evil eye*" that I will use: "the evil eye is a perverse perspective." *Merriam-Webster's Online Dictionary* defines the "*evil eye*" as "an eye or glance held capable of inflicting harm."[1] According to the *Columbia Encyclopedia*, the evil eye is principally "a Sicilian and Mesoamerican superstition, although it is known in other cultures."[2] According to the Native American version of the term, a person who stares fixedly at a pregnant woman or a child or who is too admiring or physically affectionate with children may produce a malicious effect on their lives, whether or not by intent. In rural Sicily, any person or animal was considered vulnerable to the evil eye, and many individuals wore protective amulets or charms to nullify its effects.

Blinded by the Enemy

The word *occult* means "to conceal or cause to disappear from view—to be secret, mysterious, supernatural." The Bible explains that we can be blinded by the deceptive ways of the enemy, but God gives us access to revelation that will uncover that which has been kept secret (see 2 Corinthians 4:3–4, 6). The enemy likes to hide. He plans strategies to divert us from accomplishing God's will and entering into our heavenly Father's blessings. Many of us have a hard time *seeing* the enemy's snares, which are strategically planted along our path. Thus we *step into* his tangled web and spend much of our time struggling to free ourselves. There are several snares that the enemy lays: generational iniquity, covetousness, superstition, spiritism, magic and sorcery. Instead of being blinded by the evil eye, one must learn to BLIND the EVIL EYE!

Freemasonry

Freemasonry is the most common structure or secret society in our culture. The evil eye linked to Freemasonry is signified by the Eye of Horus. This is an ancient Egyptian symbol of protection, royal power and good health. The eye is personified in the goddess Wadjet. It is also known as "the Eye of Ra."

Horus was the ancient Egyptian sky god who was usually depicted as a falcon, most likely a lanner or peregrine falcon. His right eye was associated with the sun god, Ra. The eye symbol represents the marking around the eye of the falcon, including the "teardrop" marking sometimes found below the eye. The mirror image, or left eye, sometimes represented the moon. In one myth, when Set and Horus were fighting for the throne after Osiris's death, Set gouged out Horus's left eye. The majority of the eye was restored by either Hathor or Thoth (with the last portion possibly being supplied magically). When Horus's eye was recovered, he offered it to his father, Osiris, in hopes of restoring his life. Hence, the eye of Horus was often used to symbolize sacrifice, healing, restoration, protection and prosperity.

Freemasonry has fully admitted that the Eye of Horus is its root symbol. If you turn your American one dollar bill over to the back side, you can observe the Great Seal. The unfinished pyramid with the EYE hovers over a New World Order. This order is ready and waiting to bring change to the world ahead. This connects Freemasonry to the same goals of Nimrod, which were eventually passed on to those in charge of building the Tower of Babel.

I want to help us get disconnected from wrong worship types so that we redeem our bloodline, build His Church according to the pattern of the Lord and advance the Kingdom. This chapter will help many of you who have been defiled by its workings in your bloodline. Let me suggest how to remove these snares and unveil the evil eye in relationship to Freemasonry.

A Testimony of Freedom

Through the years, I have helped many people deal with iniquitous issues in their bloodlines. I find that those linked with the secret society of Freemasonry have been some of the most arduous. These structures keep people from worshiping the Lord freely. Linda Heidler's story is one of victory. I remember her sharing with me how the beginning of her deliverance occurred:

I attended a conference on "How to Minister Deliverance." Selwyn Stevens from Australia was ministering on Freemasonry. As he finished his session he said, "Now we're going to pray and break the power of Freemasonry from those who are here." All of a sudden I was in a panic and thought, *I've got to get out of here right now. I've got to leave this room. I cannot stay in here.* Then I thought, *Oh no, I've got it. Whatever he's about to break the power of and cast out is in me.* I stayed as he went through the steps of renunciation and the repentance and the Lord ministered powerfully to me. At that time I really didn't know the power of Freemasonry. I remembered my father mentioning Freemasonry, but I never remembered him going to a meeting. He had a Masonic ring and we had a Masonic bible, but that was really all I knew about it. I did not know that even that level of involvement in Freemasonry could affect me. I didn't know the structure of Freemasonry and how it's designed to capture people, to capture families, to capture cities, to capture nations. I did not understand that it is a structure designed to take territory.[3]

Steps to Captivity

In Freemasonry, the steps in the initiation ceremony are prophetic acts that are part of a well-designed, well-thought-out system whose purpose is to capture the soul, the spirit and the body of a person. It is also designed to gain control of their identity, their destiny and their value. It's designed to take their whole being. Each step in the initiation requires the person to relinquish part of themselves to Freemasonry.

Many of the steps in Freemasonry are the same as the steps in making a biblical covenant. This is an ungodly covenant but it works the same way as a godly covenant. There are incidents in the initiation ceremony that will affect the children and the children's children. This is an issue of a bloodline covenant.

God said that He would honor His covenant with Abraham on to Isaac, on to Jacob, and on to his sons. God said that He would honor His covenant with David so that he would always have a man on the throne. It's not hard to see how covenants travel through the bloodline.

There are several steps of preparation before the Freemasonry initiation begins. Each of these is designed to capture a portion of the initiate. The first of these steps is that the initiate takes his clothes off and is given pajamas and one slipper to wear during the initiation. Clothing is linked with your identity and represents your mantle of authority. When David and Jonathan made a covenant, they exchanged their robes, symbolizing an exchange of identities.

In this step you are stripped of your identity and a different identity, represented by pajamas, is imposed on you. Pajamas represent an identity that is very passive and confining. You would not be dressed appropriately to go out for a job interview wearing your pajamas. Pajamas convey an identity that confines your sphere; it's connected with sleep and passivity. This identity will make you feel like you are not able to present yourself well. It will make you feel dull and unable to be alert. It will make you feel that you are not qualified or equipped to go beyond certain boundaries.

Clothing is also linked with your authority. If you see someone in a policeman's uniform holding his or her hand up at an intersection, you're probably going to stop because that uniform, that clothing, represents the authority that the person has. If you see someone in pajamas holding up their hand to try to stop traffic, you will probably think they are crazy. Their clothing does not represent the authority they are trying to exercise. In giving up your own clothing and putting on pajamas, you're relinquishing your authority. The slipper is designed to make you unsure of your footing; it is deliberately called the "slipshod slipper." Like the pajamas, this is part of capturing your confidence to move forward into your destiny.

The second thing you do is to relinquish all of your valuables: money, jewelry, keys, rings and anything else that has any value. As you enter into these first two actions, you are turning over your value as a person to the structure and system of Freemasonry. You are relinquishing and abdicating your intrinsic God-given value. From that moment forward within the Masonic structure, you have to prove that you're worth something. Your performance proves your future value. How hard you work and the sacrifices you make reflect your commitment to the structure and the system. You don't have any value apart from the value you are assigned by the system.

There are three more steps that are designed to capture the soul, the mind, the will and the emotions of the initiate. In the first of these steps, a black hood is placed over the head of the initiate. It is called a "hoodwink." This hood covers the whole head so that you cannot see. The effect of the hood is to capture everything that it covers. This act signifies the capture of your mind, your eyes, your ears, your throat, your tongue and your mouth. This is actually the act that inhibits your ability in the future to perceive the Spirit of God. The act itself veils your mind and makes you resistant to the Holy Spirit as you pursue God in your life. In this action, you have submitted your thought processes, mindset and intellect to the structure of Freemasonry.

The next step in preparation for the ceremony is that a noose called a "cable tow" is placed around the neck of the initiate. Someone holding the cable tow leads him through the ceremony. This action captures the free will of the initiate. The cable tow captures your ability to freely pursue your destiny outside of the confines related to Freemasonry. You may find yourself trying to follow God and pursue His call on your life, but something always seems to hold you back. You have lost your God-given gift of free will. You have lost the ability to be led by the Spirit. You are led by the cable tow, which will choke you if you try to resist the will of the society in your life.

In the third step of capturing your soul, a dagger is placed on the left breast. Sometimes a compass point is used and blood is drawn. The dagger is placed over your heart, prophetically the seat of your emotion, redirecting your desires to the system and structure of Freemasonry. Many people influenced by Freemasonry find that their emotions are so bound that they can't rejoice when they know joy should be released. They grieve over things they should rejoice about because their emotions have been captured. They feel blocked from experiencing the love of God or the joy of the Lord.

In these steps the identity and value of the initiate have been redefined. They no longer see themselves as who God created them to be. They no longer have a sense of their intrinsic worth and value. In addition, the soul of the initiate—the intellect, emotion and will—has come under the structure and system of Freemasonry. With these things in place, the initiation ceremony is now ready to begin.

The Initiation Ceremony!

The first step in the initiation ceremony is to bring the initiate to the door of the lodge, where he knocks. Someone will say, "Who is it?" He replies, "I am a poor soul in a state of darkness seeking the light of Freemasonry." When the initiate makes this declaration, the hoodwink is pulled off with the words, "Let there be light." This step is designed to capture the spirit of the initiate. This confession submits the spirit of the initiate to the deception of Freemasonry. What he is saying is, "I will accept the light, the revelation, of Freemasonry as truth rather than the light of the Living God, rather than the revelation of the

Holy Spirit." A spirit other than the Holy Spirit is given preeminence. Discernment is compromised and the person is captured in false worship. The human mind that is designed to receive revelation from God will now receive revelation from the spirit behind Freemasonry. They are actually deceived into believing that they are worshiping the true God. Freemasonry, like most secret societies, is a worship system. What has really happened is that the initiation breaks the first of the Ten Commandments.

At this point the initiate is ready to enter the room. He is led onto a floor that is a checkerboard of black and white tiles called a "tracing board." Prophetically this means that you may step into light and it may be good, but the next step may take you into darkness. Because of the slipshod slipper, you are not sure if your feet are going to fly out from under you. You certainly don't have feet that are shod with the preparation of the Gospel. You don't have hinds' feet that are leaping on high places, and you don't have a path that's growing brighter and brighter.

While the tracing board captures your destiny, the cable tow captures your ability to pursue your destiny. You may have vision to move forward, but because of the cable tow you are not free to pursue your destiny even if you can see what it is and you want to fulfill it. You may hear many wonderful prophetic words for your life but find yourself saying, "Oh, I can't do that." Many become discouraged and condemn themselves because they cannot seem to make any progress when the real issue is that they are trying to pursue God while being held captive by Freemasonry. If the slipshod slipper does not cause you to lose your footing, the cable tow will prevent you from going the way you want to go. Your destiny has been captured.

This is very important to understand, because any organization can lead you through these steps. These same principles will be in any religious system, even a Christian religious system that's not based on relationship. For instance, in the last apostolic season everybody had to give up everything in the shepherding movement. In God's way of giving, you give out of worship to the Lord. What you give becomes part of a structure or a model that God is creating. In Freemasonry you have to let go of the identity that God has given you. You lose your identity to be inside of the structure.

The Final Step—Curses or Blessings!

The final step in the initiation is to bring the physical body into subjection to Freemasonry. Capturing the physical body is accomplished through a series of oaths, vows and curses. Oaths are repeated to pledge loyalty to Freemasonry. Vows of personal commitment are made, and curses are pronounced should the oaths or vows ever be violated.

Curses are spoken over all your internal organs, your endocrine system, your immune system, your reproductive system, your eyes, your brain, your ears, your tongue and all of your extremities. Each increasing degree of Freemasonry has additional curses with it. The first degree mainly affects the throat, tongue and respiratory system.

Higher degrees include things like having your nose cut off, eyes gouged out, hands cut off and your body cut into quarters and thrown onto a trash heap. The curse states that you could be split in two from your throat to your groin so that all of your internal organs are exposed to the sun and given to vultures for food. Curses are spoken from having your head cut off to having your feet flayed. Head to toe and everything in between has some kind of curse spoken against it. These curses are released to come on should you ever betray or leave Freemasonry.

This creates further problems for those in Freemasonry, because God has pronounced curses and diseases against those who practice idolatry or worship the gods of Egypt. What is not made evident in the initiation is that Freemasonry incorporates the worship of all gods. It is not a Christian organization, even though it tries to present itself as one.

The stated purpose written in their doctrines for this first degree initiation is to conceal "higher truths" from the initiates. Albert Pike, one of the most prolific Masonic writers in America, in his book *Morals and Dogmas*, writes, "The Blue Degrees are but the outer court or portico of the Temple. Part of the symbols are displayed there to the Initiate, but he is intentionally misled by false interpretations. It is not intended that he shall understand them; but it is intended that he shall imagine he understands them."[4]

As you ascend in the system, worship of Greek gods, Hindu gods, Norse gods and Egyptian gods is introduced. At its core, Freemasonry is a system of false worship. When the initiate commits their spirit to Freemasonry, they are basically committing themselves to this whole system of worship.

This doesn't happen just in Freemasonry, but in all sorts of religious structures. If you don't stay focused and keep the blood-bought worship of the Lamb of God who gave us freedom, then eventually you will sacrifice to other god structures, which will infiltrate your whole being. One of the ways this is happening today is through "religious tolerance." We are told that we should be tolerant of other religions. We should not say that they're false religions. There is only One Way to total redemption. That Way is by accepting the One, Jesus of Nazareth, sent by the Father to redeem mankind.

Let Us Go, That We Might Worship!

The whole issue of Israel in Egypt was worship. The plagues were designed to show the superiority of the God of Israel over the gods of Egypt. At Passover the Lord said for them to separate themselves from the gods of Egypt. The blood on the door was the sign of those who had aligned with the God of Israel. When they left Egypt, the Bible says that there was not one feeble or sick among them. When they separated themselves from the gods of Egypt, all the diseases of Egypt left them.

After they crossed the Red Sea, the Lord revealed Himself as *Jehovah Rophe*, the God who Heals. He then declared that none of the diseases of Egypt would rest on them if they did not return to worshiping the gods of Egypt. The opposite of that is also true: If they returned to worshiping the gods of Egypt, then all the diseases of Egypt would return to them. When you review the medical advancement of ancient Egypt, you find they were very sophisticated and advanced. They had to have had medical breakthroughs because they had so many sicknesses.

In Freemasonry you are involved in worshiping the gods of Egypt, so you get the diseases that go with them. In addition to all the curses that you've pronounced on yourself, you get all the judgments of God on you, as well. You become caught in sickness, infirmity and disease. Through the initiation ceremony, you are brought into a system of false worship.

A False Covenant

Freemasonry is not only a system of false worship but also a structure of covenant. Many of the steps in the initiation ceremony are the same as those in entering a covenant relationship. The exchanges of clothing and valuables as well as pledging loyalty on penalty of death are all steps in forming a covenant. In Freemasonry you pledge your identity, your value, your strength, your loyalty, your body and your life to something other than God. You become part of a structure that will define who you are and determine your destiny.

You can't honor two covenants at the same time. Freemasonry will demand that it is your highest covenant relationship. This will bring conflict into the lives of those who are Christians. The Word of God is supposed to produce life in us, but if a false covenant is already in place, then God's Word is going to be hindered in what it can do. As you received an anti-Christ mindset by being hoodwinked, then you're going to have trouble receiving the mind of Christ. Revelation from God will be hindered.

By relinquishing your free will through the cable tow, then you will have trouble submitting to the leading of the Holy Spirit. If you have participated in a system of false worship that is cursed by God with sickness and disease, then you will not be able to receive healing by the power of the Holy Spirit.

Reclaim Your Lost Ground

Up to this point, most of the ministry that we have developed concerning Freemasonry has involved repenting on behalf of those in our generational line who have participated in Freemasonry. You can repent and renounce each of those steps, but if you don't reclaim what you relinquished, then you will stay under the influence of Freemasonry. For instance, if you repent of putting on the hoodwink and renounce that action but do not reclaim the mind that God gave you and you don't command the effects of the hoodwink to leave you, then your mindset will still remain under the influence of Freemasonry.

We must reclaim what we relinquished. When we repent for and renounce all those steps, we get ourselves out of the structure of Freemasonry, but we haven't gotten the structure out of us. The influence of the initiation will continue to have influence in all the areas that were submitted. You have to reclaim what was abdicated to bring yourself back into wholeness.

The Bible Reclaimed!

Linda Heidler tells the story of her deliverance:

> In my life as I began to do this, as God began to give revelation about reclaiming all the things that had been scattered through that initiation, I found myself coming into greater freedom and confidence. As I did this, the Lord did something very interesting that was a prophetic picture of what was happening in my life. Before my mom died she decided to sell her house and to give each of the children a portion of their inheritance. She asked each of us what things we would like from her house, so I asked for the Masonic Bible that had been in our family. I felt like I was the only one in the family who would know what to do with it. My mom gave it to me, and the first thing I did when I got it home was to take a utility knife and cut out the pages that had our family tree. All the names of my relatives, my sister, my brothers, my nieces and nephews—I pulled them out of that Bible. This was a declaration that my family was not going to be in the structure of Freemasonry anymore.
>
> After that, Chuck (as the apostolic leader of my life, and dear friend that he was to Robert and me) began to direct me. From time to time he would say that we were to do something new with the Bible. The first thing he said to do was to take the dark cover off of the Bible and to declare that new revelation was coming. We ripped the cover with the Masonic symbol from the Bible and burned it. Soon after that I was reading in Ephesians and all of a sudden it was as though the words jumped off the page and became three-dimensional to me. They began to have substance and color and they were woven together. The Lord said, "I want you to see this as the new mantle that you're going to wear." It was a mantle of wisdom and love and perseverance. It was as though I could see the colors of wisdom, love and perseverance; I could feel the texture of them. It was wonderful.
>
> As we looked at the content of the Bible we found that about a third of what was in it was not the Bible; it was Masonic

teaching, Masonic doctrines, Masonic commentary, Masonic definitions, Masonic oaths—all kinds of stuff. Before you ever got to the "Bible" these things were already interpreting it for you, defining things for you and putting the Bible in a Masonic light. All of it was like a veil of Masonic interpretation. As you read that Bible, you would be reading through a Masonic filter of Masonic definitions. Time after time, we would know when the information included in the next few pages of the layers covering the Word would need to be removed and burned.[5]

Remember, I was not having Linda burn the Word of God. The Word of God was still intact. Actually, we hadn't even gotten close to the Word of God yet. There were many layers of false revelation included before we could ever get to the first words of the canonized Word of God. We carefully processed layer after layer that was covering over the revelation of the Word of God until finally we could get to "In the Beginning. . ." I fully realized that in Freemasonry, the entire false structure of revelation preempted and had become the first revelation before the Word of God could be presented for freedom and understanding.

Every time we removed a layer, we encountered warfare! Therefore, we knew that deliverance was a process that had to be strategically approached. The Spirit of God led us step by step. Faith works in time and space. We had to know the time and place to accomplish this renunciation leading to freedom. Therefore, we were actually blinding the evil eye of Horus step by step, and Linda's eyes were becoming more and more filled with the light of His Spirit.

Remove the Next Layer and Reestablish My Timing in Your Life!

One year, just before Passover the Lord said, "Remove the next layer." When we looked at these pages, they actually stated that

Masons would adhere to the Roman calendar and celebrate the Resurrection of Jesus at Easter according to the time that had been determined and decreed by Constantine. This was directly contrary to the biblical celebration of Passover, the time when God had determined each year for acknowledgment of crossing over and resurrection. We had no idea that this decree existed, but by the Spirit, we had moved in perfect timing to remove this layer of false doctrine.

As we did this, we remembered that a few years earlier we had celebrated the Resurrection at Passover rather than at Easter. We got so much criticism. Many religious leaders as well as part of the Body had expressed anger. This explained why. We had defied the Masonic root that's in the bloodline of most of the denominations of America.

One thing that we encounter many times is that people say, "I don't need deliverance from anything Masonic because there's no history of Freemasonry in my family." However, the way Freemasonry is designed, you can be under its influence without ever having been part of a Masonic lodge.

Freemasonry in Established Society

In the Western part of the United States, as new areas of the country were being settled, Masons would seek to be the first ones to move and stake claim to the land. They would build the first building. The government would operate from that building. Masons would then build the school, where most churches gathered. Masons made it one of their priorities to occupy as many pulpits as possible, so many of the pastors of a region were Masons.

The civic leaders were Masons; the bankers were Masons; the businessmen were Masons; the schoolteachers were Masons. The society reflected Masonic values. Business relationships were determined by Masonic rules. They had a secret hand-shake for doing business that would allow you to be favored in the community. If you were a Mason, you could progress and prosper more quickly than if you refused to participate. A corrupted form of Freemasonry practices are also found in Mafia activities.

The roles and identities of men and women were set by Masonic standards. There was a whole other organization for women called Eastern Star. It was supposed to show you how to be a godly woman.

Therefore, even if you had no family history in Freemasonry, if you lived in a community like the one I just described, then you lived under a Masonic structure. Freemasonry defined your culture, your mindset, your belief system, and your identity. Your life would have been influenced by a system of Freemasonry whether you were ever in it or not. Most people need deliverance from the influence of Freemasonry. It may not be to the degree that someone who has been directly involved would, but if you've lived in that culture and under that structure, it has influenced you.

The point of all of this in Freemasonry is to construct and maintain a structure of false worship. Every false worship system is held in place by the worship of those who are in it. If the worshipers stop worshiping, the system and the structure will fall; it's only kept in place by those who continue to stay in the structure and serve the system.

Worship Is the Ultimate Goal of All Deliverance!

Worship is the ultimate goal of all deliverance. God wants us delivered so we're not oppressed, but more importantly, He wants us delivered so we can worship. That was what He said in Egypt. His people were oppressed in Egypt, but He didn't say, "Set My people free because they are so oppressed by those wicked Egyptians." He said, "Set My people free that they might worship Me." As long as you are kept captive under a system of false worship, then you are not free to worship the Lord with all your heart and soul and mind and strength. If your heart and soul and mind and strength have been captured in another system, you're not going to be free to worship. To fully separate we must remove ourselves from the structure by repenting, renouncing, and receiving the power of the Holy Spirit.

Many have been through individual or corporate deliverance, where you repent and renounce Freemasonry in your generational line. That is how you separate from the structure. That is how you get out of the structure, but also you have to get the structure out of you. Israel came out of Egypt, but never got Egypt out of them.

Many who have repented and renounced Freemasonry still have struggles with identity. They still have struggles hearing God and getting revelation. They have trouble submitting their will and following the Lord. They struggle with confidence in pursuing their destiny. They still have struggles from the effects of what happened in the initiation ceremony. The structure is still in them. They still have the mindset; they still have the identity; they are still unable to see, hear or speak by the Spirit.

We get the structure out of us by sending back what we received and reclaiming what we gave up. For instance, if one has renounced and repented of the hoodwink, the Masonic mindset is not going to automatically go away. Once a person has broken agreement with the hoodwink, they can send away the spirit behind the force that has been flowing through their blood. This starts the process of the renewal of their mind. The mindset received from Freemasonry will no longer have any right to continue to hold that person captive.

A Time to Minister to Others!

We are set free so we can minister to others. Ministering this way has brought freedom to more people than almost anything I have ever done. It's brought freedom to me personally. Realizing the power to reclaim and experience a divine recovery of what was given away in the steps of that ceremony (or any initiation) will change your outlook on who you really are and who you were destined to become. You will begin to see your future. Use the following prayer to do just this!

Here is an example of how we pray when we minister to people corporately. If you know that you have Freemasonry in your bloodline or you recognize the influence of Freemasonry in your life, you can pray this for yourself.

In the name of Jesus, we declare that we have repented and renounced of saying that we would exchange the light of Freemasonry for the light of the Gospel, the true Light that came into the world that brought life to men. Now we reclaim the ability to receive revelation from the Holy Spirit of God. We reclaim the light of the Gospel coming into us that will bring life into our lives. And we tell every spirit of false light that it is no longer welcome. We don't want you anymore—leave! Holy Spirit, come and bring us revelation of light and life and truth of the Gospel.

We also call back the sense of value we let go of when we turned all our valuables over to Freemasonry. We call back the intrinsic worth that God gave to us. We are precious because we are His. We are His handiwork; we are His masterpiece. He assigned a value to us. He said, "I am willing to pay the life of My Son for them. That's how valuable they are." Now we call the apprehension of that value back to us. We are not unworthy. We do not have to prove that we have worth; we don't have to perform well or work hard to know that we have value. We have value because God made us. We are His, and we will not believe anything that tells us we have to prove our worth or prove our value. We call that sense of value back. We call our destiny back to us, and where we have felt uncertain, where we've felt like we can't see, where we felt like we don't know what we're stepping into, we call back the light that is going to show us the way.

We throw off the slipshod slipper. God makes our feet to be prepared with the good news of the Gospel. In warfare and in battle we will take our stand securely and we will take territory. We are going forward prepared with Good News. We also declare that our destiny is determined by God. It is not uncertain, light or dark. God has a good plan for us. He's prepared good works for us to walk in. He has written our days in His book and will lead us in the way we should go. Our path will grow brighter and brighter as we move forward. We call our destiny back to us. We will walk in it and fulfill it.

We call our identity and our authority back to us. Where we have felt inadequate, inappropriate or not able to present ourselves well, where we have felt passive or apathetic, or lethargic—we throw all of that away. We throw off the identity that was imposed on us through our initiation into Freemasonry. We call back our God-given identity. He created us with gifts and talents and abilities that equip us to fulfill our destiny. He created us as individuals who are not to be judged as inferior because we are not like someone else. We will be who He created us to be.

We throw off the hoodwink and call back the full use of our minds, our eyes, our ears, our mouths, our tongues, our throats and all else affected by the hoodwink. We claim our right to hear, to see, to perceive the things given to us by God. Any way that the action of the hoodwink has blocked people from being able to pray in tongues is broken. We are free to speak by the Spirit. Our tongues and throats are released from the control of the hoodwink. We send the mindset imposed on us by Freemasonry away. Our minds will receive revelation from the Holy Spirit. We will know, discern and comprehend truth, and it will make us free.

We throw off the cable tow, and we call back our free will. God gave us free will and we take it as His gift. We are free to follow the leading of Holy Spirit. We are free to pursue the destiny God created for us. We are free to choose, and we choose to submit to the Lord Jesus Christ. We choose to submit to the Word of God. We are free from a false worship system that prevented us from fully obeying the Lord.

We pull the dagger off of our breast and declare that our emotions are free. We are free to know the joy of the Lord. We will receive the revelation of the love of God spread abroad in our hearts. We will be able to feel compassion. We declare that as we call our emotions back, God's people will begin to operate in such a release of the compassion of the Lord that we will see healings and miracles like Jesus did. He was moved with compassion for those who were sick, and He healed them.

We call physical health back to our bodies. We break the power of the curses and vows and oaths that were taken to bring physical harm, infirmity and diseases. We call into ourselves the blessing of health. We declare that by His stripes we are healed. In the Kingdom of Light, God does not give us sickness, infirmity or disease. We reclaim every part of our physical bodies to be used in worship. Our bodies will not be subject to a system of false worship. They will be instruments of worship to the True and Living God.

In ministry, following a prayer like this, we then make declarations like the following to declare our freedom.

I declare that I have repented of all participation in the ceremonies of Freemasonry.

I have renounced the spiritual transactions that took place in those ceremonies.

I have reclaimed my God-given identity, worth and destiny.

I have reclaimed my soul, my mind, my emotions and my will.

I have reclaimed my physical body.

I have reclaimed my spirit.

I have broken covenant with a false religious spirit of Freemasonry.

I now submit myself body, soul and spirit to the Living God, the God of Israel, the Maker of heaven and earth, and I fully enter into covenant with Him.

I now position myself in active resistance to the devil, and according to the Word of God he must run away.

I claim my right to every blessing of God in place of the curses that have been affecting my life. The Word of God says that the blessing of God will overtake me; healing, prosperity, favor, protection, power, wisdom and all the blessings of God are now free to come to me and my family.

I am unhindered by any connection to false worship, and I now freely enter into a new level of worship of the true and living God, and of Jesus, His only Son, with all of my heart and soul and mind and strength.

*I will go to new realms of worship in the Spirit and will join
     with angels in worshiping the Lord.*

*I will ascend directly into the throne room and descend in
     war to win every battle against my adversary.*

Hallelujah! Those who are free are free indeed.

Appendix B

Prayer of Release for Freemasons and Their Descendants

If you were once a member of a Masonic organization or are a descendant of someone who was, we recommend that you pray through this prayer from your heart. Don't be like the Masons, who are given their obligations and oaths one line at a time and without prior knowledge of the requirements. Please read it through first so that you know what is involved. It is best to pray this aloud with a Christian witness or counselor present. We suggest a brief pause following each paragraph to allow the Holy Spirit to show you any related issues that may require attention.

Father God, Creator of heaven and earth, I come to You in the name of Jesus Christ, Your Son. I come as a sinner seeking forgiveness and cleansing from all sins committed against You and others made in Your image. I honor my earthly father and mother and all of my ancestors of flesh and blood, and of the spirit by adoption and godparents, but I utterly turn away from and renounce all of their sins. I forgive all of my ancestors for the effects of their sins on me and my children. I confess and renounce all of my own sins. I renounce and rebuke Satan and every spiritual power of his affecting me and my family.

In the name of the Lord Jesus Christ, I renounce and forsake all involvement in Freemasonry or any other lodge, craft or occultism by my ancestors and myself. I also renounce and break the code of silence enforced by Freemasonry and the occult on my family and myself. I renounce and repent of all pride and arrogance, which opened the door for the slavery and bondage of Freemasonry to afflict my family and me. I now shut every door of witchcraft and deception operating in my life and seal it closed with the blood of the Lord Jesus Christ. I renounce every covenant, every blood covenant and every alliance with Freemasonry or the spiritual powers behind it made by my family or me.

In the name of Jesus Christ, I renounce and cut off witchcraft, the principal spirit behind Freemasonry, and I renounce and cut off Baphomet, the Spirit of Antichrist and the spirits of Death and Deception. I renounce the insecurity, the love of position and power, the love of money, avarice or greed and the pride that would have led my ancestors into Masonry. I renounce all the fears that held them in Masonry, especially the fears of death, fears of men and fears of trusting, in the name of Jesus Christ.

I renounce every position held in the lodge by any of my ancestors or myself, including "Master," "Worshipful Master" or any other. I renounce the calling of any man "Master," for Jesus Christ is my only Master and Lord, and He forbids anyone else from having that title. I renounce the entrapping of others into Masonry, and observing the helplessness of others during the rituals. I renounce the effects of Masonry passed on to me through any female ancestor who felt distrusted and rejected by her husband as he entered and attended any lodge and refused to tell her of his secret activities.

First Degree

I renounce the oaths taken and the curses and iniquities involved in the First or Entered Apprentice Degree, especially their effects on the throat and tongue. I renounce the Hoodwink blindfold and its effects on spirit, emotions and eyes, including all confusion, fear of the dark, fear of the light and fear of sudden noises. . . . I renounce the secret word, BOAZ, *and its Masonic meaning. . . . I renounce the mixing and mingling of truth and error . . . and the blasphemy of this degree of Masonry. . . . I renounce the cable tow noose around the neck, the fear of choking and also every spirit causing asthma, hay fever, emphysema or any other breathing difficulty. I renounce the ritual dagger, or the compass point, sword or spear held against the breast, the fear of death by stabbing pain and the fear of heart attack from this degree. . . . I now pray for healing of . . .* [throat, vocal cords, nasal passages, sinus, bronchial tubes, etc.] *and for healing of the speech area, and the release of the* Word of God *to me and through me and my family.*

Second Degree

I renounce the oaths taken and the curses and iniquities involved in the Second or Fellow Craft Degree of Masonry, especially the curses on the heart and chest. I renounce the secret words SHIBBOLETH *and* JACHIN *and all their Masonic meaning. . . . I cut off emotional hardness, apathy, indifference, unbelief and deep anger from me and my family. In the name of Jesus Christ, I pray for the healing of . . .* [the chest/lung/heart area] *and also for the healing of my emotions, and I ask to be made sensitive to the Holy Spirit of God.*

Third Degree

I renounce the oaths taken and the curses and iniquities involved in the Third or Master Mason Degree, especially the curses on the stomach and womb area. I renounce the secret words TUBAL CAIN *and* MAHA BONE *and all their Masonic meaning. . . . I renounce the Spirit of Death from the blows to the head enacted as ritual murder, the fear of death, false martyrdom, fear of violent gang attack, assault or rape and the helplessness of this degree. I renounce the falling into the coffin or stretcher involved in the ritual of murder. . . . I renounce the false resurrection of this degree, because only Jesus Christ is the Resurrection and the Life. (I also renounce the blasphemous kissing of the Bible on a witchcraft oath. I cut off all spirits of death, witchcraft and deception.) In the name of Jesus Christ, I pray for the healing of . . .* [the stomach, gallbladder, womb, liver and any other organ of my body affected by Masonry], *and I ask for a release of compassion and understanding for me and my family.*

Holy Royal Arch Degree

I renounce and forsake the oaths taken and the curses and iniquities involved in the Holy Royal Arch Degree,

417

especially the oath regarding the removal of the head from the body and the exposing of the brains to the hot sun. (I renounce the Mark Lodge, and the mark in the form of squares and angles, which marks the person for life. I also reject the jewel or talisman, which may have been made from this mark sign and worn at lodge meetings.) I renounce the false secret name of God, JAHBU-LON, and declare total rejection of all worship of the false pagan gods, Bul or Baal, and On or Osiris. I also renounce the password AMMI RUHAMAH and all its Masonic meaning. I renounce the false communion taken in this degree, and all the mockery, skepticism and unbelief about the redemptive work of Jesus Christ on the cross of Calvary. I cut off all these curses and their effects on me and my family in the name of Jesus Christ, and I pray for the healing of . . . [the brain, the mind, etc.].

Eighteenth Degree

I renounce the oaths taken and the curses, iniquities and penalties involved in the Eighteenth Degree of Masonry, the Most Wise Sovereign Knight of the Pelican and the Eagle and Sovereign Prince Rose Croix of Heredom. I renounce and reject the Pelican witchcraft spirit, as well as the occultic influence of the Rosicrucians and the Cabbala in this degree.

I renounce the claim that the death of Jesus Christ was a "dire calamity," and also the deliberate mockery and twisting of the Christian doctrine of the Atonement. I renounce the blasphemy and rejection of the deity of Jesus Christ, and the secret words IGNE NATURA RENOVATUR INTEGRA *and its burning. I renounce the mockery of the Communion taken in this degree, including a biscuit, salt and white wine.*

Thirtieth Degree

I renounce the oaths taken and the curses and iniquities involved in the Thirtieth Degree of Masonry, the Grand Knight Kadosh and Knight of the Black and White Eagle. I renounce the secret passwords STIBIUM ALKABAR, PHARASH-KOH and all they mean.

Thirty-First Degree

I renounce the oaths taken and the curses and iniquities involved in the Thirty-First Degree of Masonry, the Grand Inspector Inquisitor Commander. I renounce all the gods and goddesses of Egypt, which are honored in this degree, including Anubis with the jackal's head, Osiris the sun god, Isis, the sister and wife of Osiris and also the moon goddess. I renounce the Soul of Cheres, the false symbol of immortality, the chamber of the dead and the false teaching of reincarnation.

Thirty-Second Degree

I renounce the oaths taken and the curses and iniquities involved in the Thirty-Second Degree of Masonry, the Sublime Prince of the Royal Secret. . . . I renounce Masonry's false trinitarian deity AUM, and its parts: Brahma the creator, Vishnu the preserver and Shiva the destroyer. I renounce the deity of AHURA-MAZDA, the claimed spirit or source of all light, and the worship with fire, which is an abomination to God, and also the drinking from a human skull in many rites.

York Rite

I renounce and forsake the oaths taken and the curses and iniquities involved in the York Rite Degrees of Masonry. (These include Mark Master, Past Master, Most Excellent Master, Royal Master, Select Master, Super Excellent Master, the Orders of the Red Cross, the Knights of Malta and the Knights Templar degrees. I renounce the secret words JOPPA, KEB RAIOTH and MAHER-SHALAL-HASH-BAZ. I renounce the vows taken on a human skull, the crossed swords and the curse and death wish of Judas—having the head cut off and placed on top of a church spire. I renounce the unholy communion and especially drinking from a human skull in many rites.)

Shriners (Applies Only in North America)

I renounce the oaths taken and the curses, iniquities and penalties involved in the Ancient Arabic Order of the Nobles of the Mystic Shrine. I renounce the piercing of the eyeballs with a three-edged blade, the flaying of the feet, the madness and the worship of the false god Allah as the god of our fathers. I renounce the hoodwink, the mock hanging, the mock beheading, the mock drinking of the blood of the victim, the mock dog urinating on the initiate and the offering of urine as a commemoration.

Thirty-Third and Supreme Degree

*I renounce the oaths taken and the curses and iniquities
involved in the supreme Thirty-Third Degree of Freemasonry, the Grand Sovereign Inspector General. . . . I
renounce and utterly forsake The Great Architect of the
Universe, who is revealed in this degree as Lucifer, and
his false claim to be the universal fatherhood of God.
I renounce the cable tow around the neck. I renounce
the death wish that the wine drunk from a human skull
should turn to poison and the skeleton whose cold arms
are invited if the oath of this degree is violated. I renounce
the three infamous assassins of their grand master, law,
property and religion, and the greed and witchcraft involved in the attempt to manipulate and control the rest
of mankind.*

All Other Degrees

*I renounce all the other oaths taken, the rituals of every
other degree and the curses and iniquities involved.
These include the Allied Degrees, The Red Cross of
Constantine, the order of the Secret Monitor, and the
Masonic Royal Order of Scotland. I renounce all other
lodges and secret societies, including Prince Hall Freema-
sonry, Grand Orient Lodges, Mormonism, the Order of
Amaranth, the Royal Order of Jesters, the Manchester
Unity Order of Odd Fellows, Buffalos, Druids, Forest-
ers, the Loyal Orange, Black and Purple Lodges, Elks,
Moose and Eagles Lodges, the Ku Klux Klan, the Grange,
the Woodmen of the World, Riders of the Red Robe,
the Knights of Pythias, the Mystic Order of the Veiled
Prophets of the Enchanted Realm; the women's Orders*

421

of the Eastern Star, Ladies Oriental Shrine, and White Shrine of Jerusalem; the girls' Orders of the Daughters of the Eastern Star, Job's Daughters, and Rainbow; and the boys' Order of DeMolay, and their effects on me and all my family.

(I renounce the ancient pagan teaching and symbolism of the First Tracing Board, the Second Tracing Board and the Third Tracing Board used in the ritual of the Blue Lodge. I renounce the pagan ritual of the "Point within a Circle" with all its bondages and phallus worship. I renounce the occultic mysticism of the black-and-white-mosaic-checkered floor with the tessellated border and five-pointed blazing star. I renounce the symbol "G" and its veiled pagan symbolism and bondages. I also renounce the false claim that Lucifer is the Morning Star and Shining One, and I declare that Jesus Christ is the Bright and Morning Star of Revelation 22:16.)

I renounce the All-Seeing Third Eye of Freemasonry or Horus in the forehead and its pagan and occult symbolism. . . . I renounce all false communions taken, all mockery of the redemptive work of Jesus Christ on the cross of Calvary, all unbelief, confusion and depression (and all worship of Lucifer as God). I renounce and forsake the lie of Freemasonry that man is not sinful, but merely imperfect, and so he can redeem himself through good works. I rejoice that the Bible states that I cannot do a single thing to earn my salvation, but that I can only be saved by grace through faith in Jesus Christ and what He accomplished on the cross of Calvary.

I renounce all fear of insanity, anguish, death wishes, suicide and death in the name of Jesus Christ. Jesus Christ conquered death, and He alone holds the keys of death and hell, and I rejoice that He holds my life in His hands *now. He came to give me life abundantly and eternally, and I believe His promises.*

I renounce all anger, hatred, murderous thoughts, revenge, retaliation, spiritual apathy, false religion, all unbelief, especially unbelief in the Holy Bible as God's Word, and all compromise of God's Word. I renounce all spiritual searching into false religions and all striving to please God. I rest in the knowledge that I have found my Lord and Savior Jesus Christ and that He has found me.

I will burn or destroy all objects in my possession that connect me with all lodges and occultic organizations, including Masonry, witchcraft and Mormonism, and all regalia, aprons, books of rituals, rings and other jewelry. I renounce the effects these or other objects of Masonry, including the compass and the square (the noose or the blindfold), have had on me or my family, in the name of Jesus Christ.

All participants should now be invited to sincerely carry out in faith the following ten actions:

1. symbolically remove the blindfold (hoodwink) and give it to the Lord for disposal;

2. in the same way, symbolically remove the veil of mourning, to make way to receive the joy of the Lord;

3. symbolically cut and remove the noose from around the neck, gather it up with the cable tow running down the body and give it all to the Lord for His disposal;

4. renounce the false Freemasonry marriage covenant, removing from the fourth finger of the right hand the ring of this false marriage covenant, giving it to the Lord to dispose of it;

5. symbolically remove the chains and bondages of Freemasonry from your body;

6. symbolically remove all Freemasonry regalia, including collars, gauntlets and armor, especially the Apron with its snake clasp, to make way for the Belt of Truth;

7. remove the slipshod slippers to make way for the shoes of the Gospel of Peace;

8. repent of and seek forgiveness from having walked on all unholy ground, including Freemasonry lodges and temples, and any Mormon or other occultic/Masonic organizations;

9. symbolically remove the ball and chain from the ankles;

10. proclaim that Satan and his demons no longer have any legal rights to mislead and manipulate the person seeking help.

Holy Spirit, I ask that You show me anything else that I need to do or to pray so that my family and I may be totally free from the consequences of the sins of Masonry, witchcraft, Mormonism and all related paganism and occultism.

Pause, while listening to God, and pray as the Holy Spirit leads you:

Now, dear Father God, I ask humbly for the blood of Jesus Christ, Your Son and my Savior, to cleanse me from all these sins I have confessed and renounced: to cleanse my spirit, my soul, my mind, my emotions and every part of my body that has been affected by these sins, in the name of Jesus Christ.

(I renounce every evil spirit associated with Masonry and witchcraft, and all other sins, and I command in the

name of Jesus Christ for Satan and every evil spirit to be bound and to leave me now, touching or harming no one, and to go to the place appointed for you by the Lord Jesus, never to return to my family or me. I call on the name of the Lord Jesus to be delivered of these spirits, in accordance with the many promises of the Bible. I ask to be delivered of every spirit of sickness, infirmity, curse, affliction, addiction, disease or allergy associated with these sins I have confessed and renounced. I surrender to God's Holy Spirit and to no other spirit all the places in my life where these sins have been.) I ask You, Lord, to baptize me, fill me anew with Your Holy Spirit now according to the promises in Your Word. I take to myself the whole armor of God in accordance with Ephesians 6 and rejoice in its protection as Jesus surrounds me and fills me with His Holy Spirit. I enthrone You, Lord Jesus, in my heart, for You are my Lord and my Savior, the Source of eternal life. Thank You, Father God, for Your mercy, Your forgiveness and Your love, in the name of Jesus Christ, Amen.[1]

Notes

Chapter 1: Spiritual Life, Liberty and Freedom

1. James Strong, *The New Strong's Exhaustive Concordance of the Bible* (Nashville, Tenn.: Thomas Nelson, 1990), refs. 2198 and 2222.

2. Ibid., ref. 4053.

3. *The American Heritage Dictionary of the English Language,* 4th ed., s.v. "liberty."

4. Ibid., s.v. "freedom."

5. Robert D. Heidler, *Experiencing the Spirit* (Ventura, Calif.: Renew Books, 1998), 51, 54. [Italics in original.]

6. Ibid., 88.

Chapter 2: Becoming Aware of Spiritual Darkness

1. C. Peter Wagner, *Warfare Prayer* (Ventura, Calif.: Regal Books, 1992), 61.

2. Noel and Phyl Gibson, *Evicting Demonic Intruders* (West Sussex, England: New Wine Press, 1993), 47.

3. Ibid., 48–49.

4. Alice and Eddie Smith, *Spiritual Housecleaning* (Ventura, Calif.: Regal Books, 2003), 48.

Chapter 3: The Jewelry Box

1. C. Peter Wagner, *Hard-Core Idolatry: Facing the Facts* (Colorado Springs, Col.: Wagner Publications, 1999), 17.

2. C. Peter Wagner, *Breaking Strongholds in Your City* (Ventura, Calif.: Regal Books, 1993), 65.

3. *The American Heritage Dictionary of the English Language,* 4th ed., s.v. "culture."

Chapter 4: Spiritual Discernment

1. Francis Frangipane, *Discerning of Spirits* (Cedar Rapids, Iowa: Arrow Publications, 1991), 6.

2. Gary D. Kinnaman, *Overcoming the Dominion of Darkness* (Old Tappan, N.J.: Chosen Books, 1990), 133–134.

3. *The American Heritage Dictionary of the English Language*, 4th ed., s.v. "perceive."

4. Ibid., s.v. "fetish."

Chapter 5: A Demonic Foothold in the Land

1. *The American Heritage Dictionary of the English Language*, 4th ed., s.v. "foothold."

2. Other entry points for demonization include victimization, rejection, trauma, witchcraft, occult, fraternal orders (including Freemasonry) and cursing. An excellent study on this topic as it relates to issues of land is Bob Beckett's *Commitment to Conquer* (Grand Rapids, Mich.: Chosen Books, 1997).

3. *The American Heritage Dictionary of the English Language*, 4th ed., s.v. "topographical."

Chapter 6: Overthrowing Generational Curses

1. Cindy Jacobs, *The Voice of God* (Ventura, Calif.: Regal Books, 1995), 64.

2. Chuck D. Pierce and Rebecca Wagner Sytsema, *Possessing Your Inheritance* (Ventura, Calif.: Regal Books, 1999), 172–173.

3. Ibid., 174.

4. *The American Heritage Dictionary of the English Language*, 4th ed., s.v. "curse."

5. John Eckhardt, *Identifying and Breaking Curses* (Chicago: Crusaders Ministries, 1995), 1.

6. Ibid., 10.

7. Pierce and Sytsema, *Possessing Your Inheritance*, 175–176.

8. For further study on Freemasonry, we recommend reading chapter 10 of Noel and Phyl Gibson's *Evicting Demonic Intruders* (West Sussex, England: New Wine Press, 1993).

9. Dean Sherman, *Spiritual Warfare for Every Christian* (Seattle, Wash.: Frontline Communications, 1990), 107; Cindy Jacobs, *The Voice of God* (Ventura, Calif.: Regal Books, 1995), 65–67.

10. Penny Jackson, e-mail message to Chuck Pierce, April 19, 2004.

Chapter 7: Protecting Our Children from Spiritual Darkness

1. Larry Christenson, *The Christian Family* (Minneapolis, Minn.: Bethany House Publishing, 1970), 15.

2. *The American Heritage Dictionary of the English Language*, 4th ed., s.v. "order."

3. Ibid., s.v. "occult."

4. Frank D. and Ida Mae Hammond, *A Manual for Children's Deliverance* (Kirkwood, Mo.: Impact Christian Books, 1996), 81.

5. See *A Manual for Children's Deliverance* for a more complete list of games and toys to watch for.

6. Graham and Shirley Powell, *Christian, Set Yourself Free* (Kent, England: Sovereign World Ltd., 1983), 165.

Chapter 8: Ten Steps to Protecting Your Home from Spiritual Darkness

1. Pat Robertson, "Spiritual Answers to Hard Questions," *The Spirit-Filled Life Bible* (Nashville, Tenn.: Thomas Nelson, 1991), 1997.

2. Charles H. Kraft, *Defeating Dark Angels* (Ann Arbor, Mich.: Servant Publications, 1992), 43.

3. Bob Beckett has written about staking a whole community in his book *Commitment to Conquer* (Grand Rapids, Mich.: Chosen Books, 1997), which is an excellent resource for further study.

4. Jack Hayford, *Glory on Your House* (Grand Rapids, Mich.: Chosen Books, 1991), 94–104.

Appendix A: Delivered to Worship—Reversing the Effects of Freemasonry

1. *Merriam-Webster's Online Dictionary*, s.v. "evil eye," accessed January 12, 2011.

2. The Columbia Encyclopedia, sixth ed., s.v. "evil eye," quoted at Bartleby.com, http://www.bartleby.com/65/ev/evileye.html (accessed February 16, 2005).

3. Personal communication, January 15, 2016.

4. Albert Pike, *Morals and Dogma of the Ancient and Accepted Scottish Rite of Freemasonry,* Charleston, 1871: 819. (For more info go to: http://www.sacred-texts.com/mas/md/img/title.jpg.)

5. Personal communication, January 15, 2016.

Appendix B: Prayer of Release for Freemasons and Their Descendants

1. This prayer is taken from Dr. Selwyn Stevens, *Unmasking Freemasonry—Removing the Hoodwink* (Wellington, New Zealand: Jubilee Publishers, n.d.).

Copying of this prayer is both permitted and encouraged, provided reference is made to where it comes from: Jubilee Resources, PO Box 36–044, Wellington 6330, New Zealand (ISBN 1877203–48–3). Copies of *Unmasking Freemasonry* as well as this prayer can be found at http://www.jubileeresourcesusa.org.

Written testimonies of changed lives and healings are welcome. If additional prayer and ministry are required, or information is required about other spiritual deceptions, please contact Jubilee Resources. For reasons of distance, Jubilee Resources may refer you to someone based closer to you.

Charles D. "Chuck" Pierce serves as president of Global Spheres, Inc. (GSI) in Corinth, Texas. This is an apostolic, prophetic ministry that is being used to gather and mobilize the worshiping Triumphant Reserve throughout the world. GSI facilitates other ministries as well, and participates in regional and national gatherings to develop new Kingdom paradigms. Peter and Doris Wagner complete the leadership team of this new wineskin. Chuck also serves as president of Glory of Zion International Ministries, a ministry that aligns Jew and Gentile. He is known for his accurate prophetic gifting, which helps direct nations, cities, churches and individuals in understanding the times and seasons in which we live.

Chuck has a degree in business from Texas A&M, master's work in cognitive systems from the University of North Texas, and a D.Min. from the Wagner Leadership Institute.

He has authored or co-authored over twenty books, including *Possessing Your Inheritance*, *The Future War of the Church*, *The Worship Warrior*, *Restoring Your Shield of Faith*, *The Rewards of Simplicity* and *God's Unfolding Battle Plan*.

Chuck and his wife, Pam, live in Denton, Texas, and have six children and nine grandchildren.

Rebecca Wagner Sytsema currently serves as director of Children of Destiny, and also works as a freelance author and editor. She has co-authored eight Christian books, including *Possessing Your Inheritance* and *The Future War of the Church*. She and her husband, Jack, live in Florida with their three sons, Nicholas, Samuel and Trey.

More from
Chuck D. Pierce

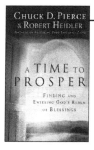

Discover the biblical model for work, worship and giving—and understand how this pattern prepares you to give and receive blessings. Now is the time to claim your inheritance and your portion and dwell in the realm of God's blessing.

A Time to Prosper (with Robert Heidler)

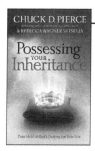

God longs for His people to prosper and to accomplish all He has planned for them. He wants to take you to a place of restoration, hope and abundant life. This book will show you how to embrace what God has destined for you—and your legacy.

Possessing Your Inheritance (with Rebecca Wagner Sytsema)

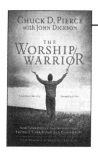

Pierce and Dickson unfold a biblical model of worship, revealing how to ascend to God's throne room in worship and descend in His power to declare His will in our lives, our cities and the nations. Discover how to push back the kingdom of darkness and recover God's blessings through worship.

The Worship Warrior (with John Dickson)

✅Chosen

More from
Chuck D. Pierce and
Rebecca Wagner Sytsema

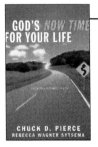

Why do so many believers fall short of their divine calling? Here you'll find dynamic, life-giving answers to help you reach your potential and find God's direction for your life, your family and your territory.

God's Now Time for Your Life

With the accuracy of this prophetic vision now realized, the revised edition of *The Future War of the Church* offers updates on Pierce's prophetic words early in the millennium, revealing what has come to pass. This book will leave you in no doubt that the Lord is still calling His people to advance His Kingdom, using worship, prayer and spiritual warfare to overcome the world's pervasive lawlessness and violence.

The Future War of the Church

Printed in Great Britain
by Amazon

42401538R00246